CONTENTS

KT-573-793

INTRODUCTION

This *Handbook* has become more condensed as the BUFVC expands. The Information Service, Off-Air Recording Back-Up Service, publications, courses and events still lie at the heart of the Council's work. The BUFVC has also gained funding from the Joint Information Systems Committee (JISC), the Research Support Libraries Programme (RSLP) and the Arts and Humanities Research Board (AHRB) for several new national initiatives – the Managing Agent and Advisory Service for UK Higher and Further Education (MAAS Media Online), British Universities Newsreel Scripts Project (BUNSP), The Researcher's Guide Online (RGO) and Television and Radio Index for Learning and Teaching (TRILT).

The *Handbook* describes all these projects, but the essays relating to network delivery of moving images are the core of the publication. They trace the thinking behind the recent development of new services and highlight the determination within the academic community to integrate moving images further within teaching and learning.

In comparison to the last edition, this *Handbook* boasts twice the number of e-mail and web addresses in the directory of organisations, but it is also more compact as the large distributors' section is now published electronically via the AVANCE database at www.bufvc.ac.uk.

Much of the BUFVC's specialist information is now available online – including the Television Index, the British Universities Newsreel Project, and Researcher's Guide Online – but this printed book is still valuable. The *Handbook* contains information about the BUFVC itself (including its history, membership, publications and services) and articles addressing important issues in the network delivery of moving images – technical considerations, associated descriptive information, copyright in content and, of course, content itself.

The articles are followed by directories of audio-visual centres in higher and further education, other relevant organisations, and education officers in television. It also includes an annotated bibliography of relevant media legislation and reports, Internet addresses that BUFVC staff have found to be useful in their work, and information about the Learning and Teaching Support Network (LTSN) and its subject centres, and the RSC (JISC Regional Support Centres).

This *Handbook* was collated by Martyn Glanville, Suren Rajeswaran and Hetty Malcolm-Smith. The BUFVC would like to thank them for all their hard work in creating this comprehensive publication.

ABBREVIATIONS & ACRONYMS

These abbreviations refer to entries contained within this Handbook.

ACU	Association of Commonwealth Universities
ADSET	Association for Database Services in Education & Training
AHDS	Arts & Humanities Data Service
AHRB	Arts & Humanities Research Board
ALCS	Authors' Licensing & Collecting Society
ALT	Association for Learning Technology
APTV	Associated Press Television
ARLIS	Art Libraries Society
ASA	Advertising Standards Authority
AsLib	Association of Information Management
ASME	Association for the Study of Medical Education
BAFTA	British Academy of Film & Television Arts
BBC	British Broadcasting Corporation
BBFC	British Board of Film Classification
BCS	British Computer Society
BECTa	British Educational Communications & Technology Agency
BECTU	Broadcasting, Entertainment & Cinematograph Technicians Union
BFFS	British Federation of Film Societies
BFI	British Film Institute
BIDS	Bath Data & Information Services
BIMA	British Interactive Multimedia Association
BKSTS	British Kinematograph, Sound & Television Society aka The Moving Image Society
BPI	British Phonographic Industry
BSAC	British Screen Advisory Council
BUFVC	British Universities Film & Video Council
BUNP	British Universities Newsreel Project
BUNSP	British Universities Newsreel Scripts Project
BVA	British Video Association
BVHT	British Video History Trust
CBA	Council for British Archaeology
CDPA	Copyright, Design and Patents Act
CD-ROM	Compact Disc – Read-Only Memory
CEI	Committee on Electronic Information
CHEST	Combined Higher Education Software Team
CILT	Centre for Information on Language Teaching and Research

CLA	Copyright Licensing Agency
COI	Central Office of Information
CTI	Computers in Teaching Initiative
CVCP	the erstwhile Committee of Vice-Chancellors & Principals of the Universities of the United Kingdom – now Universities UK
DACS	Design and Artists Copyright Society Ltd
DENI	Department for Education in Northern Ireland
DfEE	Department for Education & Employment
DNER	Distributed National Electronic Resource
DTG	Digital Television Group
DTI	Department of Trade and Industry
DVD	digital versatile disc
EAFA	East Anglian Film Archive
EBS Trust	Educational Broadcasting Services Trust
EDINA	Edinburgh Data and Information Access
ERA	Educational Recording Agency
ETmA	Educational Television & Media Association
FACT	Federation Against Copyright Theft
FAST	Federation Against Software Theft
FDTL	Fund for the Development of Teaching and Learning
FIAF	Fédération Internationale des Archives du Film (International Federation of Film Archives)
FOCAL	Federation of Commercial Audio-Visual Libraries
GLTC	Generic Learning and Teaching Centre
hbk	Hardback
HEDS	Higher Education Digitisation Service
HEFCE	Higher Education Funding Council for England
HEFCW	Higher Education Funding Council for Wales
HTV	Harlech Television
IAMHIST	International Association for Media & History
IAMS	International Association for Media in Science
ILT	Institute for Learning and Teaching
IPRs	Intellectual property rights
ISBN	International Standard Book Number
ISSN	International Standard Serial Number
ITC	Independent Television Commission
ITN	Independent Television News
ITV	Independent Television
IUHFC	InterUniversity History Film Consortium
IVCA	International Visual Communications Association
IWMFVA	Imperial War Museum Film & Video Archive

JANET	Joint Academic Network
JISC	Joint Information Systems Committee
JPEG	Joint Photographic Experts Group
KK	Kraszna-Krausz Foundation
LAN	Local Area Network
LTSN	Learning and Teaching Support Network
MAAS	Managing Agent and Advisory Service for UK Higher and Further Education
MACE	Media Archive for Central England
MAN	Metropolitan Area Network
MAP-TV	Memories Archive Programmes Television
MCPS	Mechanical Copyright Protection Society
MeCCSA	Media, Communication and Cultural Studies Association
MIRRDOC	Moving Image, Radio and Related Documentation Collections
MPEG	Motion Picture Experts Group
MU	Musicians' Union
MVC	Manchester Visualization Centre
NAG	National Acquisitions Group
NCC	National Computing Centre
NCET	National Council for Educational Technology (now BECTa)
NFT	National Film Theatre
NFTS	National Film & Television School
NFTVA	British Film Institute National Film & Television Archive
NGfL	National Grid for Learning
NIACE	National Institute of Adult Continuing Education
NISS	National Information Services & Systems
NMPFT	National Museum of Photography, Film & Television
NPA	New Producers Alliance
NRCD	National Resource Centre for Dance
NRFTA	Northern Region Film & Television Archive
NSA	British Library National Sound Archive
NWFA	North West Film Archive
OCR	Optical Character Recognition
PACT	Producers Alliance for Cinema & Television
PADS	Performing Arts Data Service
PAMRA	The Performing Artists' Media Rights Association
p&p	Postage and packing
pbk	Paperback
PCC	Press Complaints Commission
PDF	Portable Document Format
PPL	Photographic Performance Ltd

PRS	Performing Rights Society
QCA	Qualifications & Curriculum Authority
RAI	Royal Anthropological Institute
RGO	Researcher's Guide Online
RLSP	Research Libraries Support Programme
RSC	Research Support Centres
RTE	Radio Telefís Eireann
RTS	Royal Television Society
SCRAN	Scottish Cultural Resources Access Network
SEDA	Staff & Educational Development Association
SEFVA	South East Film & Video Archive
SFTA	Scottish Film and Television Archive (now Scottish Screen Archive)
SHRE	Society for Research into Higher Education
TASI	Technical Advisory Service for Images
TIC	Technology Integration Centre
TRILT	Television and Radio Index for Learning and Teaching
UCLA	University of California Los Angeles
UKERNA	United Kingdom Education & Research Networking Association
UKFAF	UK Film Archive Forum
UKOLN	UK Office for Library & Information Networking
URI	Uniform Resource Identifier
URL	Uniform Resource Locator
URN	Uniform Resource Name
UTV	Ulster Television
VADS	Visual Arts Data Service
VLV	Voice of the Listener & Viewer
VSC	Video Standards Council
WAN	Wide Area Network
WAVES	Women's Audio-Visual Education Scheme
WCT	WIPO Copyright Treaty
WFSA	Wessex Film and Sound Archive
WFTA	Wales Film and Television Archive
WIPO	World Intellectual Property Organisation
WPPT	WIPO Performances and Phonograms Treaty
WWW	World Wide Web
YFA	Yorkshire Film Archive

ABOUT THE BUFVC

The British Universities Film & Video Council (BUFVC) was established as the British Universities Film Council (BUFC) in 1948 by a group of university teachers who were pioneering the use of film for higher education and research. 16mm film was then a relatively new medium which, for the first time, made moving pictures available to teachers and researchers for use in their work.

The Council received its first grant support in 1968, when a full-time secretary was appointed. The organisation then became a grant-in-aid body of the British Film Institute (BFI). Between 1968 and 1975, the Council's staff grew to seven full-time personnel. In 1983, BUFC became BUFVC and moved from the British Film Institute into separate offices. Since then, the Council has been entirely independent, funded for a decade directly from the erstwhile Department of Education and Science (DES). Since 1993, the Council has been supported by a grant from the Joint Information Systems Committee (JISC) of the Higher Education Funding Councils received via the Open University.

One of the Founders, Thorold Dickinson (top), working at a Moviola with trainee editors in late 1930s (Courtesey of BFI stills)

The BUFVC exists to promote the production, study and use of moving image media for higher education and research. It provides a forum for the exchange of information and experience among teachers, researchers and academic support staff in higher and further education. The Council is a company limited by guarantee (number 955348), with charity status (number 313582).

INFORMATION SERVICE AND LIBRARY

At the heart of the BUFVC's activities is a specialist information service and library. The reference library holds over 3000 books, and series of some 100 periodicals and newsletters, with current catalogues from over 800 British and overseas distributors of audio-visual materials.

Its collection of journals and magazines is impressive and extensive, and includes every issue of the *Radio Times* since March 1991 (when it began listing all terrestrial television channels); over 20 years of *American Cinematographer*, and the *Journal of the Society of*

Motion Picture & Television Engineers from 1916-1986 (both collections kindly donated by the University of Newcastle); *Screen Digest* since 1972; 30 years of *Monthly Film Bulletin*; and every issue, including supplements, of *Sight and Sound*.

Information Service staff handle a wide variety of enquiries from university lecturers, television researchers, teachers, instructors and members of the public on audio-visual materials for teaching and learning. Requests range from dates of television broadcasts and distributors of feature films to source material for new television programmes and advice on health information videos for sixth-formers. The Information Service and Library are available free of charge to members. Visitors are advised to make an appointment in advance.

OFF-AIR RECORDING BACK-UP SERVICE

Since June 1998, the BUFVC has been recording all five British terrestrial television channels for 16 hours per day. The service allows

Assistant Director Geoffrey O'Brien in the off-air recording suite

member institutions to request copies if they have missed the opportunity to record programmes locally under licence. This is of particular value in covering recordings missed through transmission schedule changes and technical breakdowns.

The BUFVC is the only body in Britain holding a letter of agreement with the Educational Recording Agency (ERA) allowing the back-up recording of UK television programmes under Section 35 of the Copyright, Design and Patents Act 1988. Some 80 hours of television are added each day to the collection. An index to the material, the BUFVC Television Index, is published on www.bufvc.ac.uk.

FACILITIES

The BUFVC offers a wide range of services and facilities, with special prices for members, at its premises in central London. These include:

- Research and reading facilities for film researchers and students, including access to the British Universities Newsreel Project database (described below)
- Viewing facilities for a wide range of video formats
- Steenbeck film viewers (35mm and 16mm)
- 30-seat seminar room with video projection viewing facilities – available for courses, meetings and other events

COURSES

The BUFVC offers a number of one-day courses at its offices in central London. These are designed for the professional development of teachers, researchers and academic service providers, and cover subjects from copyright to the online delivery of moving images. Visit www.bufvc.ac.uk or see the current issue of *Viewfinder* magazine for details of upcoming courses.

ASSOCIATIONS

The BUFVC enjoys a close relationship with a number of other organisations, acting in some cases as a secretariat. For more details about the following bodies, see the Organisations section of this *Handbook*.

- British Video History Trust (BVHT)
- Council for British Archaeology/BUFVC AV Media Working Party
- UK Film Archive Forum (UKFAF)
- International Association for Media in Science (IAMS)
- InterUniversity History Film Consortium

PUBLICATIONS

VIEWFINDER

With wide-ranging information for academic staff, researchers and librarians, the BUFVC magazine *Viewfinder* explores the production, study and use of film, television and related media for higher and further education and research in up-to-the-minute feature articles and other news and comment. The supplement *Media Online Focus* carries additional information on the online delivery of moving images and related content, including databases and streamed media. *ISSN 0952-4444. Published four times a year: March, June, October and December. BUFVC Member institutions can receive multiple copies of* Viewfinder *to distribute locally to staff and students.*

THE RESEARCHER'S GUIDE: FILM, TELEVISION, RADIO AND RELATED DOCUMENTATION COLLECTIONS IN THE UK

This new publication is essentially the sixth edition of the popular *Researcher's Guide to British Film & Television Collections in the UK*, now expanded to describe over 550 film, television, radio and related documentation collections held in the United Kingdom and Ireland by national and regional archives, television companies and stock shot libraries, as well as local authorities, museums, industrial companies and private individuals. This invaluable guide also includes a directory of film and television researchers currently working in the UK.

These listings are complemented by articles on topics including copyright and clearance issues, British television franchises and production companies, setting up a media archive, using radio archives, film and broadcasting documents at the Public Record Office, and film and television research resources on the Internet. Contributors to this edition include Professor Nicholas Cull (University of Leicester), Emanuella Giavarra (Legal Adviser to European Bureau of Library, Information and Documentation Associations), Dr. Peter Lewis (London School of Economics), Barrie MacDonald (Independent Television Commission), James Patterson (Media Archive for Central England), Alex Cowen and Tony Dalton (freelance film researcher and consultants). *Edited by Jim Ballantyne, April 2001. ISBN 0-9001299715. £39 inc. UK p&p (£29 inc. p&p to BUFVC members), contact BUFVC for p&p elsewhere.*

FILM AND TELEVISION COLLECTIONS IN EUROPE: THE MAP-TV GUIDE

This indispensable guide to 1900 film and television archives in over 40 European countries from the Atlantic to the Urals. Includes large and well-known national film archives, television companies, newsreel and stock shot libraries, as well as many small and lesser known collections held by regional and local authorities, museums, business and industry, and private individuals. *Edited by Daniela Kirchner, 1995. ISBN 1857130154. 671 pages/hbk. £75 (£67.50 BUFVC members), £5.50 p&p UK, £9.50 p&p elsewhere.*

RESEARCHER'S GUIDE TO BRITISH NEWSREELS

This is the scholar's definitive guide to the British cinema newsreel companies, which draws together in three cumulative volumes 655 items abstracted from books and journals. Written by the newsreel makers themselves, as well as their critics and historians, the guide spans the life of the British cinema newsreel from 1901 to 1982. It is intended for professional researchers working in film and television, lecturers in 20th-century history, postgraduate students, archivists and reference librarians.

- Volume I: 1983; pbk, 119 pages, ISBN 0-901299-32-4
- Volume II: 1988; pbk, 47 pages, ISBN 0-901299-57-X
- Volume III: 1993; pbk, 86 pages plus chronological chart, ISBN 0-901299-65-0

Three volumes with supplementary chronological chart. £27 (£20 to BUFVC members) in UK p&p, £5.50 p&p elsewhere.

BUYING AND CLEARING RIGHTS: PRINT, BROADCAST AND MULTIMEDIA

The book to steer you through the minefield of rights clearances, with sound, practical advice on cutting costs and avoiding production delays. The authors manage the Rights Department at the Open University, which has over 25 years' experience in negotiating rights in third-party materials for re-use in broadcasts, audio-visual course materials, computer-based publications and books. *Richard McCracken and Madeleine Gilbart, 1995. ISBN 1-857130-25-1. 172 pages/hbk. £34.99 (£29 to BUFVC members), £2.50 p&p UK, £9.50 p&p elsewhere.*

THE ORIGINS OF THE COLD WAR 1945-1950

Produced by the BUFVC in association with the InterUniversity History Film Consortium, this CD-ROM examines the origins of the Cold War using eight contemporary newsreel stories, from Churchill's 'Iron Curtain' speech in 1946 to the Korean War in 1950. With new historical commentaries and background text, the CD-ROM forms a valuable and attractive teaching resource. Suitable both for PC and Apple Macintosh systems. *£95 including VAT and p&p.*

THE BRITISH UNIVERSITIES NEWSREEL PROJECT (BUNP) DATABASE

The BUNP Database is the first centralised record of British cinema newsreel releases, with details of all traceable stories distributed by British newsreels and cinemagazines between 1910 and 1979. It offers:

- 160,000 individual newsreel stories
- contents of 21 British newsreels and cinemagazines
- news coverage from 1910 to 1979
- political events of the 20th century
- fashion, sport, crime, leisure, transport, personalities and more
- newsreel stories covering the two world wars

The database is fully searchable by subject, title, event, location, date, company, cameraman and synopsis, with unique cross-searching

capabilities. The database is available online at no charge to academic users in the UK and to BUFVC members on the BUFVC Web site at www.bufvc.ac.uk/newsreels. The cross-platform CD-ROM (PC and Macintosh) comes with a detailed booklet which includes a history of the newsreels. *BUNP Database CD-ROM: £95. One copy of the CD-ROM is free to BUFVC subscriber researchers and member institutions; further copies, £65.*

www.bufvc.ac.uk

The BUFVC's Website is an essential source of up-to-date information about the Council and its activities. The latest news, upcoming events and publications are regularly featured, as well as three information sources: the AVANCE database of audio-visual materials for use in higher education; the BUFVC Television Index, an index to broadcast television, which began in July 1995 and lists documentary programmes, news and current affairs, music and drama; and the BUNP database. New features will include a Moving Image Gateway and access to the Researcher's Guide Online (RGO).

RESEARCH AND DEVELOPMENT

The BUFVC recognises that higher education in the UK is going through rapid development and radical changes. These changes are bringing about major shifts in the way in which higher education is organised and delivered.

The increasing use of computers and networks for the distribution of teaching material (including audio-visual information); the move from analogue to digital methods in audio-visual production; the expansion of broadcasting capacity through cable, satellite and digital encoding; and major developments in the application of databases – these changes offer important opportunities to BUFVC and its members. The Council maintains a constant watch on new activities and developments in this field. It takes an active role in stimulating debate concerning the implementation of new methods and acts as an information exchange for experience in higher education.

NATIONAL INITIATIVES

The BUFVC has received funding from the Joint Information Systems Committee (JISC), the Research Support Libraries Programme (RSLP) and the Arts and Humanities Research Board (AHRB) for several prestigious research initiatives and services – the Managing Agent and Advisory Service for UK Higher and Further Education (MAAS Media Online), British Universities Newsreel Scripts Project (BUNSP), The Researcher's Guide Online (RGO) and Television and Radio Index for Learning and Teaching (TRILT).

MANAGING AGENT AND ADVISORY SERVICE FOR MOVING PICTURES AND SOUND (MAAS)

The BUFVC, working in close collaboration with the Open University, is now at an advanced stage in its development of a Managing Agent and Advisory Service for Moving Pictures and Sound. The Managing Agent has the responsibility to select and clear rights in audio-visual content for delivery online to UK higher and further education. Negotiations with a number of organisations are currently underway and steering groups of academics and industry professionals are assisting in the prioritisation of material for digitisation and delivery to the sector.

Working alongside, the Advisory Service will assist teachers, researchers, support staff and the institutions to access and use this  form of content. The Advisory Service has already delivered a significant number of training courses for staff in institutions wishing to make use of the moving image and sound content in a digital environment. The service offers support to a raft of differing needs and user scenarios, from the use of off-air materials through to support for distance learners. The Advisory Service intends to offer a complete service within its resources addressing the diverse needs of the HE and FE community.

BRITISH UNIVERSITIES NEWSREEL SCRIPT PROJECT (BUNSP)

The four-year British Universities Newsreel Project (BUNP) completed its work in August 1999. The project is discussed in the article *Useless If Delayed?* (page 86), and the BUNP database is published online and on dual-platform CD-ROM (see above). The Council retains all of the issue sheets used in the creation of the project, in addition to a small but valuable collection of publications relating to newsreel history, and is continuing to gather information on British newsreels.

Thanks to a grant from the Arts and Humanties Research Board, which runs from 1999 until 2003, the BUFVC has now begun the British Universities Newsreel Script Project (BUNSP), a programme of digitising original newsreel documents such as commentary scripts, assignment sheets and cameramen's dope sheets. Around 80,000 documents are to be processed over three years in an ititiative which will greatly enhance the value of the newsreel database as an historical resource.

The bedrock of the BUNSP is a substanial collection of some 40,000 surviving files from British Paramount News, Gaumont British News and Universal News, generously deposited with the BUFVC by Reuters Television in October 1998. The collection runs from 1930 to 1958, and includes fascinating additional ephemera such as newspaper clippings (as background to the story which the cameraman was supposed to be covering), and sports programmes. Other substantial collections of dope sheets and commentary scripts exist at British Movietonenews,

British Pathé, and the Imperial War Museum Film and Video Archive. The documents will be scanned as greyscale images (including corrections, censors' marks and so on) to provide researchers with the visual equivalent of the document itself, and will be searchable by document type or keyword. The documents are being added to the database in PDF format (accessible through Adobe Acrobat Reader), and are freely available to all UK higher and further education insitutions, and to BUFVC members.

The project will greatly enhance our understanding of the newsreels and their place as unique records of the twentieth century, as well as making widely available documentation collections that have hitherto been largely unavailable to researchers.

RESEARCHER'S GUIDE ONLINE (RGO)

This new service is based on data from *The Researcher's Guide: film, television, radio and related documentation collections in the UK*. The Web-based online version will enable users to define searches by collection title, subject, index term and medium. Each record will include live e-mail and Web links, with entries regularly updated by the BUFVC's Information Service. This project is funded by the Research Support Libraries Programme (RSLP). For more information, visit www.bufvc.ac.uk, tel. +44 (0)20 7393 1508, or e-mail rgo@bufvc.ac.uk.

TELEVISION AND RADIO INDEX FOR LEARNING AND TEACHING (TRILT)

The BUFVC was awarded funding in June 2000 for this new initiative. The Television and Radio Index for Learning and Teaching (TRILT) will provide access to a comprehensive television and radio listings service under license, add cataloguing content to the data from a higher education/further education learning and teaching perspective, and deliver this online in a format which will integrate with the Distributed National Electronic Resource (DNER) of the JISC. The funding is for a three-year period.

MEMBERSHIP

There are four main types of membership:

Ordinary Membership is open to all universities and university colleges in Great Britain and Northern Ireland. All members of staff of an Ordinary Membership institution may use the services of the BUFVC. Each institution appoints one or two representatives who act as the focus for the distribution of Council information.

Associate Membership is open to overseas universities and colleges, to colleges of higher and further education, and to non-profit making organisations associated with university education either in the UK or abroad. All members of staff of an Associate Member institution may use the BUFVC's services.

Corporate Membership is open to commercial organisations which have an interest in the work of the BUFVC. All members of staff of a Corporate Member organisation may use the BUFVC's services.

Schools Membership is open to all secondary schools and sixth-form colleges (from both independent and public sectors) with an interest in the work of the BUFVC.

All members are entitled to discounts on all BUFVC services, publications and courses, and unlimited free access to the Information Service and Library.

All UK higher and further education institutions in membership will automatically have access to BUFVC's unique Off-Air Recording Back-up Service. (Educational institutions must hold an Educational Recording Agency Licence for off-air recording.)

Other types of subscriptions are available to individual researchers. Information on membership and current subscription rates can be obtained by contacting the BUFVC or visiting our Website. All applications for ordinary or associate membership should be made by letter to the Director of the BUFVC and must be formally approved by the Executive Committee. The letter should come from the Vice Chancellor, Principal, Registrar or other appropriate person and should, if possible, name the proposed representative.

BUFVC CONTACTS

British Universities Film & Video Council
77 Wells Street
London W1T 3QJ

GENERAL ENQUIRIES
TEL 020 7393 1500   FAX 020 7393 1555
E-MAIL ask@bufvc.ac.uk   WEB www.bufvc.ac.uk

Murray Weston, Director
TEL 020 7393 1505 • E-MAIL murray@bufvc.ac.uk

Geoffrey O'Brien, Assistant Director
TEL 020 7393 1503 • E-MAIL geoffrey@bufvc.ac.uk

Sergio Angelini, Library & Database Manager
TEL 020 7393 1506 • E-MAIL sergio@bufvc.ac.uk

Jim Ballantyne, RGO Co-ordinator
TEL 020 7393 1510 • E-MAIL jim@bufvc.ac.uk

Luís Carrasqueiro, Network Content Manager
TEL 020 7393 1509 • E-MAIL luis@bufvc.ac.uk

Sarah Easen, BUNSP Cataloguer
TEL 020 7393 1518 • E-MAIL sarah@bufvc.ac.uk

Anne Fleming, Head of Content, Managing Agent
TEL 020 7393 1515 • E-MAIL anne@bufvc.ac.uk

Madeleine Gilbart, Headof Contract & Rights, Managing Agent
E-MAIL maasrights@bufvc.ac.uk

Cathy Grant, Information Officer
TEL 020 7393 1507 • E-MAIL cathy@bufvc.ac.uk

Aimee Hamblyn, Administrator
TEL 020 7393 1519 • E-MAIL aimee@bufvc.ac.uk

Sandra Houlton, Courses
TEL 020 7393 1504 • E-MAIL sandra@bufvc.ac.uk

Linda Kaye, BUNSP Manager
TEL 020 7393 1518 • E-MAIL linda@bufvc.ac.uk

Hetty Malcolm-Smith, Publications Officer
TEL 020 7393 1511 • E-MAIL hetty@bufvc.ac.uk

Luke McKernan, Head of Information
TEL 020 7393 1508 • E-MAIL luke@bufvc.ac.uk

Greg Newton-Ingham, Head of Advisory Service
TEL 020 7393 1502 • E-MAIL maas@bufvc.ac.uk

Marianne Open, TRILT Cataloguer
TEL 020 7393 1501 • E-MAIL marianne@bufvc.ac.uk

John Riley, TRILT Manager
TEL 020 7393 1501 • E-MAIL john@bufvc.ac.uk

Kush Varia, Assistant to the Managing Agent
TEL 020 7393 1515 • E-MAIL kush@bufvc.ac.uk

Outside the UK, dial +44 20 instead of 020.

MOVING IMAGES ONLINE

MURRAY WESTON

Those readers familiar with the BUFVC will no doubt be aware of the Council's contribution to the Imagination/Universities Network joint pilot project with the BFI, Networking Moving Images for University Teaching & Research, which was completed in 1999. The delivery of moving images online to universities was demonstrated across the national network for the first time at a conference organised by the BUFVC at Robinson College, Cambridge, in December 1998, and a report was delivered in 1999.

In 2000, following an open tender process, the BUFVC, in partnership with the Open University, was appointed Managing Agent and Advisory Service for Moving Pictures and Sound in UK further and higher education. This article places these developments in context and attempts to set the scene for the activity which will take place during the next five years.

BACKGROUND

In 1995 the BUFVC, in association with Communication Arts, first outlined a project for the networking of moving images for university teaching and research. This paper, which was presented to the Joint Information Systems Committee (JISC), had a far-reaching effect. It proposed that four channels of British terrestrial television could be recorded in real time in MPEG1 to hard disks in four high speed Silicon Graphics servers.

The metadata/database to describe the moving image files and link to the content would be derived from the CEEFAX information delivered as part of the television service in the picture field blanking.

Once recorded, the moving image files would be moved to a slower back-end server and the entire system would provide access online to a 'buffer' of some three months of television output from the four channels. The system would be operate under Section 35 of the Copyright, Design and Patents Act 1988 and would only be accessible by students and staff in ERA licence-holding institutions.

This proposal, radical as it was for 1995, brought the BUFVC to the attention of the JISC, which was already considering the implications of developing new services to deliver online via the Joint Academic Network (JANET) and broadband backbone – SuperJANET (operating at 155mbps). The prospect of delivering time-based media to support learning and teaching was under serious discussion although the JISC did not agree to the immediate development of a service.

In December 1996, with the support of JISC, the BUFVC organised a consultation day at the National Film Theatre (NFT) in London where service-providers, producers, teachers and researchers exchanged views on how online delivery of moving pictures might best serve the needs of higher education and research. The British Film Institute had a similar interest in developing online access routes to its National Film and Television Archive (NFTVA).

The consultation meeting pointed up a number of expected issues. How would the content be selected for a service delivering moving pictures online? If the system could only handle a limited quantity of material, would key extracts from films and television programmes be the most appropriate delivery – or would it be necessary always to encode full-length productions so academic staff could make their own selection of sequences? Who would create the metadata to describe the assets, and what standards would need to be adopted? How would third party rights be cleared for this activity and how would the assets be managed? Could any of the work in this medium fall under the exceptions established in UK copyright legislation?

In 1997, with the BFI as partner, the BUFVC embarked on the development of a pilot proof-of-concept project supported by JISC via its Committee on Electronic Information (CEI). The project would be designed to test the viability of supplying moving pictures via a distributed network, to a selection of university sites. The intention was to establish the pilot using existing infrastructure in UK higher education. It would evaluate both qualitative data and quantitative/technical information (that is, data relating to traffic, appropriate forms of access, access times and so forth), with a view to scaling-up to a national service, and would test the effectiveness of the interface, search tools, delivery and likely pedagogical implications.

CONTENT

Early in the development of the project it was agreed that, for the pilot, content should be identified and prepared in three different academic subject areas – film studies, medicine and social history. Three groups of subject specialists were brought together to consider criteria for the selection of a library of ten hours' running time of moving pictures in each subject. While the long-term ambition of a fully developed network service would be to supply sufficient content and connectivity to create a rich research resource, it was very clear, in the context of the pilot, that ten hours of material in each subject area would be useful only to support teaching. The subject groups therefore focused on this in their discussions. The film studies group chose a collection of British feature film material and associated stills and poster collections. The social history group concentrated on selecting moving pictures from the 1960s, and the medicine group looked at material relating to clinical techniques, patient interviews and neurology. While much of the material selected initially for medicine had been sourced from the National Film and Television Archive and was significant historically, it soon became clear that medical schools were more interested in obtaining access to up-to-the-minute training material to ease the pressure on packed teaching timetables. So additional new material was identified part-way through the pilot in response to this need.

INTELLECTUAL PROPERTY RIGHTS

Rights in the material sourced from the National Film and Television Archive, to be held on the servers, was cleared in a conventional manner at the BFI. Other material sourced direct from owners was cleared for delivery by the BUFVC. Releasing content via networks raises issues regarding authorisation (*i.e.* verification of the identity of those accessing a service) and conditional access (*i.e.* whether the identified user should have access to the material being viewed and whether a payment should be made).

Such systems require administration to monitor activity and to identify and respond to unauthorised use. In a distributed system, the architecture must be planned carefully to allow local monitoring and data collection. Another issue at the forefront of negotiations with rights owners is the question of allowing downloading without permission or payment.

Some collections of moving pictures may be acquired specifically to encourage downloading and local use either on computer platforms or on analogue videotape. However, the great proportion of material may only be released to support real time viewing with no opportunity to download. This requires the implementation of reliable, resilient systems to stream content to the user. On busy networks which use contention-based delivery, such reliability is at a premium.

STANDARDS

Within the project, a group met to consider technical parameters and to discuss the standards for metadata, compression, server software, authorisation protocols and conditional access which might be adopted in the pilot. At the conclusion of the discussion it was agreed that there would have to be criteria established for the selection of potential pilot client sites. The key features were that:

- the sites should have a connection to the Super-JANET network;
- the sites should have server capacity of at least 100GB in place and available for use in the pilot;
- the sites should preferably be connected to high-speed MANs (Metropolitan Area Networks) serving other institutions of higher education;
- the sites be capable of providing access to staff and students working in the three subject areas selected for the pilot content.

The working group developing the pilot project decided that no more than three sites would be selected as clients. The sites would be likely to act as mirrors to a main server, receiving updates and additions overnight in a store-and-forward operation. Digitisation of material would take place at the Manchester Visualisation Centre, part of the University of Manchester. Metadata (data describing the media stored – *i.e.* the database to retrieve and access the moving picture files) adopted the Dublin Core 15-field standard and was derived from existing databases held at the BFI and the BUFVC. (Martyn Glanville's article describes Dublin Core in detail, later in this *Handbook*.) Compression standards adopted for the moving pictures were to be a mixture of MPEG1 and MPEG2 encoding.

The main perceived benefits of the distributed network model were:

- provision of access (ultimately) to large libraries of material for browsing/viewing purposes;
- the opportunity to link to and reference moving pictures alongside other digitised assets, whether text, illustration, music or sound;
- the scope to develop a fully integrated system allowing users of material also to be suppliers.

This last point would be significant in the long-term providing the distinction between the pilot being tested and parallel developments in digital television and video-on-demand. The model of broadcasting might be described as a system of supply of 'one to many'. The video-on-demand model is 'one to many, when the many want it'. The distributed network model could be described as 'many to many'.

OPERATION

Digitisation work started during November 1997 and selected pilot sites were ready to operate in early 1998. In December 1998, the work was demonstrated at a conference at Robinson College, Cambridge. (Two articles in this *Handbook*, 'Networking Moving Images for University Teaching and Research' and 'Copyright Clearance for Higher Education' further address issues raised at that conference.) Dr. Jim Stephenson of the Educational Broadcasting Services Trust described the demonstration in issue 35 of *Viewfinder*, the BUFVC magazine:

> *What we were seeing was the translation of computer data streamed across Britain into projected images, cinema-screen size, full-motion, full-colour. We saw the original script in the original font. We saw data relating to the film and we mouse-clicked through menus seeking bits and bobs as the moving pictures arrived at Cambridge in bits and bytes from Glasgow. This was not video or cable TV or even DVD. This was moving pictures on the Net. We saw it and it worked.*

The experiments had worked and knowledge had been gathered. It became apparent that there would be no obvious 'turnkey solution' suitable for every institution and local architecture – no 'broadcast standards' model for delivery. Rights in moving picture material for online delivery were not so difficult to clear – the real challenge was in preparing the material, and organising and creating coherent metadata to agreed standards. This 'Cinderella story' of the moving image world would be likely, one day, to be seen as the most strategically valuable in online services development. A full report of the pilot was published via the Joint Information Systems Committee (see www.jisc.ac.uk:8080/curriss/collab//#c4).

The demonstration of the pilot and the consideration of 'next steps' brought forward discussion about the aim of this work long-term. Why spend significant resource in developing online delivery?

It was soon after the Robinson College meeting that the JISC published a new five-year policy paper. This focussed on content delivery and the development of a Distributed National Electronic Resource – (DNER). The integration of moving images in this resource was seen as an important development and funds would be released to take existing work further.

PRESSURES FOR DEVELOPMENT

There has been a growing recognition among university teachers and students in all faculty disciplines that moving picture and sound material is of significant value in their work. This is not simply a function of the increase in the numbers of courses, such as media studies, which clearly have special needs. Teaching and learning styles across the board in higher education are changing radically and will soon rely heavily on good quality resources delivered efficiently.

UK higher education has installed and maintains one of the best national computer network facilities in the world – JANET and Super JANET – and, with the help of the JISC, a range of specialist services is being delivered via the network. The time was right to experiment with establishing a service that would provide moving pictures via the network. For the BUFVC, which has been working since 1948 to encourage wider access and use of moving pictures in university teaching and research, this was an important experiment. Despite more than fifty years of activity, the full integration of moving images and sound alongside text as a scholarly resource has not been achieved.

The neglect and disregard shown to moving pictures can be contrasted with the way in which we have favoured text as a resource for learning. The efforts made to identify, abstract, catalogue, index and store text for scholars greatly overshadow similar efforts made for moving pictures. Without proper catalogues and abstracts for books and journals, access to written works would have been far more difficult, and it is unlikely that learning and literacy would ever have moved out of the grip of the religious orders.

Moving pictures have been caught in a limbo which would appear almost as restrictive as the protection of religious orders. There is still not a 'filmography' equivalent of the British National Bibliography, and there is no system of statutory deposit for national collections. Even when copies of works have been deposited voluntarily for posterity, contractual complications can mean that they are stored away with little chance of being viewed regularly by students and scholars. Nor is there any system of distributed access, as there is with books through libraries and interlibrary loans. All of these issues, but especially the question of access, have conspired against the wider scholarly use of some of the most influential media of the twentieth century.

We now find ourselves at a turning point. There are technologies available to assist in storing, controlling and providing remote automated access to large quantities of moving picture assets. The higher and further education communities are making the integration of time-based media with text and other resources a policy of the new Distributed National Electronic Resource, and the general policies of museums and archives are beginning to extend access to collections using online systems.

However, there are real threats to the delivery of content on such online systems which would benefit teaching and scholarship. Controlling interests in rights have taken steps which could undermine *bona fide* access to content for non-commercial research and teaching purposes. Most of these steps being taken by rights owners and their agents, through the World Intellectual Property Organisation (WIPO) and the legislation of the European Union, have been to protect legitimate commercial rights. However, the side-effect of these moves is that the established route to access to content for non-commercial use, which falls within the 'three-step test' of the Berne Convention, and is expressed as exceptions to copyright in national laws, may be threatened by the new European Directive currently making its way through the European Parliament.

At the time of writing there is no clear view of what the future holds with regard to exceptions to copyright online and the *modus operandi* which will develop following the implementation of the proposed Directive. (See page 75 of Emanuella Giavarra's article, 'Educational use of multi-media materials: the legal framework' for more information on this and related issues.)

In 2000, the BUFVC, in partnership with the Open University, was appointed Managing Agent and Advisory Service for Moving Pictures and Sound for UK higher and further education. The Managing Agent will identify, select and clear for release appropriate moving image and sound resources. The Advisory Service will provide assistance to users with advice on technology and tools to make best use of the content in learning, teaching and research. Further details of these developments will be released via BUFVC's Website at www.bufvc.ac.uk.

The Joint Information Systems Committee of the Higher Education Funding Councils is supporting this work and is co-ordinating the activities of many related services around the UK as part of the Distributed National Electronic Resource; see www.jisc.ac.uk/dner for more information.

NETWORKING MOVING IMAGES FOR UNIVERSITY TEACHING & RESEARCH

MIKE CLARK

In December 1998, the BUFVC held the first in a series of conferences at Robinson College, Cambridge, to demonstrate the delivery of moving images online; the introduction to Murray Weston's article, which immediately precedes this one, more fully explains this initiative. This is the edited transcript of the speech given on that day by the Chairman of the BUFVC, Mike Clark, Director of the GeoData Institute, University of Southampton.

I would like to talk about the 'dazzle factor' in moving images, and the pot of gold at the end of the rainbow which we are now creating, and calling 'networked moving images'.

I would like to begin with an analogy. A phrase that I cannot get out of my mind is *Don't Shoot the Pianist* – when I retire and make my masterpiece, I am going to call it *Don't Clap the Projectionist*. To borrow loosely from Shakespeare, 'a phrase which must give us pause, give us pause perhaps to temper our enthusiasm'. Now, I have gone through my entire life encouraging enthusiasm – the last thing I want to do is damp it, but to temper it might be appropriate as we come towards the end of such a truly innovative meeting. Temper it so that our feelings may be mildly shaken but certainly not stirred. What I want to do is temper our enthusiasm for technology by realising what it is.

If you visit BUFVC's headquarters, just off Oxford Street, in the display window you will find a wonderful, monstrous piece of equipment with cogs, wheels and chains, and great big metal handles, that you would need a JCB to move. None of this laptop/palmtop business – it is an 'antique' film projector. I think it is worth contemplating that beautiful piece of equipment and the projectionist who presumably oiled it.

Can you imagine an era when you *oiled* your delivery mechanism? I think of 1939, when that projector was released. The clouds of war were gathering but the people were captivated – to get away from reality, they cheered the hero and they booed the villain, and the one they completely and utterly ignored was the projectionist up there in the box at the back, and that wonderful piece of delivery equipment.

What does that tell us? It tells us something about a paradox. We are all here eulogising technology and delivery. Then somebody gets up and says, 'I've got more bandwidth in my Vauxhall Astra van than the whole lot of you have got in all your technology.' I think *that* must give us pause – but certainly not enough to lose our enthusiasm for the technology nor our joy at the vision and the commitment of the Joint Information Systems Committee (JISC) in putting this capability before us, because it does have an inevitability about it.

I think what we have seen today is truly wonderful, but pause for one moment and think about all the other blind alleys there have been. Think about the film loop, think about tape-slide. Think about all the ways in which we thought heaven was about to descend upon us. This time, we must be different; we must not go up those blind alleys again. In order to escape a near century of fits and starts and false starts, we must remember one single underlying message – that no matter how much we invest in the delivery mechanism, the value, the ultimate return on investment, lies in *content*. Content is the creativity; content is the illumination, the knowledge, the trigger of all the things that make this worthwhile.

We are destined, like engine drivers, to rejoice in our technology. But as people get off our train, they rush past the engine and they never say 'thank you'. They might abuse us if we are late just as they abuse the computer department if the network goes down, but they never say 'thank you'. So it is our judgement – that what we are doing is quintessentially important for higher education – that has to carry us through.

What sorts of images should be the priority on these new networks, what images do we want to deliver? As an earth scientist, I could say certain things. I could say 'quality': go for quality, not for popularisation. This service will dumb down; within a decade, it will have dumbed down to the absolute drains. But there is no reason for JISC to fund that – that will happen in other ways.

We have to fund quality, and I would fund things that we cannot deliver in other ways. Through our Off-Air Recording Back-Up Service (see 'About the BUFVC, page 1), BUFVC is able to record and keep almost everything that comes from the terrestrial channels, because of our negotiating skills with the rights owners. Go for the quality, go for the special and, if necessary, build the business case on special audiences.

As an end-user academic, I do not need a million hours of video, any more than my students need the total freedom of the British Library. We need to focus on what is required for a particular course. By and large, I know what I would like most of my students to focus on – one or two will go off in different directions, and will ultimately earn those Nobel Prizes, but we have to cope with those few in different ways.

At one level, I could talk about quality, about specialisation. At another level, I will simply say: do not be so unutterably silly as to ask 'What moving images should we put on this service?'. We have learnt something, surely, from the last 70 years. They told us that sound was not necessary in moving pictures – sound was just for special occasions, the big productions. Then they said the same about colour – that black and white is the proper way to project images, and we will only put a few special things in colour. And we are saying much the same now about movement – movement is not important, let's just select those little things that we want to see moving. But movement is quintessential to imagery.

Networked services will ultimately be extremely broad. Our problem is the transition phase – building a business case, prototyping and getting people used to using the new methods of delivery. For the next three to five years, we will have a problem prioritising; after that, we will all look back at these days and laugh.

So, what sort of online service would you like? As an end-user, I want one that works. I do not have the luxury of coming in for an hour before my lecture to set up. I have 200 students to get out of this theatre and another 200 to get in 10 minutes. The theatre could be anywhere on campus, it could be changed at the last minute, and I have got to be there. I want end-user delivery that operates.

So, just as content is core to this argument, so is the ability to deliver to the end-user, whether in a lecture theatre, or a carrel, or a workstation complex. In a five-star university like mine, we have a superfluity of bums and very few seats to put them on, so if you want high configuration graphics workstations, then there will be a huge number of bums for each one. Our bottleneck is not going to be the bandwidth of the delivery into the institution, but the bandwidth of the delivery to a single pair of eyes and ears. I think we have to address these problems in parallel if we are going to succeed.

My third point is that rights are everything. I spent a huge amount of time with my team building an electronic library, meticulously clearing copyright for two of my major course modules. I cleared it for University of Southampton students for on-campus use – and, of course, within four years the students wanted to use it off-campus. Now we have five different colleges where other people want to use the material, too. Our original effort has proved worthless, but to start again and clear all of that material is a major operation.

Rights, if they are going to be cleared, are going to be cleared by organisations like BUFVC, who are prepared to come to a technology conference and say that it is no good having the technology if we do not have the right to use it. We have to develop systems in parallel – the technology to deliver, the technology to receive, the right to receive.

Who cares about all of this? BUFVC. We have been caring about this for an astonishing length of time. The basic issues of getting moving images into higher education have been with us for half a century. We are experienced in this and that is why I believe that the partnership that has now developed between JISC and BUFVC is incredibly timely. We have to work together if we are going to get what we need.

Not least, we have enormous experience in the pedagogical issues related to the use of moving images. It is no if good lecturers know how to receive images, if they have no idea how to build them into their teaching or actively into their research.

So it is with huge pride that we welcome this Christmas child, the pilot project for Networking Moving Images. I want to nurture it, I want it to grow, I want it to get through those difficult teenage years and mature to the point where it is self-sustaining.

I have three closing comments for you. The first is to rejoice in the *technology* – it is close to magic as far as I am concerned. It is like the Starship Enterprise, all warp drives and transporters. It's a neat idea, that we will soon actually be able to pull down movies into any of these lecture theatres. All of that is incredible but, to amortise the return on investment, we have to think about *content*, about end-user delivery, about pedagogical creativity. How is this actually going to help us build through our TQA (Teaching Quality Assessment], our RAE (Research Assessment Exercise], and get somewhere?

I think the final and single most important issue is *rights*. Rights ultimately could be the barrier that would prevent this development from being successful. It will not be bandwidth – bandwidth will be a footnote in the Bill Gates memorial volume. We have the wit to solve the problem of bandwidth, but I am waiting for the licence that allows any one of my students to look at any moving image anywhere, any time, for any purpose. I confidently believe that BUFVC will arrange the writing of that licence in the same year that the publishers announce that they are giving free textbooks in perpetuity to all students.

So remember these two days, they are 'mission critical'. They are pivotal. This is one of those special times when you feel that a new era is about to dawn. Let us thank the Lord that we are launching it in partnership, the technology and the users together.

WHAT IS THE DUBLIN CORE ?

MARTYN GLANVILLE

Metadata is the descriptive information used to find individual resources; it was devised with World Wide Web resources in mind to provide context to searches. The emerging standard known as the Dublin Core, a set of 15 basic elements of information which can be used to describe a huge variety of digital objects, from Web pages to virtual reality.

This article looks at the application of the Dublin Core to film and moving image resources. Text on the application of the set to moving image resources was provided by Catherine Owen at the Performing Arts Data Service.

METADATA

The simplest useful definition of metadata is 'structured data about data'. This general definition of course covers a vast range of possibilities ranging from a human-generated textual description of a resource to machine-generated data that may be useful only to software applications.

The term metadata has been used only in the past 15 years, and has become more common with the popularity of the Web. But the underlying concepts have been in use for as long as collections of information have been organised. Library catalogues represent a well-established variety of metadata that have served for decades as collection management and resource discovery tools.

THE DUBLIN CORE

The Dublin Core Metadata Initiative began in 1995 to develop conventions for resource discovery, *i.e.* how we find things on the Web. The focus of initial discussion was electronic resources. It was clear at the outset, however, that the semantics of resource discovery should be independent of the medium of the resource, and that there are obvious advantages in using the same semantic model across media.

Thus, considerable attention has been invested in making the Dublin Core sufficiently flexible to represent resources (and relationships among resources) that exist in digital and traditional formats.

The Dublin Core is a metadata element set intended to facilitate the discovery of electronic resources. Put another way, it is a set of consistent descriptive terms which can be applied to a whole range of media.

ELEMENT DESCRIPTIONS

The list of elements and their general definitions given below were finalised in December 1996. The elements and their names are not expected to change substantially from those on list, though the application of some of them is currently experimental and subject to varying interpretation from implementation to implementation.

In the element descriptions below, the label is specified to make the syntactic specification of elements simpler for encoding schemes.

1. Title
Label: TITLE
The name given to the resource by the CREATOR or PUBLISHER.

2. Author or Creator
Label: CREATOR
The person or organisation primarily responsible for creating the intellectual content of the resource. For example, authors in the case of written documents, artists, photographers, or illustrators in the case of visual resources.

3. Subject and Keywords
Label: SUBJECT
The topic of the resource. Typically, subject will be expressed as keywords or phrases that describe the subject or content of the resource. The use of controlled vocabularies and formal classification schemas is encouraged.

4. Description
Label: DESCRIPTION
A textual description of the content of the resource, including abstracts in the case of document-like objects or content descriptions in the case of visual resources.

5. Publisher
Label: PUBLISHER
The entity responsible for making the resource available in its present form, such as a publishing house, a university department, or a corporate entity.

6. Other Contributor
Label: CONTRIBUTOR
A person or organisation not specified in a CREATOR element who has made significant intellectual contributions to the resource but whose contribution is secondary to any person or organisation specified in a CREATOR element (for example, editor, transcriber, illustrator).

7. Date
Label: DATE

The date the resource was made available in its present form. Recommended best practice is an eight digit number in the form YYYY-MM-DD.

8. Resource Type
Label: TYPE

The category of the resource, such as home page, novel, poem, working paper, technical report, essay, dictionary.

9. Format
Label: FORMAT

The data format of the resource, used to identify the software and possibly hardware that might be needed to display or operate the resource.

10. Resource Identifier
Label: IDENTIFIER

String or number used to uniquely identify the resource. Examples for networked resources include Uniform Resource Locators (URLs) and Uniform Resource Names (URNs), when implemented. Other globally unique identifiers, such as International Standard Book Numbers (ISBN) or other formal names would also be candidates for this element in the case of offline resources.

11. Source
Label: SOURCE

A string or number used uniquely to identify the work from which this resource was derived, if applicable. For example, a PDF (Portable Document Format) version of a novel might have a SOURCE element containing an ISBN number for the physical book from which the PDF version was derived.

12. Language
Label: LANGUAGE

Language(s) of the intellectual content of the resource.

13. Relation
Label: RELATION

The relationship of this resource to other resources. The intent of this element is to provide a means to express relationships among resources that have formal relationships to others, but exist as discrete resources themselves. For example, images in a document, chapters in a book, or items in a collection.

14. Coverage

Label: COVERAGE

The spatial and/or temporal characteristics of the resource.

15. Rights Management

Label: RIGHTS

A link to a copyright notice, a rights-management statement, or a service that would provide information about terms of access to the resource.

RESOURCE DISCOVERY WORKSHOPS

A series of resource discovery workshops were organised by the UK Office for Library and Information Networking and the Arts and Humanities Data Service, to concentrate on the application of these 15 elements to moving image resources. A subsequent report concluded that the Dublin Core model is generally adequate to describe such resources.

APPLICATION OF THE 15 ELEMENTS

The next pages discuss the 15 elements as applied to moving image resources

1. TITLE

The name given to the resource by the Creator or Publisher.

Multiple Titles

Films may have multiple titles. The usual convention would be to use the title of the main country of release. There may be alternative titles (*e.g.* a different title used for release in the USA or UK: *The Madness of George III, The Madness of King George*). Remakes of films may have the same title as the original, or different subtitles, *e.g. Bladerunner – The Director's Cut.*

Format of Main Title

Issues such as the use of definite article, *e.g.* Sleeping Beauty [The]

Series Titles

Television series can present difficulties. For example, *Hancock's Half Hour* (the title of the series) vs 'The Blood Donor' (an episode in the series). Users might expect to find 'The Blood Donor'. Similarly, in newsreels, individual stories are often titled. Some series episodes do not have individual titles (*e.g. Dallas, Coronation Street*). Television cataloguing uses part numbers and original transmission dates to identify individual episodes. Qualifiers useful to this element might be:
- main
- alternative
- series
- episode

2. AUTHOR OR CREATOR

The person(s) or organisation(s) primarily responsible for the intellectual content of the resource. For example, authors in the case of written documents, artists, photographers, or illustrators in the case of visual resources.

This label presents difficulties. If, for the present purposes, we read 'artistic' or 'creative' for 'intellectual', the problem is that there is a multiplicity of creative input into moving image media. The provision of a single name (main author entry) implies a hierarchy of artistic responsibility and authorship that would be hotly debated in film studies' circles.

Films

In films the convention is to cite the director as principal 'author'.

Television

The situation here is problematic. Users searching for television drama, for example the BBC's *Middlemarch*, might expect to find a main author entry for George Eliot rather than Anthony Page.

Filmed Stage Performances

The situation here is equally difficult. Should a record for a video of a staged performance of *The Seagull* cite Peter Hall (as director) or Chekhov (playwright)? Should a record for the ballet *The Sleeping Beauty* cite Tchaikovsky as composer, the director of this particular stage production, the choreographer or the director of the edited television version?

In the discovery workshops, there was much discussion of how this element should be used in conjunction with Element 6 – Other Contributors. Following the recommendations of the Performing Arts Data Service (PADS) Sound Resources workshop and discussion within the Arts & Humanities Data Service, Element 6 should be merged with the current element with a tagging scheme describing roles of contributors. This is discussed more fully below.

3. SUBJECT

The topic of the resource, or keywords or phrases that describe the subject or content of the resource. The intent of the specification of this element is to promote the use of controlled vocabularies and keywords. This element might include scheme-qualified classification data (for example, Library of Congress or Dewey Decimal schema) or scheme-qualified controlled vocabularies (such as Medical Subject Headings or Art and Architecture Thesaurus descriptors) as well.

General libraries would use a scheme such as the Library of Congress classification scheme here. Specialised archives, such as the National Film and Television Archive (NFTVA), do not use established subject schemes as they find them too restrictive and not adequate to cover television. There are two major concerns with the element Subject:

(i) the element is likely to become overloaded and a catch-all for subject indexing, keywords and genre classification, partially due to the inadequacy of other elements for moving image resource description;

(ii) potential overlap with other elements (specifically Element 14 – Coverage, Element 8 – Type and Element 13 – Relation).

An example of a working solution to defining Subject for film and television resources was provided by Alex Noel-Tod's University of East Anglia subject catalogue of video holdings for film and television studies. This listing is designed to answer queries related to the way film and television studies is taught at UEA. Here are some extracts from the subject listing:

- Actors and Actresses
- American Cinema: The Silent Era
- British Cinema: 1920-1949
- Comedy: American Feature Films and TV Drama
- Science Fiction and Fantasy Films and TV Drama
- Second World War in Feature Films and TV Drama
- Shakespeare in Film and TV Versions

The subject listing covers:

- Provenance (country of production)
- Genre
- Period
- Topic
- Personalities (actors and actresses)

Adaptations

With the exception of Personalities (which would be covered in the newly enlarged Contributors element) and Period (partially covered under Element 7 – Date), all the other categories are likely candidates for inclusion under subject.

Provenance – Country of production is an important search term for film and television resources. It is very awkward to use under Element 14 – Coverage, and would be better placed here.

Genre – The consensus recognised genre as an extremely important search term for moving image resources which is not adequately covered elsewhere in the element set and should be included here, even though existing schemes for genre classification are not entirely satisfactory.

Period – Specific dates (of production or release) would be included in Element 7 – Dates, but a time period as it relates to style (such as the Silent Era) would be included here. Again, this stylistic interpretation is better suited to this element than Element 14 – Coverage.

Topic – Aside from the difficulties of indexing fiction – what's the subject of *Middlemarch*, for example? – users might expect to find a title associated with the content, *e.g.* a television adaptation of a Dickens novel may cite Dickens here and the name of the work concerned. This potentially overlaps with Element 13 – Relation. This element may also be interpreted to include the topic of the drama itself, *e.g.* robbery, ethnic or sexual conflict.

Although for fictional works this multi-faceted approach to Subject is acceptable, there may be problems for documentary, for example, an interview between Peter Hall and Richard Eyre on the history of the National Theatre. The genre may be 'interview' or 'discussion' (describing the format of the show); the subject indexing might be several terms describing the content of the debate (*e.g.* architecture, finance, commissioning) while the keyword/key phrase might be National Theatre and Great Britain.

4. DESCRIPTION

A textual description of the content of the resource, including abstracts in the case of document-like objects or content descriptions in the case of visual resources ...

This would be the location for a synopsis, which could also include the interpretative subject/content information not easily dealt with in Element 3 – Subject, above. Less interpretative information to be included here might be a statement of certification as awarded by the British Board of Film Classification.

5. PUBLISHER

The entity responsible for making the resource available in its present form, such as a publisher, a university department, or a corporate entity. The intent of specifying this field is to identify the entity that provides access to the resource.

This is another case where there are multiple interpretations of the word 'publisher'. In moving image resources, there are a number of 'entities responsible for making the resource available in its present form', so the definition is particularly confusing with regard to film. For example, an archive or a distributor may provide access to a film;

providing access is different from publishing. There are production companies and broadcasting organisations, and each of these entities has a different role in the process.

A definition of Publisher for the present purposes will incorporate the various roles and as such is acceptable. Other important information here is place of release or broadcast (= publication).

6. OTHER CONTRIBUTORS

Person(s) or organisation(s) in addition to those specified in the Creator element who have made significant intellectual contributions to the resource but whose contribution is secondary to the individuals or entities specified in the Creator element (for example, editors, transcribers, illustrators, and convenors).

As mentioned above, this element will be merged with Element 2 – Author or Creator. The given description of this element does not suit moving image resources well and is obviously conceived with book resources in mind (editors, transcribers, illustrators, etc.). The concept of a contribution of secondary importance, and the hierarchy it suggests, is problematic. It can be argued (and was!) that, for example, in a film the director is the individual who is finally responsible for bringing the complex totality of a movie together. It can equally be argued that each contributor has a vital role to play: in the film of Joe Orton's play *Loot*, for example, is Orton a secondary creative contributor? Is Shakespeare secondary in the Branagh film of *Much Ado About Nothing*?

Another problem is the sheer numbers of creative personnel associated with bringing into existence a moving image resource. The NFTVA can list as many as 250 people on production credits, all of whom, it can be argued, have a significant creative input. Obviously there is a line to be drawn here with regard to high-level resource description: the Dublin Core is not meant to carry a full archive record. However, it is probably more difficult to find a suitable cut-off point for film resources than any other type of resource.

Roles

There is a recent European legal definition of the creators of a film constructed for rights management purposes, as follows:
- director
- writer of screenplay
- writer of original work (if an adaptation)
- composer of music

This definition would account for Orton and Shakespeare in the problematic examples above; the facility easily to distinguish the writer of an original from a writer of a filmed resource was also seen as vital), but still has worrying omissions for users, excluding, for example, members of the cast, cinematographer, editor.

Whatever decision is made as to the extent of coverage of this element set, it will be necessary to include a description of the role of each of the contributors to be included, for example:

Title: THE SOUND OF MUSIC
Contributors: Wise, Robert (director)
Chaplin, Saul (producer)
Lehman, Ernest (screenwriter)
Rodgers, Richard (composer)
Hammerstein, Oscar (lyricist/songwriter)
Andrews, Julie (performer)
Plummer, Christopher (performer)
Parker, Eleanor (performer)

The roles suggested here by no means represent a definitive list. Experience from the NFTVA suggests, for example, that the assignment of a 'performer' tag is not sufficient: users need often to search on the name of the role being played (for example, Julie Andrews playing Maria in the example above). This degree of detail would be impossible to represent in an implementation of the Dublin Core for moving image resources, but this example does reflect those detailed needs of film researchers.

These additional role fields are gradually becoming commonplace and the template decided upon for the Imagination/Universities Networking Moving Images project has been used effectively on current collections, such as the catalogue of the Scottish Screen Archive (the former Scottish Film and Television Archive), thus proving its viability.

7. DATE

The date the resource was made available in its present form.

This element needs some refinement. Various dates might be associated with a film: dates of production, release, distribution and copyright may all be different and may have all to be qualified and clearly indicated in the Dublin Core.

In filmed versions of stage performances, it may also be desirable to include, along with the date of the production under consideration, the date of first performance. So a date record for the production of Euripides' *Bacchae* mentioned above may be as Date: 1996 (this production); 406 BC (first performance).

8. TYPE

The category of the resource, such as home page, novel, poem, working paper, technical report, essay, dictionary. It is expected that Resource Type will be chosen from an enumerated list of types.

As noted above, there is potential for confusion between this element and Element 3 – Subject. If Element 3 deals with the slippery notion of genre, this element should describe the type of moving image resource in a less interpretative way. Not forgetting to state the obvious, the two basic categories here would be film and video (as the basic handling media for moving image resources). These could be refined to include some classifying description of the nature of a resource, according to an existing scheme, such as:

Film:
- feature
- musical
- animated
- documentary
- silent
- short
- of staged/other performance

Television broadcast:
- drama
- serial
- documentary
- of staged/other performance

Some questions arise with the classification of filmed or broadcast versions of staged theatrical, dance or musical performances. Here it would be desirable to note the type of performance being recorded (*e.g.* play, opera, dance and type of dance, ballet) which would have to go into Element 3 – Subject; information about whether, for example, the recording of the performance had been edited would probably be best placed under Element 4 – Description.

9. FORMAT

The data representation of the resource, such as text/HTML, ASCII, PostScript file, executable application, or JPEG image. The intent of specifying this element is to provide information necessary to allow people or machines to make decisions about the usability of the encoded data (what hardware and software might be required to display or execute it, for example). As with Resource Type, Format will be assigned from enumerated lists such as registered Internet Media Types. In principle, formats can include physical media such as books, serials, or other non-electronic media.

This is a non-controversial element: in the case of a digitised moving image resource, the file type, size, resolution, compression type and player information would be supplied. In the case of describing a non-digital resource, there is no difference in the principle of supplying information necessary for playback, for example:

Format:
- 35mm film, colour and sound
- 35mm film, black and white, silent
- VHS, colour and sound

A note of running time fits more naturally into this element than elsewhere (see discussion under Element 14 – Coverage) and should be included here.

10. IDENTIFIER

String or number used to uniquely identify the resource. Examples for networked resources include Uniform Resource Locators (URLs) and Uniform Resource Names (URNs) (when implemented). Other globally unique identifiers, such as International Standard Book Numbers (ISBN) or other formal names would also be candidates for this element.

This is another non-controversial element. Whichever of the various identifiers (video recording identifiers, broadcast identifiers, ISBNs) are available should be used here.

11. SOURCE

The work, either print or electronic, from which this resource is derived, if applicable. For example, an HTML encoding of a Shakespearean sonnet might identify the paper version of the sonnet from which the electronic version was transcribed.

Again, the description for this element betrays a text-based view of the world and would be applied most comfortably as an edition identifier. The description also implies the use of this element for transcription, *e.g.* transportation into another medium with only superficial changes of format, not content.

A record for a digitised version of a moving image resource would cite the non-digital version from which it was made. The closest parallel when describing non-digital resources with moving image data would be a 'transcription' of a movie or broadcast to a video format. Thus the record for a video copy of the feature film *Loot* would cite the 35mm feature film as its source (not the original play – this would be cited under Element 13 – Relation).

12. LANGUAGE

Language(s) of the intellectual content of the resource. Where practical, the content of this field should coincide with the Z39.50 three-character codes for written languages.

There may be more than two languages used in a moving image resource that is subtitled, so a tag would be a valuable addition here. Otherwise this presents no problems.

13. RELATION

Relationship to other resources. The intent of specifying this element is to provide a means to express relationships among resources that have formal relationships to others, but exist as discrete resources themselves. For example, images in a document, chapters in a book, or items in a collection. A formal specification of Relation is currently under development.

This element could be used in two ways: to handle the relation of parts to a whole, *e.g.* episodes to series, clips to the whole work as suggested in the description above or vice versa; and in a wider sense to cite original (often textual) sources.

The use of this element to describe a textual source could be particularly useful in an interdisciplinary context. An obvious example in this category would be a movel such as Michael Ondaatje's *The English Patient*; a less obvious one, which would benefit an interdisciplinary searcher, might be *Romeo and Juliet* cited in relation to *West Side Story*.

14. COVERAGE

The spatial location and temporal duration characteristic of the resource. Formal specification of Coverage is currently under development.

There was much discussion and concern about this element. The two sub-elements under the umbrella of Coverage, 'spatial location' and 'temporal duration' (both of which seem tautologous) are potentially extremely important to moving image resources: translated into moving image terms, users want to know the country of production and the running time of a resource.

However, the vocabulary used ('coverage') doesn't have an appropriate resonance for moving images, and is often used in broadcasting in quite a different context, for example in the sense of 'news or current affairs coverage'. Another interpretation of coverage for a dramatic, fictional work might suggest the location of the drama itself: for example, the city of Thebes in Euripides' *Bacchae*, or deep space for *Star Trek* – surely not the spirit of the element and not of primary importance for users.

What is important for searching moving image resources is their provenance, or country of production. Users need to search, for example, for British or Italian films. There was concern expressed that this important searching information is shoe-horned into the element. To add to these difficulties, provenance itself can be a complicated subject: for example, the NFTVA records the country that funded a movie (for example, *The English Patient* with predominantly British actors and a British director is not a British film in this sense, having been funded in the USA).

Running time (translated from 'temporal duration') is of primary importance, but doesn't fit comfortably under the element Coverage. It would be more usual to cite running time as part of Element 9 – Format. Feedback from workshop participants suggested that there seems no sensible way of using this element consistently and usefully.

15. RIGHTS MANAGEMENT

The content of this element is intended to be a link – a URL or other suitable URI (Uniform Resource Identifier) as appropriate – to a copyright notice, a rights-management statement, or perhaps a server that would provide such information in a dynamic way. The intent of specifying this field is to allow providers a means to associate terms and conditions or copyright statements with a resource or collection of resources. No assumptions should be made by users if such a field is empty or not present.

The inclusion of this element presents few problems, although, again, there will often be several agencies involved. The execution of rights management in digitised moving image resources presents vast problems which will require considerable attention in the future.

CONTRIBUTORS AND CONTACTS

The Dublin Core Element Set was obtained from the Dublin Core Website, http://purl.oclc.org/dc. The site is the major public entry point to the Dublin Core, with areas such as workshop links and documents, working group issue lists and related documents, a bibliography of Dublin Core publications, links to implementation projects, standards documents, working papers, and frequently asked questions.

Text on the application of the set to moving image resources was provided by Catherine Owen at the Performing Arts Data Service (www.pads.ahds.ac.uk), and the Editors would like to thank her for her kind assistance. The full report of the Resource Discovery Workshops can be found on the PADS Website at: www.pads.ahds.ac.uk/padsMovingImageWorkshopCollection.

COPYRIGHT CLEARANCE FOR HIGHER EDUCATION

MURRAY WESTON

This is the edited transcript of a talk given at the Networking Moving Images for University Teaching and Research meeting, described in Murray Weston's introductory article, 'Moving Images Online' (page 11).

Copyright clearance for moving pictures is something with which the British Universities Film & Video Council (BUFVC) has dealt for a great many years. The problems do not change, but the knowledge of how to circumvent problems increases daily.

One of the important facilities which BUFVC offers is the Off-Air Recording Back-Up Service (see 'About the BUFVC', page 1), which is testimony to the way in which we can operate within the framework of copyright law to lever a service which is valued by the educational community and seen to be non-threatening to the rights owners. I would like to make the case now for such a systematic approach to copyright clearance on behalf of higher education.

With any discussion of copyright, you have to start with a definition, because many people are not entirely clear about the subject.

DEFINITIONS OF COPYRIGHT

Copyright is a property right, and it applies to various creative works – literary, dramatic and musical, as well as film. It is important to recognise that copyright, like any other property, can be sold, hired or leased, so the original creator may not be the present owner.

Consider this example. Some students, not long ago, rang a famous pop group and asked to use one of band's tracks in an end-of-course video production. The group were delighted and, in fact, helped the students to incorporate the music into the production. However, both the band and the students were in breach of copyright because the band had previously sold the rights to their music, and were not in a position to give permission for its use. This is the case for many recording artists – much of the Beatles' music is owned by Michael Jackson, for instance. First of all, you have to be able to trace ownership, because rights are commonly bought and sold, and the obvious place is not always where the rights reside.

In the case of film and television, there is no central registry which actually tracks the ownership for all the material produced. In fact, we have no statutory deposit in the UK, and no unified catalogue. This means, in effect, you are on your own in accumulating knowledge of rights ownership. Any recorded moving pictures – and they are all defined as 'film' in law, whether film, video, television recordings or moving pictures from a hard disk, however artistic or trivial – carry the same rights. Thus, a broadcast television programme is protected in the same way as an amateur film, and there is really no such thing as copyright-free material.

However, rights can be waived, and in some countries there are arrangements which allow certain types of films or recordings to be in the public domain. In the USA, for instance, NASA waives rights because it regards material which is made with public expenditure as 'public domain', which is owned by the nation and may be re-used without further rights payment. Occasionally, people in Britain talk about public domain, but this is not a native term under UK law.

In Europe, legislation came into effect on 1 January 1997 with regard to the harmonisation of copyright 'term' – that is, the length of time a work is protected. (See Emanuella Giavarra's article, 'Educational use of multi-media materials: the legal framework' for more information on this and related issues.)

The legislation, which meant a major change for the UK, followed the German model. It extended the copyright term to 70 years after the death of the author, in the case of literary works, and for film, 70 years after the death of the last of four people who may have contributed to a production – the director, scenarist, the designer and the music composer. So, only 70 years after the last of those four is dead, can you use the material without fear.

Previously under UK law, term for film had been 50 years after first distribution or public performance, which is a great deal shorter than the new European term. Perhaps the worst aspect of this change was that the Directive was retrospective. In other words, you might have used a sequence made by some silent film producer of the early 1900s, legitimately edited into a television programme on 31 December 1996, transmitted it on 1 January 1997, and actually then found yourself in breach of copyright. There was no proper transitional arrangement as far as one understood it – and it was a hell on wheels. UK law is at least pragmatic, and our intellectual property laws have never been applied retrospectively.

Copyright law is quite complicated, but is made more complicated because of contract law which meshes with it, and sometimes overrides it. However, it is well worth getting a copy of the Copyright, Design and Patents Act 1988, which is actually a good read. It is important to remember that you also have to read the two previous Acts for a comprehensive account of current UK copyright law.

People sometimes talk about 'renewing' copyright. The only way to achieve this is to produce a new work out of an old one. For instance, the animated film *Snow White*, produced in 1937, was very close to becoming clear of copyright in the UK. However, the Walt Disney company always ensured that prints had to be returned after use as part of the contract of distribution. If a new version of the film were then released – perhaps recoloured, or with a new soundtrack – then the copyright term started again, because this would be regarded as a new product.

Knowledge of the Copyright, Design and Patents Act 1988 is only one part of the current UK legislation, because none of the UK Acts was retrospective. The relevant UK Acts are dated 1911, 1956 and 1988, so if you are looking at a film which was made after 1911 but before 1956, you have look to at the 1911 Act to know where you stand. There have always been transitional arrangements in the period between an Act of Parliament, receiving Royal Assent and the date of its implementation. The 1988 act was, for example, not implemented until 1 August 1989.

For comprehensive understanding, it is also now necessary to track changes in European law and their effect on UK legislation. The new EU Directive on Copyright and Related Rights may affect us in what are called copyright exceptions – in particular, the educational exceptions. (See page 75 for a fuller discussion of this Directive.]

There is so-called 'fair dealing' within the UK copyright law, which allows for permitted acts which do not infringe copyright; education has certain special permitted acts or exceptions. These could be affected greatly by some of the changes currently being proposed in European law. The good news is the process of European legislation is on-going and lengthy, and it takes some time for draft proposals to become law. The bad news is that most lobbying for change is done by rights owners rather than consumers or users, which means that the current discussions are rather one-sided.

RIGHTS CLEARANCE

Let us for a moment move on to consider the process of rights clearance. It is important to understand that different media require different approaches to achieve copyright clearances for new uses –

knowledge of text does not really help you with the clearance of rights in film. Each particular creative work is separately defined in the 1988 Copyright Act, and has a different 'term', rules and ownership.

For instance, there is copyright in a published work: the typography (that is, the actual physical layout of the type on the page in a book), is quite separate from the author's right in selecting the words on that page. Copyright in a published work only lasts for 25 years after its first publication. So when you photocopy a page, you can actually be breaching more than one right – the right in the published work, the typographical layout, and perhaps also illustrations and photographs with attendant rights, as well author's rights. (In higher education, through arrangements with the Copyright Licensing Agency to allow photocopying, there is a process which provides payment back to the copyright holders – publishers, authors and rights owners – via a licensing scheme.)

In a similar manner, a film generally represents the work of a bundle of creative contributors. There may be composers, musicians, designers, artists, actors and writers. Each will have a contract. Each contract may be slightly different in the rights assigned, and each will be likely to have moral rights either held or waived.

It can be a most complicated task to trace ownership, as each film production will have different arrangements with contributors. Most producers aim to buy out all rights – all rights for all uses in the world, the universe, in any medium yet to be invented and so on. Producers want (if not demand) these rights, as it is the only way that they feel they can take control. However, with 'big' artists they may have to yield on certain points, and these artists can retain individual rights.

EDUCATIONAL EXCEPTIONS

Educational exceptions relating to the use of moving pictures were only properly addressed in the 1988 Act. However, like all exceptions in UK intellectual property law, these are not retrospective, so only film productions released from 1989 onwards are subject to the 1988 Act.

Associated with the 1988 Act are special Statutory Instruments, which are important documents with regard to definitions applying within some of the educational exceptions. At three pounds each, these are probably the most expensive sheets of paper you can buy from The Stationery Office; they explain what an 'educational establishment' is. When these educational exceptions came in, all sorts of places claimed (probably quite rightly) to be educational establishments – public libraries, nursing training centres in hospitals and so forth – but proved not to be 'educational establishments' as defined in the Statutory Instruments. Civil engineering and construction companies with training sections could claim to be educational establishments, but they are not covered under the Statutory Instrument definition. So, the Statutory Instruments provide a very specific definition of what an 'educational establishment' is.

I should add here that, even though an exception exists, it is often necessary to enter a dialogue with those parties who represent rights owners who may be affected by the use of the exception. This is one of the reasons why BUFVC took care to obtain a formal letter of agreement with the group representing broadcasting rights owners before setting up the Off-Air Recording Back-Up Service. If you actively make use of an exception, even though it is in the Act, you may attract criticism from rights owners and possibly even legal action challenging your activities.

Indeed, our own off-air recording back-up service went to Queen's Counsel, but because we had our letter of agreement, the plaintiffs had to challenge their own representative committee of rights owners, because they had signed a Letter of Agreement with us, and so they bore the cost of the legal advice. At the highest level in media-related businesses, there are executives who will not understand educational exceptions and will be prepared to spend money challenging legitimate activities. We must avoid that situation as much as possible.

I will now work through some of the relevant sections within the 1988 Act which are exceptions likely to assist formal education.

SECTION 30: FAIR USE

Section 30 allows for fair use for criticism, review and news reporting. However, a number of these uses have caused trouble within the broadcasting industry itself, for instance with news reporting. The BBC used sequences recorded from Sky Television's live coverage of football matches (the goals, anyway) and transmitted these as part of its news programmes, without payment to Sky. The BBC held the view that sports matches were news and, on these grounds, claimed exception. This caused a rumpus because it was within the Act, but the exercising of the exception in a highly competitive field meant that other business relationships would be likely to suffer. The matter was resolved by the two parties coming to an accommodation. This is why I say, even if it is in the Act, you have to be careful.

There is also scope for use of material using the defence of 'criticism and review'. Channel 4's programme on *A Clockwork Orange* was an interesting piece of case law.

Stanley Kubrick had not allowed, since about 1974, any copies of *A Clockwork Orange* to be distributed in the UK. Anyone can go to Paris and see it in a cinema or buy a videodisc, but it had not been, nor could be, shown in the UK. Then some bright spark from an independent production company, who obviously knew something about UK law, bought a copy of the videodisc, selected and copied some eight minutes or so (at least 10% of the total running time), and put these extracts into a critical television programme without formal permission and payment.

It went to court and Channel 4 was big enough to defend its position. It maintained that its use of the material was fair, for the purposes of criticism and review. To the surprise and consternation of almost every film distributor in the UK, Channel 4 won the case. But even though that opened the door for every broadcaster in Britain to use all sorts of bits of film from all sorts of different people, this didn't happen.

So, once again, uses which are allowed within the law are also subject to underlying business relationships, which could be damaged in the long term. This is more about politics than the law.

SECTION 32: INSTRUCTION IN FILM-MAKING

Section 32, item 2, states that there is no infringement if the material is used in the course of instruction for the making of films and soundtracks, provided that the copying is done by a person giving or receiving instruction. This is a very important and useful (if not essential) exception for film schools and practical media courses.

However, it would be an infringement if, for an end-of-course production, a student had recorded a television programme off-air, re-cut it, added a new soundtrack, and then showed it to a *general audience*. If the showings took place within the course itself, between teaching staff and students, this use would be fair.

Section 32, item 3, allows copying for the purposes of examination. You can, for example, make a compilation film, using other people's work, for viewing as part of a final-year exam. Such a compilation, prepared specifically for examination, could include all manner of works. However, it would not be permitted to publish research work prepared in this way without appropriate clearances for use of the third-party materials included.

SECTION 35: OFF-AIR RECORDING

Section 35, which deals with off-air recording, was a major advance for the education community, and is the important Section for us.

The drafting of Section 35 in the 1988 Act, for the first time placed the onus of responsibility on the *broadcasters* to develop an off-air recording licence for education. I say that quite aggressively because we had waited 20 years and more for them to organise non-theatrical clearance of general television programmes for use post-transmission.

BBC Enterprises (as was) received a great deal of criticism over this. One person would ring up after the transmission of a *Horizon* programme and ask for a copy, and BBC Enterprises would reply, 'That would cost £10,000 to clear the non-theatrical rights, and we're not going to do it'. Then another person would ring up and get a similar answer – and so on. Thus, BBC Enterprises never properly developed the potential market for post-transmission sales; they did produce copies of certain programmes which might have had a market, but their selection was not good, and they generally cleared the rights on material *post hoc*, rather than ensuring post-transmission distribution for educational use (non-theatrical clearances) in all production contracts.

Paradoxically, when Section 35 came in, on 1 August 1989, BBC Enterprises discarded nearly all its sub-masters of the non-theatrical cleared material, thinking that off-air recording would wipe out the market for sales. Of course, there is still a market, even though there is an enormous amount of recording off-air for use in teaching.

Section 35 allows educational establishments to record any sort of broadcast in the UK – cable, satellite, terrestrial and radio. It does not distinguish between analogue or digital formats, or anything like that. Educational establishments can record any of these items, make copies and keep them forever in a university, college or school as long as they are used for 'the educational purposes of the establishment'. There are some grey areas around the business of off-air recording, but by and large people are pretty sensible, and I do not think that this exception has been debilitating to rights owners' interests.

The only condition within Section 35 concerns licences signed by the Secretary of State at the Department of Trade and Industry (DTI). There are two of these: one covers a transactional licence for Open University transmissions, so that users pay a fee per programme per year to retain copies, the other relates to the Educational Recording Agency (ERA) licence, which covers all other television programmes made and transmitted by Channel 4, Channel 5, ITV and BBC television channels. This costs approximately £1.20 per student, per full-time equivalent student head in UK higher education, and there is now no institution which does not pay that licence.

SECTION 70: TIME-SHIFTING

Section 70 of the Act relates to time-shifting for private and domestic use, which is important to mention here even though it does not specifically relate to education. Under Section 70, anyone can time-shift broadcasts for private and domestic use. However, technically, domestic users are not permitted to create a library of off-air recordings at home – the law simply says that you can use the recording facility for time-shifting. When the Bill was going through Parliament, one draft actually specified that users had to wipe the recordings after just three weeks. Then someone asked, 'Who's going to check that then?', so the wording was left as it stands, and lots of people do of course create libraries at home.

SECTION 75: DESIGNATED ARCHIVES

Section 75 allows for activities by 'designated archives'. This is quite useful, in allowing a designated archive to record off-air. Institutions like the Imperial War Museum, the National Film and Television Archive (NFTVA), and one or two others work under this section to record material specifically for preservation. They can make one copy, and a duplicate viewing copy, and provide access to *bona fide* researchers.

EDUCATIONAL COPYRIGHT AGREEMENTS

The real complications in the interpretation of copyright come with the merging of contract law with copyright law.

From my point of view, copyright law is relatively simple. There are certain things you can do which may be creative, and are covered by copyright: writing a letter, for example, or recording yourself playing the guitar. It is your right to control who makes copies of such items. By the same token, if you want to use existing material, you have to know if the person who made what you are trying to copy has actually given you permission to do so. This is fairly simple, really.

The problem with contracts is that copyright may be bought, sold, hired or leased – and it can also be split into pieces.

We sell a book called *Buying and Clearing Rights: Print, Broadcast and Multimedia* by Richard McCracken and Madeleine Gilbart (see page 5). They are in charge of the Open University's Rights Clearance Department, which employs some 25 people working full-time to clear rights for higher education. In this book is a picture of a slice of cake with a knife in it, representing rights which can be sliced into different layers.

For example, rights may be split up and sold by territory and/or medium of distribution – so that, for a film, someone might take the non-theatrical rights (that is, the right to show it to non-fee-paying audiences such as students in university classes), someone else will take the rights for home video, and another will go off with the rights for broadcast sales. These contracts may only apply in the UK, so that there are a similar set of rights in Holland, where someone else again may hold exclusive rights for so many years. Should someone come along with a new digital medium, and want to start using that, those who own the exclusive rights on the original products can then object.

So it is not always the original copyright owner who is objecting. It is those business relationships down the line which are going to cause the trouble. There may be exclusive arrangements and agreements, which you cannot get around. If the man at Warner Brothers says 'no', that's *it*. If someone in the UK has all the rights to a film and does not want to exploit them, you cannot get that film, and *that's* it.

So there is always a history to ownership, as demonstrated by the 1911, 1956 and 1988 Acts. You have to know all that legislation, and you have to know all of the business relationships which went on down the line. Where did the non-theatrical rights to *Battleship Potemkin* go? How did Hendring Associates get hold of the home video rights?

Although this is the type of information you have to know, very often it is not written down. That is why there is a sort of black art in rights clearance, and film researchers have created a profession of knowing where the information is. Experienced researchers really know their stuff and serve the industry and academia as well. We really must take a leaf out of these professionals' books.

What would happen if institutions all tried to negotiate their own route through this particular jungle? Imagine that they all have their video servers, they all want to start delivering films, and they all plan to negotiate access to use this material. What would happen? The owners would start to set up an auction, in effect – and I do not think this would be good for higher education in terms of cost or control.

Negotiating rights clearance has to be much more focused. We have to bring the knowledge and history of what has gone before to bear on these new discussions. Some of this knowledge lies with the British Film Institute (BFI) for feature film distribution, some with the BUFVC for the non-theatrical rights, some in other places for specialist material.

CLEARING RIGHTS IN HIGHER EDUCATION

A lot of higher education organisations will be pushing for rights to access and use the same moving image material. Without focused discussions, the costs of clearance will definitely go up – there is no doubt about that. We need to keep the whole higher education structure together if we can. What I am suggesting will be difficult. I know higher education is anarchic and practically ungovernable.

At another presentation I gave, someone from a university said, 'We have our own archive, we can use that'; I replied, 'You may own a little bit of the material in your archive, but it will not be very much'. Very few archives actually own the underlying rights for much of the material they store – perhaps 5% of their holdings, with the rest deposited on trust.

We are lucky in higher education as we have a defined user group, which will be helpful in negotiations with rights owners. The group is already defined by Statutory Instruments for the exceptions in the Copyright, Design and Patents Act. We must use this to our advantage.

However, I regularly receive telephone calls from people in higher education desperate for advice on what they can and cannot copy or use under the current legislation – especially Section 35. Teachers do not know the exceptions, nor how to work within them, even ten years after the implementation of the last Act. I am suggesting that we should develop a focused and co-ordinated approach to rights clearance and training which would also inform people properly about permitted acts and exceptions.

In negotiating new agreements, it is also helpful to know about past agreements, both formal and informal. For example, the Inter-University History Film Consortium (IUHFC) has had an arrangement with Reuters Television and Visnews dating back to 1968, which must be taken into account in any future discussions.

THE WAY FORWARD

I believe the higher education sector needs a focused strategy and a group of experienced individuals to work on this area with regard to moving images. Such a group would initially need to meet *in camera*, for commercial reasons, and would need money to support this work.

So the way forward is to establish a strategic plan. This is critical. We are proposing to walk through a minefield: there is a path, but we need to bring together all those who have walked this path before, or we will not succeed.

We have to consider the views of the rights owners. We have to show ourselves to be non-threatening to their interests and their income; negotiations via third parties should be avoided. There is no doubt that the rights owners will obtain some income from this, if not in the early days of setting up the service, then later as this service develops.

We need to establish an acceptable authorisation system, to provide some sort of audit trail, to identify users and levels of use in UK higher education (and also further education, if further education is to be included). The dream ticket would be a smart card which users could swipe at a workstation. Students would have one card with codes which would allow a certain amount of access to a certain number of services for specified period of time. Staff would have another which might allow them to receive more content of greater value.

The ERA licence scheme requires licence-holders to provide an account of all the material recorded off-air by staff in their institutions. In a university, it is very difficult to account for every recording made off-air during a year, as the 1988 Act allows staff independently to record television programmes off-air at home and use those tapes in teaching and research. However, the ERA obtains a reasonably good estimate from its licensees and makes a return to rights owners based on that estimate. This is what we must be prepared to do for rights owners in the world of online delivery.

For immediate gains, we need to target those collections which will be of value to higher education, and which may be cleared without major difficulty. Some collections will be less difficult to clear than others: if we start by clearing rights on a critical mass of easily cleared material, and demonstrate that this work is non-threatening, I think we could then segue into clearing more difficult collections. By then, we will be able to prove that our activities will not be threatening but may also promote the interests of owners.

We have to draw on the past arrangements and agreements to move forward. Copyright and rights clearance contracts have a history, and we have to accommodate that and existing distribution arrangements when developing other methods of distribution.

We must also get involved with the discussions concerning new UK legislation and the developing European legislation. The educational community is pretty hopeless at lobbying in this arena – Walt Disney has an office in Brussels, but our interests do not. An American-based business is influencing European law-makers on behalf of producers, but there is no effective representation of end-users. We need to put one together; maybe JISC is a body which could encourage this.

We have to protect the interests of rights owners: we are not on 'the other side', because we are also creating rights as well. If universities are not creating intellectual property rights (IPRs), what are they doing? Universities are storehouses of intellect, knowledge and writing. We now have intellectual property rights officers in most universities who are generally responsible for protecting and exploiting the products from academic departments. Unfortunately, these rights officers rarely examine what is being done in their institution with third party works. They really ought to take an interest in this area, because proof of what is being used is actually useful in negotiations to lever more material at an equitable price.

Basically, we have to self-regulate. We have to implement appropriate authorisation systems – a modified home-grown system like Athens might be appropriate. We have to address the issue of charging and auditing as soon as possible; otherwise, we will be living on borrowed time, as we did for a year during the pilot described in 'Moving Images Online' (page 11). For a potential user group of 10,000 it may not be worth implementing a charging structure, as this not going to bring in much income and might cost too much to run. However, we could at least demonstrate a charging system to rights owners. Perhaps the whole question of access to collections is an issue of top-sliced funding.

LOOKING AHEAD

Some significant collections of moving pictures really ought to be fully owned by higher education. This sounds like a radical move but some libraries have been sold recently for relatively little money. These are commercial entities which are scholarly assets, and I do not see any reason why universities should not actually own some of them.

Take, for example, the British Pathé library, which last sold for about four million pounds. Now that it is a going commercial concern, with shareholders looking for profits. Four million pounds is not a lot of money if we think of the scholarly interest, in 100 years' time, in the 200,000 filmed stories issued by this company in British cinemas. Might it not be a good business plan actually to own resources like this within the higher education community, and to use the money generated from sales to television broadcasters to keep them going, and thus offer free use to universities? This seems like a potential win/win situation. If not yet, I think we ought to be looking at bidding for ownership of collections at some point, because this is not an inappropriate policy.

There is a way to deliver significant moving picture content online, but it is going to require strategy, knowledge and stealth. We need money – certainly not a published amount – available to us. There also needs to be careful co-ordination. We have to work within a structure which serves the interests of higher education.

That is not to say that people should not do their own thing on their own servers and build up completely different collections of material, but we have to establish a clearly defined reporting system which really allows us to clear rights for the purposes of national online network delivery of moving images.

EDUCATIONAL USE OF MULTIMEDIA MATERIALS: THE LEGAL FRAMEWORK

EMANUELLA GIAVARRA, LLM

This report, 'Educational use of multimedia materials: An examination of the legal framework', was prepared for the Joint Information Systems Committee (JISC) Multimedia Rights Working Group. The second draft, reproduced here with the generous permission of JISC, was released at the end of August 2000. This version has been updated to reflect the subsequent adoption of the EU Directive on Copyright and Related Rights by the EU Council of Ministers on 9th April 2001.

INTRODUCTION

Multimedia is the term given to the use of digital technology to facilitate the storage and use of information in a variety of forms for flexible individual access. It is the bringing together of still and moving pictures, graphics and animation, text, music and other audio and computer data, in one delivery system. Every day examples of multimedia products are CD-ROMs, computer games and services provided via the Internet.

The most difficult issue in multimedia is the enormous complexity and quantity of rights which simultaneously exist in multimedia products. These rights are mostly concerned with copyright, moral rights and rights in performances. An example of the number of rights that can exist in a song which has been recorded as a sound recording. These include, for instance:

- musical copyright
- literary copyright
- copyright in the sound recording
- performance rights
- composer's moral rights
- the lyricist's moral rights

The main concern for HE and FE institutions is the need to digitise multimedia works in their collections and to make them available to authorised users through networks. In addition, there is the need to use commercially produced multimedia products for educational purposes.

Some of these uses will be allowed by the permitted acts under copyright or related laws, but for others, clearance need to be sought. The clearance for the use of commercially produced multimedia products will usually be less difficult, as most of the allowed uses will be set out in the licensing terms that were agreed when the product was bought. Generally, the difficulties start when the licence does not seems to reflect the educational use allowed by statute, or when the FE and HE institutions wish to use the materials in ways outside the scope of the existing licence.

The JISC Multimedia Rights Working Group aims to start a dialogue with rightholders of multimedia products concerning digitisation and the use of born digital products, and to try and work towards the development of one or more standard contracts for the digitisation and usage of such multimedia products.

To this end, this report provides an overview of existing rights granted by UK copyright and related laws to owners of works in multimedia products, a list of uses permitted for educational purposes under UK copyright and related laws, and an analysis of the impact that recent international and European developments will have on UK copyright and related laws.

The focus in this report will be on multimedia aspects of copyright, moral rights, rights in performances, and the clearance of these rights.

COPYRIGHT

THE SUBJECT MATTER OF UK COPYRIGHT LAW

According to section 1(1) of the Copyright, Design and Patents Act 1988 (CDPA 1988) copyright may subsists in a variety of works. These works are:

(a)   original literary, dramatic, musical or artistic works;

(b)   sound recordings, films, broadcasts or cable programmes; and

(c)   the typographical arrangement of published editions.

For copyright to apply, these works must be recorded in writing or otherwise. 'Writing' is defined in section 178 CDPA 1988 (see page 41 note 2) as any form of notation or code. After the work has been recorded in writing or otherwise, copyright subsists immediately. Under UK law, no further notice or bureaucratic formality is required in order to obtain copyright protection.

ORIGINAL LITERARY, DRAMATIC, MUSICAL AND ARTISTIC WORKS

To acquire protection, literary, dramatic, musical and artistic works must be 'original'. Basically, an author needs to show that he has expended his own skills and effort in order to justify protection. Problems with originality are likely to arise where a work in question is a compilation or a directory. Whilst copyright clearly extends to tables and compilations, they must still be sufficiently original to merit protection. The use of parts of another work may also require the copyright owner's permission, despite the fact that the new work merits copyright protection of its own.

Literary works

Section 3(1) CDPA 1988 provides that 'literary work' means any work other than a dramatic or musical work, which is written, spoken or sung, and includes a table or compilation and a computer program. Case-law has established categories of information which may be protectable as literary works, such as examination papers, television programme listings, letters and business letters, directories and trade catalogues. On the other hand, case-law has also refused protection to certain categories of works, such as names, slogans and titles of books and magazines.

Whilst information (news) itself is not subject to copyright, the actual expressions used to report the information are protected as literary or other copyright works.

Dramatic works

Section 3 (1) CDPA 1988 defines a 'dramatic work' as including a work of dance or mime. A work cannot qualify as both a literary work and a dramatic work, although a dramatic work which contains musical elements may be protected under both dramatic and musical categories. A dramatic work is one which is capable of being performed, for example, by acting or dancing. A dramatic work is distinct from the literary elements of the work, which have their own protection.

Musical works

Section 3(1) CDPA 1988 defines 'musical work' as a work consisting of music, exclusive of any words or action intended to be sung, spoken or performed with the music. The copyright for the music of a song is distinct from the literary copyright in the lyric and, indeed, any dramatic copyright if the music is accompanied by a dance or other type of performance. Copyright in a musical work is in the composition itself. Quite separate rights arise in respect of any sound recording or broadcast of a musical work. There are separate copyrights, perhaps also in separate ownership, for music, lyrics and recording.

Artistic works

According to section 4(1) CDPA 1988, a graphic work, photograph, sculpture or collage, irrespective of artistic quality qualifies as an artistic work. A 'graphic work' includes, among others, a painting, drawing, diagram, map, chart or plan.

SOUND RECORDINGS, FILMS, BROADCASTS AND CABLE PROGRAMMES

Sound recordings and films are, in most cases, 'derivative works', *i.e.* they are based on other copyright works. Broadcasts and cable transmissions are often derivative works as they either consist entirely of previous recorded films or sound recordings, or they are live transmissions of copyright works.

The distinction between derivative works and the underlying rights is very important. The 'underlying rights' include all other rights in works which have their own copyright protection. These copyrights are then included in the derivative work which in turn has its own copyright. In addition to copyrights, there are other categories of rights, such as performers' rights and moral rights which must be considered before an existing work is used in a derivative work.

Sound recording

A sound recording is defined in section 5(1) as:

(a)   a recording of sounds, from which the sound may be reproduced; or

(b)   a recording of the whole or of any part of a literary, dramatic or musical work, from which sounds reproducing the work or part may be produced.

This is regardless of the media in which the recording is made or the method by which the sound are reproduced or produced. Copyright does not subsist in a sound recording which is a copy taken from a previous sound recording.

Films

A film is defined in section 5(1) CDPA 1988 as a recording on any medium from which a moving image may by any means be produced.

This clearly covers video recordings and has been considered wide enough to embrace new technology such as CD-ROM, interactive media and the visual aspects of computer games. Single frames of a film are protected as a part of the film and not as photographs.

Copyright does not subsist in a film which is a copy taken from a previous film.

Broadcasts

A broadcast is defined in section 6(1) CDPA 1988 as a transmission by wireless telegraphy of visual images, sounds or other information which:

a)   is capable of being lawfully received by members of the public; or

b)   is transmitted for presentation to members of the public

Copyright will not subsist in a broadcast which infringes the copyright in another broadcast or cable programme.

Cable programme

A cable programme is defined in section 7 CDPA 1988 as any item included in a cable programme service. Cable programme service is defined as a service consisting wholly or mainly in sending visual images, sound or other information by means of a telecommunication system.

Copyright does not subsist in a cable programme if it is included in a cable programme service by reception and immediate re-transmission of a broadcast or if it infringes the copyright in another cable programme or in a broadcast.

PUBLISHED EDITIONS

Copyright also subsists in the typographical arrangement of published editions. A published edition is defined in section 8 CDPA 1988 as: 'the whole or any part of one or more literary, dramatic or musical works'. These provisions are aimed at giving the publisher of a work some protection in the typesetting and formatting and arrangement of the published work.

Copyright does not subsist in the typographical arrangement of a published edition if it reproduces the typographical arrangement of a previous edition.

AUTHORSHIP AND OWNERSHIP OF COPYRIGHT

Authorship and ownership are distinct concepts in copyright. The author of a work is the person who creates it. The author of a work is the first owner of any copyright in it.

ORIGINAL LITERARY, DRAMATIC, MUSICAL AND ARTISTIC WORKS

It is usually obvious who the author is of original works. For example, the author of a piece of music is the person who composed it. Problems often arise where no share of income from the work is received by an individual who claims to be a joint author of the work. This can occur among members of a pop group, for example when, one member is the songwriter, but each member contributes to the development and sound of a song.

SOUND RECORDINGS, FILMS, BROADCASTS AND CABLE PROGRAMMES

The author of a sound recording is the producer. The authors of a film are the producer and the principal director (work of joint ownership). The producer is defined in section 178 CDPA 1988 as the person who makes the arrangements necessary for the creation of the work.

The person making the broadcast, invariably a company, is the author of the broadcast. In the case of a broadcast which is received and re-transmitted from another broadcast, the person who made the first broadcast is the person who transmits.

In the case of cable programmes, the person providing the cable programme service in which the programme is included is the author.

PUBLISHED EDITIONS

The author of the typographical arrangement of a published edition of whole or part of the work is the publisher.

COPYRIGHT INFRINGEMENTS AND PERMITTED ACTS

In the case of multimedia it is important to establish exactly what rights a copyright owner has, how those rights are infringed, and equally what defences are available to HE and FE institutions if faced with claims of infringement.

EXCLUSIVE RIGHTS AND RESTRICTED ACTS

Under the CDPA 1988 the rights owner has the following exclusive rights:

- the right to copy the work;
- the right to issue copies to the public;
- the right to rent or lend the work to the public
- the right to perform, show or play the work in public;
- the right to broadcast the work or include it in a cable programme
- the right to make adaptations to the work.

Copyright will be infringed where any of these acts are done without the permission of the copyright owner, either contractual or provided by law. An infringement of copyright can take place not only where the whole of a work has been copied, but also where something less than the whole but none the less 'substantial' has been copied.

An interesting issue is the legal position of sampling. Sampling involves taking the whole or part of a sound recording. It may be a snatch of melody or a drum beat or sound. If the sample is taken of the whole or a substantial part of the copyright work, it may infringe that copyright, even though it has its own copyright protecting. Samplers must take care not to take identifiable pieces of copyright material. Any sound recording which uses identifiable elements of other musical works or sound recordings may infringe copyright.

An accumulation of insubstantial taking may constitute a substantial part. A computer database is an example. Reg 16(2) of the Copyright and Rights in Databases Regulation 1997 specifically states that the repeated and systematic extraction or re-utilisation of insubstantial parts of a database may amount to the extraction or reutilisation of a substantial part.

The reduction in the size of a photograph to a small scale copy was held to be an infringement of copyright in Antiquesportefolio.com plc v Rodney Fitch & Co Ltd 2000/LTL 10th July 2000. The claimant had used photographs of antiques contained in a well known antiques encyclopaedia in producing a Website. Small scale copies of those photographs were used to form icons and banners.

THE RIGHT TO COPY THE WORK

Section 17 CDPA 1988 deals with the concept of copying and generally states that copying is a restricted act for all categories of copyright works. According to section 17(6) CDPA 1988, copying includes the making of copies that are transient or are incidental to some other use of the work. This applies to all copyright works as well.

Literary, dramatic, musical or artistic works

Section 17(2) CDPA 1988 provides that copying is a restricted act in relation to any literary, dramatic, musical or artistic work means reproducing the work in any material form. This includes transient and incidental copies and storing the copy in or on any medium by electronic means. Under section 178 CDPA 1988, 'electronic' means actuated by electronic, magnetic, electro magnetic, electro-chemical or electro-mechanical energy.

In the case of an artistic work, copying includes the making of a copy in three-dimensions of a two-dimensional work and the making of a copy in two-dimensions of a three-dimensional work.

Films, television broadcasts and cable programmes

Section 17(4) CDPA 1988 establishes that copying of the work as a whole or any substantial part of it infringes copyright. This also includes making a photograph of the whole or any substantial part of any image forming part of the film, broadcast or cable programme. In Spelling-Goldberg Productions Inc v B.P.C. Publishing Ltd [1981] RPC 280, the producers of 'Starsky and Hutch' were able to prevent the defendants from publishing a single frame from an episode as it infringed their copyright.

Typographical arrangements

Copying in relation to a typographical arrangement of a published work simply means making a facsimile copy of the arrangement. Section 178 CDPA 1988 offers some assistance with the meaning of 'facsimile copy', stating that it includes a copy which is reduced or enlarged in scale. It is often assumed that the word facsimile means an exact copy or duplicate of something, especially in relation to printed material and copies transmitted using 'fax' machines. According to section 17(5) by sending a fax the copyright in the typographical arrangement of the published material may be infringed, but also the copyright in a drawing that was included in the text that was faxed.

THE RIGHT TO ISSUE COPIES OF THE WORK TO THE PUBLIC

The main thrust of this restricted act is that the copyright owner can take action against anyone who issues a copy of his work to the public for the first time without his consent. Thus, a person who has put his goods into circulation anywhere in the European Economic Area cannot prevent someone, who lawfully requires the works, from reselling them or importing them into another country for resale (section 18(2) CDPA 1988). This act applies to each and every copy of the work plus the original (section 18(4) CDPA 1988). The EU Directive on Copyright and Related Rights has defined this right as the Distribution Right. The Distribution Right is a very complex right. This right only deals with the distribution of physical copies. The distribution of electronic information using networks is regulated by the proposed new Communication to the Public Right (see pages 71 to 82).

THE RIGHT TO PERFORM, SHOW OR PLAY A WORK IN PUBLIC

The performance of a work in public is an act restricted by the copyright in literary, dramatic and musical works only. Section 19(2) CDPA 1988 expands upon the meaning of performance and states that it includes delivery of lectures, addresses, speeches and sermons and, in line with modern technology, it includes in general any mode of visual or acoustic presentation, including by means of a sound recording, film, broadcast or cable programme.

Under section 19(3) CDPA 1988, playing or showing a sound recording, film, broadcast or cable programme in public is an act restricted by the copyright in the work. An important element is that the performance, showing or playing must be in 'public', a word that has been responsible for a lot of case law. From present case law, the conclusion can be drawn that for a performance not to be a public performance, it must be performed for a private individual, a closed group or an audience of a domestic nature.

THE RIGHT TO BROADCAST OR INCLUDE IT IN A CABLE PROGRAMME SERVICE

Under section 20 CDPA 1988, the broadcasting of a work or its inclusion in a cable programme service is an act restricted by the copyright in all categories of work except for the typographical arrangements of published editions. The definition of broadcasts in section 6 and 'cable programme' in section 7 CDPA 1988 are of vital importance because, if the activity concerned falls outside the definitions, such as a cable programme service run as an interactive service then there is no infringement of copyright. However, there may be other restricted acts involved in the activity such as the making of copies, including incidental or transient copies. In Shetland Times Limited v. Dr. Jonathan Wills [1997] FSR 604, operating a Website on the Internet was held to be operating a cable programme service. The defendant had included headlines from the plaintiff's Website in articles published on the Internet. According to Lord Hamilton, the headlines fell within the meaning of a cable programme, being any item included in a cable programme service.

THE RIGHT TO MAKE AN ADAPTATION TO THE WORK

In terms of the CDPA 1988, the word adaptation has some very special meaning. Making an adaptation does not simply mean the same as modifying the work. The restricted act of making an adaptation applies only to literary, dramatic and musical works. An adaptation is made when it is recorded in writing or otherwise (section 21). 'Writing' is defined in section 178 CDPA 1988 as including any form of notation or code, whether by hand or otherwise, regardless of the method by which, or medium in or on which it is recorded. 'Adaptation is defined in section 21(3) CDPA 1988 and means:

(a)   In relation to an literary work (other than computer program or a database) and dramatic work:

   (i)   a translation of the work

   (ii) a version of a dramatic work in which it is converted into a non-dramatic work and vice versa

   (iii) a version of the work in which the story or action is conveyed wholly or mainly by means of pictures in a form suitable for reproduction;

(ab) In relation to a computer program, means an arrangement or altered version of the program or a translation of it.

(ac) In relation to a database, means an arrangement or altered version of the database or a translation of it.

(b)   In relation to a musical work, an arrangement or transcription of it.

The word 'translation' takes a special meaning in relation to computer programs, under section 21 (4) CDPA 1988:

> *... a 'translation' includes a version of the program in which it is converted into or out of a computer language or code or into a different language or code, otherwise than incidentally in the course of running the program.*

PERMITTED ACTS RELEVANT TO HE AND FE INSTITUTIONS

The CDPA 1988 contains some express defences to copyright infringement, known better as the 'permitted acts' which have particular importance for HE and FE institutions. The justification for the 'permitted acts is to provide a fair balance between the rights of the copyright owner and the rights of society at large.

Generally, the permitted acts excuse activities which, although technically infringing the copyright in a work, do not unduly interfere with the copyright owner's commercial exploitation of the work.

The notion of permitting some use of a copyright work which is considered to be 'fair' is common in many jurisdictions. In the UK, fair dealing is allowed in relation to a copyright work. Fair dealing covers research or private study, criticism, review and reporting current events. Education is treated as a special case by copyright law, and there are several exceptions to infringement contained in the Act. In the two tables below, all exceptions under the CDPA 1988 that are relevant to the digitisation, use and creation of multimedia works have been grouped under their relevant headers, *e.g.*

- Permitted acts [Type of work] *Comments*

LITERARY, DRAMATIC, MUSICAL OR ARTISTIC WORKS

FAIR DEALING ETC.

- Research and private study: section 29 [Literary, dramatic, musical or artistic works, typographical arrangement] *Comments: Decompilation of a computer programs is not fair dealing but provided for under section 50B. For databases, the source must be indicated.*

- Criticism or review: section 30(1) [Any work or performance] *Comments: Must be accompanied by a sufficient acknowledgement*

- Reporting current events: section 30(2) [Any work other than a photograph] *Comments: Must be accompanied by a sufficient acknowledgement*

- Incidental inclusion in an artistic work, sound recording, film, broadcast or cable programme: section 31(1) [Any work] *Comments: Must be accompanied by a sufficient acknowledgement except in the case of a sound recording, film, broadcast or cable programme*

- Issuing to the public of copies, or the playing, showing, broadcasting or inclusion in a cable programme service: section 31(2) [Anything, the making of which was not an infringement by virtue of section 31(1)] *Comments: Musical works, words spoken or sung with music must not be deliberately included*

EDUCATION

- Copying in the course of instruction or preparation for instruction: section 32(1) [Literary, dramatic, musical or artistic works] *Comments: Must be done by person giving or receiving instruction and not copied by means of a reprographic process*

- Anything done for the purpose of examination: section 32(3) [Any work] *Comments: Making a reprographic copy of a musical work for the use by an examination candidate in performing the work is not permitted section 32(4)*

- Inclusion of a short passage in a collection intended for use in educational establishments: section 33 [Published literary or dramatic works] *Comments: Must be accompanied by a sufficient acknowledgement, see for further restrictions section 33*

- Performances before an audience of teachers at an educational establishment and pupils and other persons directly connected with the activities of the establishment: section 34 (1) [Literary, dramatic or musical works (such performance is not considered to be a public performance] *Comments: Performance must be by a teacher or a pupil*

- Reprographic copying of passages not exceeding 1% of a work in any quarter by and on behalf of an educational establishment for the purpose of instruction: section 36 [Published literary, dramatic or musical works including typographical arrangement] *Comments: Does not apply if or to the extent that licences are available*

LIBRARIES AND ARCHIVES

- Librarian may make and supply: a copy of an article in a periodical section 38 [Literary work (text) and accompanying artistic works (illustrations), including typographical arrangements] *Comments: See for quantify restrictions section 38 + section 40*

- Librarian may make and supply: a copy of part of a published edition: section 39 [Literary, dramatic or musical works including the typographical arrangement of such work] *Comments: See for quantify restrictions section 39 + section 40*

- Librarian may supply to an other library a copy of an article in a periodical: section 41 [An article in a periodical or literary, dramatic or musical works, including the typographical arrangement of such works] *Comments: see section 41 for conditions*

- Librarian may supply to an other library the whole or part of a published edition: section 41 [An article in a periodical or literary, dramatic or musical works, including the typographical arrangement of such works] *Comments: see section 41 for conditions*

- Librarian and archivist may make a copy from any item in the permanent collection of that library or archive: (a) in order to preserve and replace the item; (b) to replace a lost, destroyed or missing item of another library or archive: section 42 [An article in a periodical or literary, dramatic or musical works plus accompanying illustrations (artistic works) and include the typographical arrangement] *Comments: restriction to cases when it is not reasonably practical to purchase a copy of the item to fulfil the purpose*

- Librarian and archivist may make and supply a copy of the whole or part of a work from an unpublished document, provided that the copyright owner has not prohibited copying to the knowledge of the person making the copy: section 43 [Literary, dramatic or musical works] *Comments: See for conditions section 43*

- Making a copy of an article of cultural or historic importance or interest which cannot be exported from the UK unless a copy is made and deposited in a library or archive: section 44 [Any work]

PUBLIC ADMINISTRATION SECTION 45 – SECTION 50

COMPUTER PROGRAMS

- Making back-up copy necessary for lawful use: section 50A [Computer program] *Comments: Must be by a lawful user. A lawful user is a person having a right to use the program (whether under a licence or otherwise)*

- Decompiling a computer program by a lawful user: section 50B [Computer program] *Comments: See for conditions section 50B*

- Copying or adapting by a lawful user: section 50C [Computer program] *Comments: This can be restricted or prohibited by a term in a licence agreement*

DATABASES

- Doing anything necessary for the purposes of access to and use of the content of a database or part of a database by a person having a right to use the database: section 50 D [Databases] *Comments: Any term or condition purporting to prohibit or restrict this is void*

DESIGNS SECTION 51 – SECTION 53

TYPEFACES SECTION 54 – SECTION 55

WORKS IN ELECTRONIC FORM

- Transferee of a work in electronic form may do anything purchaser was allowed to do section 56 [Any work in electronic form] *Comments: See for conditions section 56*

MISCELLANEOUS

- Acts done in relation to anonymous or pseudonymous where it is not possible to trace the author and it is reasonable to assume that copyright no longer subsists in the work section 57 [Literary, dramatic, musical or artistic works] *Comments: Note: effects of longer duration of copyright*

- Use of a record of spoken words or material from it section 57 [Literary work]

- Public reading or recitation and the making of a sound recording, broadcast or including in a cable programme of such a reading or recitation section 59 [Published literary or dramatic work] *Comments: Accompanied by a sufficient acknowledgement*

- Copy abstracts of scientific or technical subjects published in periodicals or issue copies to the public section 60 [Literary works (abstracts are almost certain in many cases literary works themselves)] *Comments: Does not apply if a licensing scheme is in place section 143*

ADAPTATION

- Any acts in Chapter III are also allowed in respect of an adaptation: section 76 [Literary works, dramatic or musical works] *Comments: Does not infringe copyright in the work from which the adaptation was made*

SOUND RECORDINGS, FILMS, BROADCASTS OR CABLE PROGRAMMES

FAIR DEALING, ETC

- Criticism or review: section 30(1) [Any work or performance] *Comments: Must be accompanied by a sufficient acknowledgement*

- Reporting current events: section 30(2) [Any work]

- Incidental inclusion in an artistic work, sound recording, film, broadcast or cable programme: section 31(1) [Any work] *Comments: Must be accompanied by a sufficient acknowledgement except in the case of a sound recording, film, broadcast or cable programme*

- Issuing to the public of copies, or the playing, showing, broadcasting or inclusion in a cable programme service: section 31(2) [Anything, the making of which was not an infringement by virtue of section 31(1)] *Comments: Musical works, words spoken or sung with music must not be deliberately included*

EDUCATION

- Copying by making a film or a film sound track in the course of, or in preparation for, instruction in the making of films or film soundtracks: section 32(2) [Sound recording, film, broadcast or cable programme] *Comments: Must be done by a person giving or receiving instruction*

- Anything done for the purpose of examination: section 32(3) [Any work] *Comments: Making a reprographic copy of a musical work for the use by an examination candidate in performing the work is not permitted section 32(4)*

- Playing and showing before an audience of teachers at an educational establishment and pupils and other persons directly connected with the activities of the establishments for purpose of instruction: section 34(2) [Sound recording, film, broadcast or cable programme]

- Making a recording by or on behalf of an educational establishment or making a copy of such a recording for educational purposes of that establishment: section 35 [Broadcast or cable programme and any included work] *Comments: Does not apply if or to the extent that there is a certified licensing scheme under section 143; ERA Licence Scheme is in force*

LIBRARIES AND ARCHIVES

- Making a copy of an article of cultural or historic importance or interest which cannot be exported from the UK unless a copy is made and deposited in an library or archive: section 44 [Any work]

PUBLIC ADMINISTRATION SECTION 45 – SECTION 50

WORKS IN ELECTRONIC FORM

- Transferee of a work in electronic form may do anything purchaser was allowed to do: section 56 [Any work in electronic form] *Comments: see for conditions section 56*

MISCELLANEOUS

- Acts done in relation to films where it is not possible to ascertain the identity of the persons in section 13B(2) and to assume that copyright no longer subsists in the work: s 66A [Films]

- Incidental recording for the purpose of broadcasting or inclusion in a cable programme service: (a) making a sound recording or film or an adaptation; (b) taking a photograph or making a film; (c) making a copy: section 68 [Sound recording or film]

Comments: Applies where person is authorised to broadcast or include a work in a cable programme by virtue of a licence. The recording, film, photograph shall be destroyed within 28 days of first being used

- Time shifting broadcasts and cable programmes to view or listen to at a more convenient time: section 70 [Broadcasts, cable programmes and included works] *Comments: Only for private and domestic use*

- Making a photograph of the whole or any part of an image forming part of television broadcast or cable programme or making a copy of such a photograph: section 71 [Broadcasts, cable programmes and included works] *Comments: Only for private and domestic use*

- Showing or playing in public to a non-paying audience: section 72 [Broadcasts, cable programmes and included sound recordings and films]

- Making copies of television broadcasts and cable programmes, issuing copies to public for purpose of providing people who are deaf, hard hearing, physically or mentally handicapped in other ways with copies subtitled or modified for their special needs: section 74 [Broadcasts, cable programmes and included works] *Comments: Not allowed if there is a licensing scheme in place under section 143*

- Recording and making a copy of such recording for placing in an archive: section 75 [Broadcasts, cable programmes and included works] *Comments: Only for designated archives and designated classes*

STATUTORY LICENSING

- Including in a broadcast or a cable programme service a sound recording section 135 [Sound recordings] *Comments: Subject to conditions in sections 135A-C*

DURATION OF COPYRIGHT

Recently, the duration of copyright has been extended by the Duration of Copyright and Rights in Performances Regulation 1995, which came into force on 1 January 1996. The rules for determining the duration of copyright depend on the nature of the work in question, but as a basic rule of thumb, copyright lasts for the life of the author plus 70 years for literary, dramatic, musical and artistic works and film, 50 years for sound recordings, broadcasts and cable programmes, and 25 years for typographical arrangements of published editions. The recent changes to the duration of copyright in 'original works' and films have a number of implications, especially in terms extending the duration of existing copyright and reviving copyright in some works which had fallen into the public domain. This will especially effect the works of authors who died between 1925 and 1945. The ownership of extended and revived copyright is far from straightforward. The specific provisions can be found in section 12 to 15 CDPA 1988 and the 1995 Regulations).

MORAL RIGHTS

Moral rights were introduced into UK law by the CDPA 1988. Moral rights exist alongside the copyright in certain works. Moral rights , generally, remain with the author of a work or pass to the author's estate after death. Unlike copyright, moral rights cannot be assigned, although they are frequently waived. Moral rights apply to joint authors as well as to the whole or part of a work. The duration of moral rights is provided for in a fairly straightforward way in section 86 CDPA 1988. In all cases except the false attribution right, moral rights endure as long as copyright subsists in the work in question.

THE SUBJECT MATTER OF UK COPYRIGHT LAW

Moral rights are dealt with in sections 77-89 of the CDPA 1988. Moral rights are divided into four categories as follows:

(1) the right to be identified as the author or director of the work ('paternity right');

(2) the right to object to derogatory treatment of the work ('integrity right')

(3) the right to object to false attribution of a work; and

(4) the right to privacy of certain photographs and films.

Only the first two rights will be discussed in more detail.

PATERNITY RIGHT AND EXCEPTIONS

The author of a copyright in a literary, dramatic, musical or artistic work, or the director of a copyrighted film, has the right to be identified as the author or director of the work. According to section 79 of the CDPA 1988, certain exceptions apply to this right. For instance, the right is not infringed in the following cases:

(1) it does not apply to computer programs, typefaces and any computer generated works

(2) it is not infringed where any of the defences to infringement apply (for example fair dealing with the work or incidental inclusion)

(3) it does not apply to any work made for the purposes of reporting current events

(4)   it does not apply in relation to the publication in a newspaper, magazine or similar periodical, or an encyclopaedia, dictionary, year-book or other collective work of reference where the work was made for such a purpose, or the work was used with the author's consent.

INTEGRITY RIGHT AND EXCEPTIONS

The author of a literary, dramatic, musical or artistic work and the director of a film have the right not to have their work subjected to 'derogatory treatment'. Section 80 (2) defines 'treatment' of a work as meaning ' any addition to, deletion from or alteration to or adaptation of the work, other than a translation of a literary or dramatic work or an arrangement of a musical work. The treatment of a work will be derogatory if it amounts to 'distortion or mutilation of the work or is otherwise prejudicial to the honour or reputation of the author or director.

The exceptions to this right are detailed in section 81, which says that the right does not apply among others to:

(1)   computer programs or computer-generated works; or

(2)   works made for the purpose of reporting current events; or

(3)   the publication in a newspaper, magazine periodical, or an encyclopaedia or other reference work where the work was made for such a purpose, or the work was used with the author's consent.

There is no exception for fair dealing and, accordingly, despite the fact that a defence of fair dealing may be available in an action for infringement of copyright, an author or director may still have a cause of action under section 80 CDPA 1988 for breach of moral rights.

MORAL RIGHTS AND DIGITISATION

Digitisation could potentially harm the integrity and authenticity of a work. Page and content integrity and its preservation is a matter of great concern to the original author. As digitisation can introduce errors, these errors may give rise to potential liability and a moral right infringement. Besides this, digital files are subject to corruption by third parties which could violate the authenticity of the text and authorship. Therefore, it must be made clear to the outside world that digitisations from analogue originals may not be totally accurate. One way of solving this problem is by including in the digitised files a disclaimer as a part of the header information.

RIGHTS IN PERFORMANCES

THE SUBJECT MATTER OF UK LAW

The rights in performances subsists alongside and are independent from copyright (economic and moral rights).

The rights in performances were introduced in 1925 to close the loophole in copyright law. Consider the following scenario. A well known soprano gives a performance of an aria by Mozart. Unknown to the soprano, a member of the audience makes a recording of the performance and later makes copies which he sells to the public without the singer's permission. Under copyright law, there is nothing that can be done to prevent the sale of the recordings of the performance. The music and lyrics are out of copyright, so there is no infringement of the musical or literary work. The only relevance of copyright in this case is that the person who made the recording without permission owns the copyright in it as a sound recording. Had the singer agreed a recording contract with a publisher, the publisher would be unable to use copyright law to prevent the sale of the unauthorised recordings, which have a separate and independent copyright to the publishers recordings.

The CDPA 1988, considerably expanded the rights in performances in comparison with previous laws. Two separate and distinct rights were created by the 1988 Act.: a performer's right and a recording right. The nature of the rights was somewhat peculiar as the rights were not transmissible (or severely limited). The Copyright and Related Rights Regulations 1996 which implemented, inter alia, the Directive on Rental Rights and Lending Rights, changed this and granted performers full property rights which can be exploited and dealt with just as a copyright.

Rights in performances are given to performers and persons having recording rights. Rights in performances (rights of the person who sings or plays a song) should not be confused with 'performing rights'. This term is usually used to signify rights under copyright in relation the acts of performing, showing or playing a work in public (= the right to perform that song).

The meaning of 'performance'

A performance is defined in the CDPA 1988, section 180 (2) as any one of the following:
- a dramatic performance (including dance and mime);
- a musical performance;
- a reading or recitation of a literary work; or
- a performance of a variety act or any other presentation.

The performance in question must be a live performance by one or more individuals. For an performance to qualify as a 'live performance', the performance does not need to be in front of an audience.

Who qualifies as a 'performer' is not defined in the CDPA 1988. It is generally understood that the protection extends to actors, musicians, singers, dancers, etc. A new definition of 'performer' has been introduced by the WIPO Performances and Phonograms Treaty 1996 (see for more information section V).

The meaning of 'recording'

A recording is defined in section 180 (2) CDPA 1988 as being a film or sound recording made directly from a live performance, or a broadcast or cable programme including the performance or a recording made directly, or indirectly from another recording of the performance.

PERFORMERS' RIGHTS

A performer has two sets of rights in respect of live performances: property rights; and non-property rights.

PERFORMERS' PROPERTY RIGHTS

The CDPA 1988 grants performers the following full property rights:

(a) reproduction right (copy of a whole or substantial part)

(b) distribution right (right to issue works to the public)

(c) rental right and lending right

A performer's property right are infringed where someone, without the consent of the performer:

- makes, otherwise than for his private and domestic use, a copy of a recording of the whole or a part of a qualifying performance.
- issues to the public copies of a recording of the whole or a substantial part of a qualifying performances

As these rights are full property rights and assignable as such, the consent referred to should be that of the owner of the rights (rightholder). The provisions of assignment, licensing and prospective ownership are similar to those applying to copyright works.

PERFORMERS' NON-PROPERTY RIGHT

A performer's non-property rights are infringed where someone, without the consent of the performer and other than for private and domestic use:

(a) makes a recording of the whole of a substantial part of a qualifying performance directly from a live performance;

(b) broadcasts live or include live in a cable programme service, the whole or any substantial part of a qualifying performance;

(c) broadcasts or includes in a cable programme service the whole or any substantial part a qualifying performance

(d) makes a recording of the whole or any substantial part of a qualifying performance directly from a broadcasts of, or cable programme recording including, the live performance;

(e) shows or plays in public the whole or any substantial part of a qualifying performance

The performers non-property rights are not assignable or transmissible except as set out in section 192 A CDPA 1988.

RECORDING RIGHTS

Recording rights are given to a person that has an exclusive recording contract with a performer to make recordings of one or more of his performances with a view of commercial gain. Apart from being able to assign the benefit of the contract, under section 192B, the right is not assignable or transmissible.

Infringement of the rights relating to exclusive recording agreements relate to use of the whole or any substantial part of a recording without consent in the following circumstances amongst others:

(1) showing or playing in public; or

(2) broadcasting or including in a cable programme;

Consent should be sought from either the person with the benefit of the recording rights or the performer may consent to the making of the recording (section 186 CDPA 1988).

DEFENCES AND EXCEPTIONS

The CDPA 1988 provides in section 189 and Schedule 2, for a number of permitted acts which may be done in relation to a performer's right. These are similar to the permitted acts done in relation to copyright works. The table on the next page contains an overview.

DURATION

The duration of rights in performances is 50 years from the end of the calendar year in which the performance takes place or if during that period a recording of the performance is released, 50 years from the end of the year of release. A recording is first released when it is first published, played or shown in public, broadcast or included in a cable programme service (section 191 CDPA 1988).

EXCEPTIONS TO INFRINGEMENT OF RIGHTS IN PERFORMANCES (CDPA 1988, SCH 2)

EXCEPTIONS	COMMENTS
FAIR DEALING, ETC	
Criticism, review and reporting current events	No exception for research and requirement for acknowledgement
Incidental inclusion of performance or recording	As with copyright, deliberate inclusion is outside the exception
EDUCATION	
• copying in the course of instruction, preparation for instruction, in the making films or film sound-tracks, provided it is done by a person giving or receiving instruction • playing or showing of a sound recording, film, broadcast or cable programme at an educational establishment for the purpose of instruction before an audience of teachers and pupils • make a recording of a broadcast or cable programme or a copy of such recording for educational purposes	
LIBRARIES AND ARCHIVES	
Copy required as a condition of export	Long list of exceptions for libraries and archives under copyright are missing for performances
PUBLIC ADMINISTRATION (PARAS 8-11)	Similar to copyright exceptions but not so many
WORKS IN ELECTRONIC FORM	
Transfer of copies in electronic form	Allows the making of further recordings in connection with the use of the recording and back-up copy in some cases
MISCELLANEOUS (PARAS 13-21)	

• recordings of spoken words
• recordings of folk songs
• club and society purposes
Broadcasts/cable programmes
• Incidental recording for:
  - supervision and control
  - free public showing/playing
  - reception/retransmission
  - subtitled copies for hard of hearing, etc
  - recording for archival purposes
Lending of copies by
• Educational establishments (para 6A)
• Libraries and archives (para 6A)
• Order of the Secretary of State (para 14A)
	These are very similar to the copyright exceptions

INTERNATIONAL AND EUROPEAN DEVELOPMENTS

WIPO TREATIES 1996

In order to curb the growing concern about the safeguarding of rights of authors, performers and producers in the digital environment. The World Intellectual Property Organisation (WIPO) held a Diplomatic Conference from 2 to 20 December 1996 in Geneva, which lead to the adoption of the WIPO Copyright Treaty (WCT) and the WIPO Performances and Phonograms Treaty (WPPT) on 20 December 1996.

WIPO, an intergovernmental United Nations organisation with headquarters in Geneva, is responsible for the promotion and protection of intellectual property throughout the world through co-operation amongst States, and for the administration of various multilateral treaties dealing with the legal and administrative aspects of intellectual property. The number of states that are members of WIPO is presently 159, including all the economically important countries of the world.

Both the WCT and WPPT are based on existing international treaties, namely the Berne Convention for the Protection of Literary and Artistic Works (as revised in Paris on 24 July 1971) and the Rome Convention for the Protection of Performers, Producers of Phonograms and Broadcasting Organizations of 26 October 1961. The British government signed the two treaties on 20 December 1996. The EU Directive serves as the law implementing the two WIPO treaties into UK legislation.

WIPO COPYRIGHT TREATY 1996

The WIPO Copyright Treaty (WCT) governs the protection of literary and artistic works. One important new right and two new offences were introduced by this Treaty: the communication to the public right, and the offences towards technical measures and electronic rights management. Moreover it clearly extended the remit of the limitations and exceptions under copyright to the use of works in digital form, as in many countries' national laws the status of such limitations and exceptions was ambiguous.

THE COMMUNICATION TO THE PUBLIC RIGHT

This right was introduced to cover on-demand transmission over networks, as no national legislation on copyright and related rights provided for a specific right for this activity. In legal terms, it is generally accepted that the well-established distribution right, which only applies to the distribution of physical copies, does not cover the act of transmission. In addition, the reproduction right (right to copy) does not cover the act of transmission as such, but only the reproductions which take place in this context. The Communication to the Public Right is discussed further below.

OBLIGATIONS CONCERNING TECHNICAL MEASURES AND RIGHTS MANAGEMENT

The WCT in Article 11 obligates any ratifying Member State to provide in their national legislation adequate legal protection and effective legal remedies against circumvention of technical measures to control access and for the removing or altering of electronic rights management information. This obligation is also discussed further below.

LIMITATIONS AND EXCEPTIONS

The WCT contains a very important statement concerning the status of the limitations and exceptions to the right of reproduction (right to copy) in relation to the use of works in digital form. The Agreed Statement to Article 1.4 reads as follows:

> *The reproduction right, as set out in Article 9 of the Berne Convention, and the exceptions permitted thereunder, fully apply in the digital environment, in particular to the use of works in digital form.*

The exceptions for copying under the CDPA 1988 are all based on Article 9 of the Berne Convention. However, this does not mean that these exceptions automatically can be transferred to the use of works in digital form. They still need to pass the 'three step test' of Article 9(2) of the Berne Convention, which means that:

- the limitations and exceptions are confined to 'special cases';
- the limitations or exceptions do not conflict with the normal exploitation of the work;
- the legitimate interests of the author are not unreasonably prejudiced.

The WCT in Article 10 subsequently extended the limitations and exceptions to other rights than the right of reproduction to, for instance, the Communication to the Public Right. The Agreed Statement to Article 10 WCT further allows Contracting States to devise new exceptions and limitations that are appropriate in an digital network environment. Of course, any new or reformulated exception must still comply with the three step test of Article 9(2) of the Berne Convention.

WIPO PERFORMANCES AND PHONOGRAMS TREATY 1996

The WPPT protects the rights of performers of literary or artistic works and of phonogram producers. It does not cover audio-visual fixations of performances, since the Member States were not able to reach an agreement on this topic. The WPPT introduced a set of new rights, such as moral rights of performers, the right of making available of fixed performances and phonograms and it extended existing rights to material in digital form.

Article 2 of the WPPT introduced a list of definitions that aim to extend the meaning of existing definitions:

(a) 'performer's are actors, singers, musicians, dancers, and other persons who act, sing, deliver, declaim, play in, interpret, or otherwise perform literary or artistic works or expressions of folklore;

This definition of performers widens the present definition by including 'other persons', persons who 'interpret' and the extend the right to 'expressions of folklore'.

(b) 'phonogram' means the fixation of the sounds of a performance or of other sounds, or of a representation of sounds, other than in the form of a fixation incorporated in a cinematographic or other audio-visual work;

This definition has been extended to cover phonograms that are not fixations of sounds. Phonograms may be reproduced for instance using digital technology that fixes data which can be used to generate sounds.

(c) 'fixation' means the embodiment of sounds, or of the representations thereof, from which they can be perceived, reproduced or communicated through a device;

The representatives at the Diplomatic Conference declined to extend the definition of fixations to fixations of images or representations thereof.

(d) 'producer of a phonogram' means a person, or the legal entity, who or which takes the initiative and has the responsibility for the first fixation of the sounds of a performance or other sounds, or the representations of sounds;

Only adds one element to the definition of Article 3 (c) of the Rome Convention, i.e, 'representation of sounds'.

(e) 'publication' of a fixed performance or a phonogram means the offering of copies of the fixed performances or the phonogram to the public, with the consent of the rightholder, and provided that copies are offered to the public in reasonable quality;

This definition includes one additional element, which is the consent requirement such that a performance or a phonogram cannot be published without the consent of the relevant rightholder.

(f)   'broadcasting' means the transmission by wireless means for public reception of sounds or of images and sounds or of the representation thereof; such transmission by satellite is also ' broadcasting where the means of decrypting are provided to the public by the broadcasting organisation or with its consent;

New in the definition of broadcasting is the transmission of the representations of sounds or of images and sounds and includes satellite broadcasting. Transmission of encrypted signals qualifies as broadcasting as well.

(g)   'communication to the public' of a performance or a phonogram means the transmission to the public by any medium, otherwise than by broadcasting, of sounds of a performance or the sounds of the representations of sounds fixed in a phonogram. For the purposes of Article 15, 'communication to the public' includes making the sounds or representations of sounds fixed in a phonogram audible to the public.

The distinction between 'broadcasting and 'communication to the public' has been maintained by simply excluding broadcasting from the scope of communication to the public.

MORAL RIGHTS OF PERFORMERS

The WPPT grants the performer in Article 5 a new right to claim to be identified as the performer of his performances (either live of fixed in phonograms), and may object to any distortion, mutilation or other modifications of his performances that would be prejudicial to his reputation. This applies even after the transfer of those rights.

RIGHT OF REPRODUCTION

Articles 7, 11 and 16 WPPT deal with the Right of Reproduction of performers (the direct or indirect reproduction of their performances fixed in phonograms) and producers of phonograms (the direct or indirect reproduction of their phonograms) and the limitations and exceptions to this right. Both Article 7 and 11 extend the right to reproductions in 'any manor or form'.

Article 16 WPPT provides Contracting Parties to include in their national legislation the same kind of limitations and exceptions with regard to the protection of performers and producers of phonograms as they provide for protection of copyright in literary and artistic works. The meeting adopted an interesting Agreed Statement, which reads as follows:

The reproduction right as set out in Art. 7, 11, and the exceptions permitted thereunder through Art. 16, fully apply in the digital environment, in particular o the use of performances and phonograms in digital form. It is understood that the storage of a protected performance or phonogram in digital form in an electronic medium constitutes a reproduction within the meaning of these Articles.

RIGHT OF MAKING AVAILABLE OF FIXED PERFORMANCES AND PHONOGRAMS

The Right of Making Available of Fixed Performances and Phonograms in Article 10 and Article 14 WPPT is similar to the Right of Communication to the Public of authors in Article 8 WCT. This right will be further explained in the section below, concerning the EU Directive on Copyright and Related Rights.

OBLIGATIONS CONCERNING TECHNOLOGICAL MEASURES AND RIGHTS MANAGEMENT

The same applies here. The obligations are identical to the obligations in Article 11 WCT.

The implementation of the WCD and the WPPT for the Member States of the EU, including the UK is stipulated in the EU Directive on Copyright and Related Rights, discussed below.

DRAFT EU DIRECTIVE ON COPYRIGHT AND RELATED RIGHTS

The draft EU Directive on the harmonisation of certain aspects of copyright and related rights in the Information Society was published by the European Commission on 10th December 1997. After three years of negotiations within the Council of Ministers and the European Parliament, the Directive was finally adopted by the Council of Ministers on 9th April 2001. (The text referred to here is that of the political agreement reached on 9 June 2000, which was slightly amended by the European Parliament on 14th February 2001. The final text of the EU Copyright Directive is published in the *Official Journal* in May 2001.)

The European Parliament claims that this Directive has been the most lobbied Directive in its history. The discussions were held up due to major differences amongst the representatives of the fifteen Member States on the scope of the exceptions to copyright and the scope of the legal protection of technical measures.

The Directive aims to adjust and complement the existing legal framework, with particular emphasis to new products and services containing intellectual property (both online and on physical carriers such as CDs, CD-ROMs and Digital Video Discs).

The Directive also implements the obligations of the WIPO Copyright Treaty 1996 and the WIPO Performances and Phonograms Treaty 1996 as discussed in the previous section. After implementation into UK copyright law, these obligations will apply in the UK.

The issues covered by the Directive are:

- Right of Reproduction
- Right of Communication to the Public
- Legal Protection of Technical Measures and Rights Management Information
- Distribution Right

The Right of Communication to the Public and the Legal Protection of Technical Measures and Rights Management Information are new features, once implemented, in UK copyright legislation.

RIGHT OF REPRODUCTION

The Directive contains a very broad definition of the Right of Reproduction. It provides for an exclusive right to authorise or prohibit direct or indirect, temporary or permanent reproduction by any means and in any form, in whole or in part. This right is granted to:

a) authors, for their works;

b) performers, for fixations of their performances;

c) phonogram producers, for their phonograms

d) producers for their first fixations of films, in respect of the original and copies of their films;

e) broadcasting organisations for fixations of their broadcasts, whether those broadcasts are transmitted by wire or over the air, including by cable or satellite.

The definitions of the various terms can be found in Article 2 of the WIPO Performances and Phonograms Treaty 1996 and are summed up in the previous section.

It is interesting to note that this definition of the Right of Reproduction was rejected at the WIPO Diplomatic Conference 1996 on the grounds that it would extended the right of reproduction to each and every (invisible) transient and incidental copy made during transmission over networks.

The Commission eased the pain by introducing a mandatory exception to the Right of Reproduction in Article 5(1), which provides for an exception for temporary acts of reproduction ...whose sole purpose is to enable use to be made of a work or other subject matters. This includes caching and browsing.

Article 5 contains also other exceptions to the Right of Reproduction. These exceptions are optional, and whether they are implemented in UK law will depend on the UK government. According to the Commentary on Article 5, the UK government is not allowed to provide for any exceptions other than those enumerated in Article 5'. The closed list of exceptions of Article 5 contains only one mandatory exception (Article 5 (1)). This means that this list will replace the existing permitted acts allowed under the CDPA 1988.

With respect of multi-media works the following (optional) exceptions to the Reproduction Right in Article 5 are of importance:

Article 5.2.a reproductions on paper (except sheet music), fair compensation

Article 5.2.b analogue and digital reproductions on any medium by a natural person for private use for ends which are neither directly or indirectly commercial, fair compensation

Article 5.2.c specific acts of reproduction by publicly accessible libraries, educational establishments, museums or archives, which are not for direct or indirect economic or commercial advantage

Article 5.2.d ephemeral recordings of works made by broadcasting organisations and preservation of these recordings in official archives

Article 5.2.e reproductions of broadcasts by social institutions, fair compensation

Article 5.3.a illustration for teaching or scientific research, for non-commercial purposes, fair compensation

Article 5.3.b uses for the benefit of people with a disability

Article 5.3.c reproduction by the press, communication to the public of published articles on current economic and political topics, broadcasts of works or use in connection with the reporting of current events

Article 5.3.d quotations for purposes such as criticism or review

Article 5.3.e use for purposes of public security or reporting of an administrative, parliamentary or judicial procedure

Article 5.3.f use of political speeches, extracts of public lectures or similar works

Article 5.3.h use of works, such as works of architecture or sculpture located in public places

Article 5.3.i incidental inclusion of a work or other subject matter

Article 5.3.j use for purpose of advertising public exhibitions or sale of artistic works

Article 5.3.n use by the communication/making available for the purpose of research or private study, to individual members of the public by dedicated terminals on the premises in respect of reproductions made by establishments referred to in para. 5.2.c of works and other subject matter not subject to purchase or licensing terms which are contained in their collections

Article 5.3.o use in certain other cases of minor importance where exceptions already exist under national law, provided that they only concern analogue uses and do not affect the free circulation of goods and services within the Community, without prejudice to the other exceptions and limitations contained in this Article.

All these exceptions are subject to the 'three step test' of Article 5.5 of the Directive. This means that the exceptions can only apply in (1) certain special cases, (2) as long as they do not conflict with the normal exploitation of the work or other subject matter, (3) and as long as they do not unreasonably prejudice the legitimate interests of the right holder.

RIGHT OF COMMUNICATION TO THE PUBLIC

This new exclusive right was first introduced by the WIPO Copyright Treaty 1996 and the WIPO Performances and Phonograms Treaty 1996. There is still a lot of confusion about the extent and application of this right. The Explanatory Memorandum to the draft EU Directive on Copyright and Related Rights explains that the communication to the public' (the 'making available to the public') precedes the stage of its actual transmission.

In other words, the storage of material with the (future) aim to offer it on a publicly accessible site may amount to a 'communication to the public'. The draft EU Directive grants the exclusive right to authorise or prohibit the communication/making available to the public to:

a) for authors, of their works;
b) for performers, of fixations of their performances;
c) for phonogram producers, of their phonograms
d) for the producers of their first fixations of films, in respect of the original and copies of their films;
e) for broadcasting organisations, of fixations of their broadcasts, whether those broadcasts are transmitted by wire or over the air, including by cable or satellite.

The draft EU Directive allows for the following optional exceptions:

Article 5.3.a illustration for teaching or scientific research, for non-commercial purposes, fair compensation

Article 5.3.b uses for the benefit of people with a disability

Article 5.3.c reproduction by the press, communication to the public of published articles on current economic and political topics, broadcasts of works or use in connection with the reporting of current events

Article 5.3.d quotations for purposes such as criticism or review

Article 5.3.e use for purposes of public security or reporting of an administrative, parliamentary or judicial procedure

Article 5.3.f use of political speeches, extracts of public lectures or similar works

Article 5.3.h use of works, such as works of architecture or sculpture located in public places

Article 5.3.i incidental inclusion of a work or other subject matter

Article 5.3.j use for purpose of advertising public exhibitions or sale of artistic works

Article 5.3.n use by the communication/making available for the purpose of research or private study, to individual members of the public by dedicated terminals on the premises in respect of reproductions made by establishments referred to in para. 5.2.c of works and other subject matter not subject to purchase or licensing terms which are contained in their collections

Article 5.3.o use in certain other cases of minor importance where exceptions already exist under national law, provided that they only concern analogue uses and do not affect the free circulation of goods and services within the Community, without prejudice to the other exceptions and limitations contained in this Article.

All these exceptions are also subject to the 'three step test' of Art. 5.5 of the Directive.

FAIR COMPENSATION

Instead of 'equitable remuneration', which is the basis for many existing remuneration schemes in the EU, the Council of Ministers agreed under pressure of the UK delegation on the words 'fair compensation'. 'Equitable remuneration' implies that in return for the exception there must be a payment. 'Fair compensation' not only requires that the compensation must be 'fair' but must compensate for real loss. Indeed, compensation need not be financial. These concepts are reflected in Recital 35, which makes the following important statements:

1. that where rightholders have already received payment in some other form, such as part of a licence fee, no specific or separate payment may be due.
2. that the level of fair compensation should take full account of the degree of use of technological protection measures.
3. that in certain situations where the prejudice to the rightholder would be minimal, no obligation for payment may arise.

The last of these statements is very important as it creates an opportunity to challenge any future levy or other remuneration legislation. The UK government delegation will almost certainly use this wording to curb requests from the industry for the introduction of levies in relation to timeshifting.

Less positive is Recital 36 which gives the UK government the free hand to extend the provisions for fair compensation for rightholders to the exceptions in the Directive which at the moment do not require such compensation.

LICENSING

The legal solution for activities other than the ones listed as an exception can be found in the Explanatory Memorandum to the Directive. The Memorandum states 'with respect to the use of digitised material by libraries, online as well as offline, initiatives are on-going in a number of Members States, notably the UK, where library privileges are most developed, to arrive at more flexible contractual solutions'.

This shift in focus of attention from a bundle of exceptions which has developed over many years in the print-on-paper environment towards contractual licensing solutions, especially accompanied with a broad protection of (new) rights of the rightholders is one that should make HE and FE institutions wary.

Contract law is dominated by the concept of freedom of contract - that is to say the parties to a contract are free to negotiate the terms of use of copyrighted materials or indeed waive the rights that the copyright law grants them. Negotiations with a holder of an exclusive right could turn out to have a harsh result for the information purchaser.

LEGAL PROTECTION OF TECHNICAL MEASURES AND RIGHTS-MANAGEMENT INFORMATION

This kind of protection was discussed for the first time in the framework of the WIPO negotiations on certain questions on copyright and related rights. The WIPO Performances and Phonograms Treaty 1996 (WPPT) and the WIPO Copyright Treaty 1996 (WCT) contain parallel provisions on "technological measures" and on "obligations concerning rights management information". The first prohibits the circumvention of technical measures that are used by holders of copyright or related rights in connection with the exercise of their rights, the latter prohibits the removal and altering of certain electronic rights management information attached to a work or other subject matter.

These obligations have been implemented and subsequently extended in Art. 6 of the Directive. This article entitles rightholders to protect their works against the circumvention of any effective technological measures. However, where rightholders have not taken voluntary measures to give the beneficiaries of certain exceptions access to their protected works, the UK government can take appropriate measures to enable users to benefit from the exceptions concerned.

The expression 'technological measures' is broadly defined in Article 6 of the Directive and refers to any technology, device or component that, in the normal course of its operation, is designed to prevent or restrict acts, in respect of works or other subject matter, which are not authorised by the right holder. Technological measures shall be deemed 'effective' where the use of a protected work is controlled by the rightholders through application of an access control or protection process, such as encryption, scrambling or other transformation of the work or other subject matter or a copy control mechanism, which achieves the protection objective.

Art. 6.4 of the Directive is very important as it balances the potential technical monopoly of information by rightholders. Several doubts have been raised concerning the effectiveness of this article as Art. 6.4 does not provide an outright permission to circumvent a technical block for lawful uses by a lawful user (a user exercising an exception). The provision puts the obligation on the right holder to make available the means of benefiting from that exception through the use of voluntary measures or agreements which accommodate such exceptions. If they fail to do so, the UK government is entitled to step in and take 'appropriate measures'.

This protection mechanism only applies to the exceptions provided for in Article 5.2a, 2c, 2d, 2e, 3a, 3b or 3e. It is worrying that this has not been extended to the exceptions in 5.3.f, i and j. The legal protection of technical measures is retrospective, but only for the Directive on the legal protection of databases which was implemented in the UK copyright legislation in 1998.

According to Article 6.4 fourth paragraph, the circumvention by lawful users will not be allowed if the work was made available on demand on agreed contractual terms. In other words, where content is delivered online subject to contractual terms rightholders will be permitted to block technically any copying of such content, irrespective of whether such copying is allowed by law or not. Recital 52a tries to clarify that this provision only applies to interactive on-demand services, in such a way that members of the public may access works or other subject-matter from a place and at a time individually chosen by them.

Besides the protection of technical measures in Art. 6, Art. 7 requests Member States to provide adequate legal protection against any person who, without authority, removes or alters electronic rights management information or distributes, imports, communicates with the public or makes available copies to the public or other subject matter from which electronic rights management information has been removed or altered without authority.

DISTRIBUTION RIGHT

The distribution right refers exclusively to fixed copies that can be put into circulation as tangible objects. The European Commission already harmonised the distribution right for certain categories of works such as computer programs and databases.

During the preparations and adaptation of the WIPO Copyright Treaty 1996 and the WIPO Performances and Phonograms Treaty 1996 all potential Contracting Parties to the Treaties agreed to establish a distribution right for tangible objects in order to provide for a coherent level playing field for the distribution of protected material and for the need to draw a clear line between electronic (communication to the public right) and tangible distribution (distribution right) of protected material. The provision can be found in Art. 6 of the WIPO Copyright Treaty 1996 and Art. 8 and 12 of the WIPO Performances and Phonograms Treaty 1996. The articles only establishes the right, but do not provide for a national or international exhaustion of the distribution right, but leaves it to the Contracting Parties to determine the conditions under which the exhaustion of this right applies.

Pursuant to the WIPO Copyright Treaty 1996, the Directive provides in Art. 4 for a nearly identical worded exclusive distribution right. For the smooth functioning of the Internal Market, the European Commission included in Art. 4 of the Directive a provision that the distribution right should be exhausted within the Community only when the first sale or other transfer of ownership of the object is made by the right holder or with his consent in the Community. According to Art. 5.4, Member States are allowed to provide for an exception to the right of distribution to the extend justified by the purpose of the authorised act of reproduction.

ENTRY INTO FORCE OF THE WIPO TREATIES 1996 AND EU DIRECTIVE

The WIPO Treaties 1996 will be enforceable in the UK once the UK government ratifies and implements the two Treaties in its national legislation. The UK, as member of the EU, is expected to ratify the two Treaties, together with the other 14 members states of the EU during or after the implementation of the EU Directive on Copyright and Related Rights.

The Directive allows the UK government to implement the Directive into the national copyright law within a period of eighteen months. Once implemented, the Directive will be enforceable within the UK.

CLEARANCE OF RIGHTS

The clearance for the use of a multimedia work can be very complex as numerous rights may exists at the same time. Another complicating factor is that it is often not clear who the owner is of a specific right. An author or performer typically assigns a number of rights, but also retains several rights. For instance, in the case of a literary work, an author will usually have assigned the following rights to the publisher:

(1)   to publish an abridged version;

(2)   to agree serialisation rights;

(3)   to publish cartoon and picture book versions;

(4)   to prepare recording or talking versions;

(5)   to translate the work;

(5)   to dramatise the work;

(6)   to make and show or exploit a film, TV or radio version of the work.

The author in many cases retains the film, television and video rights in their work. Another complicating factor is where the author and the publisher differ about who owns what rights. This is especially important for the clearance for the digitisation of multimedia works. Who does one ask for authorisation to digitise the work? Does one ask the author, the publisher or their respective collecting societies? In the case of the collecting society, this will depend on the extent of the legal mandate they have been given by their members or what rights were assigned to them.

Although moral rights were only introduced into UK law by the CDPA 1988, it is important that when rights are acquired in underlying works, the moral rights of the author are not ignored and are dealt with in the licence. Moral rights cannot be assigned, though they can be waived.

Collecting societies can certainly simplify the rights clearance process. In cases where no collecting society exists, authorisation needs to be sought from the copyright owner direct. This can be a very time consuming exercise. A more efficient mechanism is required for this.

The collecting societies differ per sector. Some of the well-known collecting societies and their clearance remit are listed below.

Authors' Licensing & Collecting Society (ALCS)
The ALCS is the British rights management society for all writers. Its principal business is to distribute fees to writers whose work has been copied, broadcast or recorded.

Copyright Licensing Agency (CLA)

The CLA grants non-exclusive licences to third parties enabling them to photocopy and/or electronically copy all or parts of published works. The income from this is collected by the CLA and split between authors and publishers.

Design and Artists Copyright Society Ltd (DACS)

DACS is the copyright and collecting society for visual artists in the UK. It is the only organisation in the UK that deals solely with copyright and artists' rights and that collects royalties due for visual artists' secondary rights.

Educational Recording Agency (ERA)

ERA administers the ERA Licensing Scheme which gives educational establishments the right to record off-air for educational purposes any radio and television broadcasts and cable programmes.

The Mechanical Copyright Protection Society (MCPS)

The right to record a work is a separate right from the performance right in a song. The MCPS grants licences to record companies and other bodies who wish to record or re-record works. MCPS also deals with licensing of songs for inclusion on videos, CD-ROMS etc.

Performing Rights Society (PRS)

PRS administers the rights to perform a work in public, broadcast it or include it in a cable programme service. Its members consists of writers and publishers. The PRS has the benefit of a full assignment of the performing rights in the works of its members. The PRS licences (usually in the form of blanket licences) the performing rights in its works in return for a royalty.

Photographic Performance Ltd (PPL)

This organisation was established by record companies and record producers to control broadcasting and public use of recordings. Members assign to PPL the usage rights in their works. PPL negotiates and issues licences for the broadcasting and public performances of sound recordings in a similar way as the PRS. Fees are based upon the value to the user derived from the recordings.

British Phonographic Industry (BPI)

The BPI acts as a trade association for the record industry and represents the industry in negotiations relating to the payment of sessions musicians and covering the rate of mechanical royalties paid to composers when their works are recorded.

Trade Unions and representative organisations

Some trade organisations have developed standard licences for their members to be used to regulate the exploitation of their rights. These organisations are very important players within the industry and could be partners in the dialogue intended by the MRWG. A selection of the most important trade unions is noted below:

EQUITY

Equity is the performers' union, representing actors, singers, dancers, choreographers, stage managers, theatre directors and designers, variety artists, television presenters, walk-on and supporting artists, stunt performers and directors and theatre fight directors throughout the UK. Equity negotiates minimum terms on behalf of it members. As well as negotiating in traditional television and film works, Equity negotiates individual agreements for the use of its members' services in developing other media such as interactive CD-ROM games.

Musicians' Union (MU)

The MU is the only trade union in the UK which solely represents musicians. The MU has produced a number of standard contracts for its members.

The Performing Artists' Media Rights Association (PAMRA)

PAMRA is a joint venture between Equity, the actors' union, and the MU. It was set up to collect income which is due to performers when their performances are broadcasts or communicated to the public.

Video Performances Ltd (VPL)

VPL was established by record companies and producers of music videos to regulate the broadcasting and performance of music videos.

CONCLUSIONS

Even though UK law allows for certain exceptions for the reproduction of a part or the whole of a multimedia product, clearance needs to be sought in most cases if the HE and FE institution intends to make the materials available to authorised users through their networks. This right is covered by the so called 'communication to the public right'. This right was introduced by the WIPO Treaties in 1996 and included in the EU Directive on Copyright and Related Rights. The negotiation of a licence for the digitisation and the use of multimedia products is very complex as so many different rights and works may be involved.

USELESS IF DELAYED ?
NEWSREEL RESEARCH AT THE BUFVC

LUKE McKERNAN

The four-year British Universities Newsreels Project (BUNP) culminated in the launch in March 2000 of the BUNP database on CD-ROM and on the Web. Luke McKernan, Head of Information at the BUFVC, recounts the history of newsreel research at the BUFVC and describes the next stage, the British Universities Newsreel Scripts Project (BUNSP).

'Useless if Delayed' was the notice printed on the cans of the British Movietone News newsreel. It indicated the urgency of their business, and the ephemeral nature of news itself. Yet, long after the newsreels finally bowed out of British life, the films and their production have established for themselves a lasting historical importance. Their commitment to the news of the moment has bequeathed something of considerable value to historians of the 20th century, which can only grow in importance in the years to come. The BUFVC has long recognised this importance, and supplying information on newsreels and encouraging research into their production are key features of its work.

The newsreels ran in British cinemas between 1910, with the launch of Pathé's Animated Gazette, and the final demise of British Movietone News in 1979. For most of those 69 years they were a major news medium whose output was viewed by millions, and which played a significant part in shaping opinions and in offering cinema audiences a particular view of the world. It was in 1969, the year before Pathé News closed, that the Slade Film History Register was set up, with the idea of creating a central registry of film material likely to be of interest to historians. The newsreels were central to this project, and when the Register passed into the control of the BUFVC in 1974 there was already a substantial collection of newsreel issue sheets (records of the contents of each individual newsreel issue) and an index to some 30,000 newsreel stories.

The work to augment and promote this collection continued at the BUFVC. The issue sheets in the Slade Film History Register were published as a set of microfiche in 1984. Data gathered concerning the newsreels were made available in three volumes of the *Researcher's Guide to British Newsreels*, edited by James Ballantyne, and pub-

A sample of original documents from the Second World War

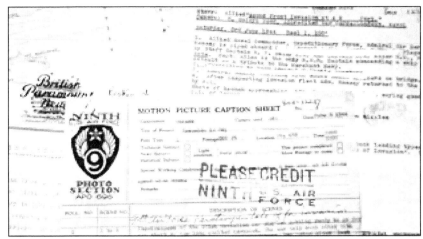

lished in 1983, 1988 and 1993. Two editions of a poster charting all of the British newsreels and cinemagazines, their start and finish dates, and current ownership were produced. The BUFVC was also co-organiser of two major conferences on newsreels, under the title "The Story of the Century!", held in 1996 and 1998.

THE BRITISH UNIVERSITIES NEWSREEL PROJECT

In 1995 the BUFVC's interest in newsreel research took a considerable step forward with the formation of the British Universities Newsreel Project (BUNP). Funded for four years by the Higher Education Funding Council for England, this project, under Dr. Nicholas Hiley, aimed at producing a computerised database of all of the newsreel issue sheets in the Slade Film History Register. The project enjoyed the full support of the newsreel libraries British Movietonews, British Pathé and the ITN Archive (a collection previously held by Reuters Television and before that by Visnews). As the project progressed, further data were added from the National Film and Television Archive (NFTVA) and the Imperial War Museum's Film and Video Archive. The result was published in March 2000 as a cross-platform (PC and Apple Macintosh) CD-ROM and as part of the BUFVC Website (www.bufvc.ac.uk/newsreels), accessible to UK higher education, further education, and BUFVC researcher members only.

The BUNP database holds details of some 160,000 individual newsreel stories taken from around 24,000 separate newsreel issues. It covers, with only a few gaps for the earlier years, all the major British newsreels – British Movietone News, British Paramount News, Empire News Bulletin, Gaumont British News, Gaumont Graphic, Pathé Gazette and Pathé News, Topical Budget and Universal News – some wartime newsreels (The Gen, Worker and Warfront, etc.) and cine-magazines such as Pathé Pictorial and Pathétone Weekly. The data for each newsreel item includes title, issue number, library number, release date, synopsis, keywords, location, length, cameraman and other technical staff, where these details exist on the original documentation. The fields are all fully searchable, and allow for great flexibility and sophistication in search requests.

As an example of how the database is constructed, one can look at the British Movietone News coverage of the Hindenburg disaster in May 1937. There are three Movietone items for that month which are brought up using the search term 'Hindenburg'. One is a report of the disaster soon after it happened that used library footage (the famous actual footage of the airship exploding had yet to reach Britain), one the film of the explosion shown ten days later, and one item on the subsequent enquiry. The second item gives the issue number (415A), the release date (20 May 1937), the Movietone library number (5366), and tells us that it was the first of eight stories in that issue. The title of the item was DISASTER; the commentator was Ivan Scott. No cameraman's name is listed – the source is given only as 'American'. The description offers Movietone's own card title, a three-line description apparently taken from the commentary, and a short shot list that tells us that we see scenes of the airship in flight, the ship in the air on fire and falling to earth, scenes after the fire, and the skeleton of the airship. The film could be found by searching on any of the words in the description, but there are also four keywords: Aviation, Disasters and Accidents, United States of America, and Dirigibles. The length is given at 97 feet (just over one minute), cut from an original 278 feet shot. Cross-searching reveals that it was followed by an item on the King of Denmark's Silver Jubilee.

The data can also sorted in chronological order, so that the researcher can see when a story first came before the British cinema-going public, and how it then developed. Thus it is possible to discover that the newsreels first reported the Holocaust with HORROR IN OUR TIME, in Gaumont British News Nº 1181, released on 30 April 1945, and ATROCITIES – THE EVIDENCE, in British Movietone News Nº 830. The original issue sheet gives no description, but has been keyworded under Concentration Camps, Germany, Prisoners of War, Buchenwald, and Belsen. Further searching under Belsen reveals a total of 25 stories produced by the five main newsreels (Gaumont British, Movietone, Paramount, Pathé, Universal). Patterns in the news agenda can be traced. There are 313 items on the Spanish Civil War, but the subject wanes as a topic of newsreel interest from 91 items out of a total of 5840 issued in 1936, to 86 out of 6354 in 1937, and 64 out of 5878 in 1938. One may also discover that, despite its infamy, only one of the newsreels was able to report on the bombing of Guernica (Gaumont British News N° 350, release date 6 May 1937).

The BUNP database is certain to prove a major resource for academics researching aspects of British history, the development of the news media, or simply locating footage for use in coursework packages or in teaching. It is also going to prove of great value to researchers seeking footage for historical television programmes. However, it not only assists in locating footage, but is also a constant reminder of how the newsreels were produced, and how such knowledge gives us a purchase on these familiar yet frequently misunderstood films. The information on the issue sheets reveals how the newsreels were constructed to a set pattern, how and when they were released, and how they were packaged. It illuminates the films themselves. This aspect of the BUNP is to be enhanced by its second stage, that of adding further documentation to the existing records.

THE BRITISH UNIVERSITIES NEWSREEL SCRIPTS PROJECT

The BUNP has now been awarded further funding by the Arts and Humanities Research Board to carry on the work of documenting the newsreels by adding commentary scripts, cameraman's dope sheets (his description and comments on the footage), assignment sheets, shot lists and other original documentation to the database.

The British Universities Newsreel Scripts Project (BUNSP) runs from 1999 to 2003, and its bedrock is a substantial collection (some 40,000 documents) of surviving files for British Paramount News, Gaumont British News and Universal News, generously deposited with the BUFVC by Reuters Television in October 1998. The collection runs from 1930 to 1958 (though there are some regrettable gaps, notably for some of the war years), and includes fascinating additional ephemera such as newspaper clippings (on the story the cameraman was supposed to film) and sporting programmes. Other substantial collections of dope sheets and commentary scripts exist at British Movietonews, British Pathé and the Imperial War Museum Film and Video Archive. The BUNSP as a whole will entail scanning and keywording of more than 100,000 documents, each of which is to be added to the existing record on the database.

The documents will be scanned as an image (including corrections, censors' marks, etc.), giving researchers the equivalent of the document itself, and then keyworded for subject access. An original plan to use OCR (optical character recognition) when scanning the documents was rejected as impractical.

The BUNSP will greatly enhance our understanding of the newsreels, and make widely available disparate documentation collections that have hitherto been mostly hidden from researchers. The British Paramount News documents come in files, each relating to a single issue of the newsreel. A typical example is British Paramount News Nº 1355, release date 24 February 1944, which contains:

1. An issue sheet for the full issue, with the story titles
2. A shot list for KING & MONTY SEE ENGLAND BEAT SCOTS
3. A newspaper clipping relating to the football story
4. The cameraman's dope sheet for the football story
5. The commentary script for the football story
6. A shot list for HOW THE R.A.F. 'OBLITERATE'
7. A detailed description from the Royal Air Force of one of its own films describing an air raid over Mannheim
8. The commentary script for the RAF story
9. A shot list for YANKS PLAY HOST TO THEIR MAJESTIES
10. A newspaper clipping relating to the royal story
11. A second newspaper clipping relating to the royal story
12. The commentary script for the royal story
13. A shot list for B.B.C. MAKES BIG PROGRAMME CHANGEOVER
14. A script for radio story with original dialogue only (for Tommy Handley)
15. The cameraman's dope sheet for the radio story
16. The commentary script for the radio story

The cameramen's dope sheets are filled with illuminating details. For British Paramount News Nº 1080 (release date 7 July 1941), cameraman Jack Harding notes: 'EXCLUSIVE & MOST SECRET: Note. Two shots must not be used of Mr Churchill. First close up where he drops his hat & picks it up. Second walking shot & he spits a little of the leaf of his cigar out as passing camera' (Churchill had been watching some army exercises). The cameramen frequently complain of the difficulties in getting their story. Jimmy Gemmell's report on people sleeping in the Underground during the war for issue 1018 (release date 2 December 1940) states: 'This story was most difficult to do owing to the confined area, lights fusing every now and then, the humidity cause[d] by the dampness and my lights, and the communistic tendencies, and apart from all that I am still happy in my work.'

There are also records from the cameramen present at notable historic events. Jim Wright's dope sheet for the capture of the Italian town of Cassino, for British Paramount News № 1364 (release date 27 March 1944) is filled with the drama of the moment: 'Today I was the first and only war Correspondent to enter the town of Cassino ... The town is completely devastated by the colossal air bombing and artillery shelling to which it has been subjected and due to the German machine gunners it was not prudent to expose myself too much to climb up on top of the heaps of rubble with a view to obtaining general views of the desolation, as it was I was under mortar fire which I filmed.'

Other intriguing artefacts within the collection include some music cue sheets. For example, that for British Paramount News № 2300 (release date 16 March 1953) gives composer, publisher and timings for each musical selection used throughout the newsreel, and, for example, reveals that for the story 300 PERISH IN CYCLONE WEEK-END, Paramount showed a rather cynical humour in selecting themes from the films LOST WEEKEND, FIVE GRAVES TO CAIRO and ACE IN THE HOLE. Of the newsreel records inherited by the BUFVC from Reuters Television, it is British Paramount News that has the most detailed information.

The commentary scripts give the words of the commentators to each of the newsreel stories, with the final additions and deletions made before recording written on the script. Thus the Gaumont British News item on the death of Stalin (№ 2001, release date 5 March 1953) reveals a generally positive view of the man, recalling his wartime alliance with Britain and America. Among the small corrections for style on the script, a whole line is deleted which compares Stalin's rise to power to that of Hitler's, and another line saying that the Three Powers have drifted apart but his successor may find greatness by 'rekindling those war-time bonds of friendship', is replaced by a simple statement that all of Russia mourns the passing of Stalin.

FUTURE DEVELOPMENTS

The BUNSP will add considerably to our understanding of the newsreels, in the presentation of material previously inaccessible, and in a form searchable across many fields. The completed database will provide the necessary scholarly apparatus for understanding the newsreels as a phenomenon, and in particular understanding the existing newsreel footage.

The database as it stands (that is, based on the issue sheets data) has been published as a CD-ROM and on the Internet. There will be further editions of the CD-ROM, with possible specialist editions on particular aspects (e.g. the Cold War, Sport, Science, World War II). The material from the Scripts Project will be added to the database and published on the Internet as it becomes available, with a completion date in 2003.

Online links with the actual footage are a possibility for the future, and discussions are going ahead with the newsreel companies.

Research from the project will be published in the form of conference papers and articles in academic journals, and it is planned that the BUFVC will publish a British newsreels reader, edited by Luke McKernan, the current head of the Newsreel Project. A key part of the newsreel research has been the compilation of a biographical database of over 600 British newsreel staff, which will be published in its entirety on the newsreel website by the end of 2001. BUNP research data will also contribute towards the autobiography of newsreel cameraman John Turner, which the BUFVC is planning to publish.

The overall aim is to make full use of the research information yielded by the Newsreel Project, and to contribute towards the publications necessary to support the newsreels as a subject of academic study in the future.

For further details, contact Luke McKernan, Head of Information at the BUFVC, TEL 020 7393 1508 or E-MAIL newsreels@bufvc.ac.uk. The Website can be found at www.bufvc.ac.uk/newsreels

AUDIO-VISUAL CENTRES IN HIGHER & FURTHER EDUCATION

This section lists a selection of audio-visual centres and departments in universities, as well as a small number in colleges, schools and other establishments in the United Kingdom and Ireland.

Every effort has been made to complete and verify these listings; to register updates, changes or new entries, please contact the BUFVC at 77 Wells Street, London W1T 3QJ, UK., TEL 020 7393 1500, FAX 020 7393 1555, E-MAIL publications@bufvc.ac.uk, WEB www.bufvc.ac.uk.

ABERDEEN CITY COUNCIL: SERVICES TO SCHOOLS & CENTRES

Summerhill Education Centre, Stronsay Drive, Aberdeen AB15 6JA • TEL 01224 346021 • FAX 01224 346243 • CONTACT Alex Hunter, Assistant Director of Education • E-MAIL ahunter@rmplc.co.uk

Provides a centralised educational resources service for Aberdeen city; a curriculum resources and information service providing library resources; an education department and multimedia service providing maintenance and repair of educational audio-visual and computer holdings; ICT; curriculum development; equipment and materials for special needs; a graphics and photographic service.

ANGLIA POLYTECHNIC UNIVERSITY

Media Production, Cambridge Campus, East Road, Cambridge CB1 1PT • TEL 01223 363271 x 2206 • FAX 01223 352900 • CONTACT Roderick Macdonald • E-MAIL r.m.macdonald@anglia.ac.uk • WEB www.mpd.anglia.ac.uk

Media Production develops and supports the use of audio visual media in traditional and open learning and teaching throughout the university. It operates the university's graphic design and photography services, and contributes to the teaching programme in areas such as educational technology, multimedia and video production. The department also offers video production services, including both studio and location work, on a commercial basis. Video-conferencing facilities up to ISDN 6 are available for hire in Cambridge and Chelmsford.

ANGLO-EUROPEAN COLLEGE OF CHIROPRACTIC

Anglo-European College of Chiropractic, Parkwood Road, Bournemouth BH5 2DF • TEL 01202 436200 • FAX 01202 436312 • CONTACT Brendan Johnston • E-MAIL bjohnston@aecc-chiropractic.ac.uk • WEB www.aecc-chiropractic.ac.uk

Provides audio-visual support, including slides and video production for academic courses.

ASTON UNIVERSITY

Aston Media, Aston Triangle, Birmingham B4 7ET • TEL 0121 359 3611 x 4099 • FAX 0121 359 6427 • CONTACT Judith Mackay, Head, Television and Multimedia • E-MAIL j.mackay@aston.ac.uk • WEB www.excellence.aston.ac.uk

Aston Media is a television and multimedia production centre providing a unique television/video production and post-production service for the university and external companies and organisations. Facilities include three custom-built lecture studios equipped to record corporate seminars, training courses and lectures. The technical support available ranges from rostrum cameras for creating on-the-spot lecture overheads, an ISDN 6 video conferencing suite which can transmit from any of the lecture studios, to both linear and non-linear post-production editing suites, all incorporating sophisticated graphics capabilities. Filming off-site with a mobile production crew is also available. All services and recordings are produced to broadcast standard. A VHS duplication bank is able to record and distribute multiple copies of any master tape. Designing Websites and CD-ROMs also falls with the centre's multimedia brief.

BBC PRODUCTION AT MILTON KEYNES

Perry Building, Walton Hall, Milton Keynes MK7 6BH • TEL 01908 655269 • FAX 01908 655643 • CONTACT Ian Rosenbloom, Head of Production • E-MAIL Ian.Rosenbloom@bbc.co.uk

Produces television, video, CD-ROM and audio-visual material for the Open University, as well programmes for other BBC outlets such as BBC Knowledge, and external business such as for the Department for Education and Employment and other training establishments.

BOLTON INSTITUTE OF HIGHER EDUCATION

Media Services, Deane Street, Bolton BL3 5AB • TEL 01204 528851 • FAX 01204 399074 • CONTACT Arun Newell

Media Services employs graphic designers, video specialists and educationalists. Production of educational training and promotional materials can be carried out using a wide range of media including text, graphics, computers and both studio and location video.

BOURNEMOUTH UNIVERSITY

Dorset House Library, Talbot Campus, Fern Barrow, Poole BH12 5BB • TEL 01202 595463 • FAX 01202 595475 • CONTACT Lorna Kenny • E-MAIL lkenny@bournemouth.ac.uk • WEB www.bournemouth.ac.uk/academic-services

Maintains and promotes the use of videotapes within the university. Its collection numbers about 2000 and includes Open University programmes, commercially produced videotapes and off-air recordings. Production is carried out by the university's media services.

BRUNEL UNIVERSITY

Media Services, Uxbridge UB8 3PH • TEL 01895 203236 • FAX 01895 203158 • CONTACT Keith Buckman, Media Services Manager; Colin Burgess, Media Teaching Consultant • E-MAIL Media-info@brunel.ac.uk • WEB www.brunel.ac.uk/depts/media

Media Services is involved in the production of teaching and learning materials for academic departments. It offers video and location recording on DVC Pro; sound recording facilities and multimedia; and contributes to the teaching of two undergraduate film and media degree courses within the university. It also maintains a lecture room and provides AV services.

BUCKINGHAMSHIRE CHILTERNS UNIVERSITY COLLEGE

Media Services, Queen Alexandra Road, High Wycombe HP11 2JZ • TEL 01494 522141 x 5069 • FAX 01494 450774 • WEB www.bcuc.ac.uk

Off-air television recording for video library. Technical support for degree-level video production courses.

CHELTENHAM & GLOUCESTER COLLEGE OF HIGHER EDUCATION

Media Department, Media Centre, Pittville Campus, Albert Road, Pittville, Cheltenham GL52 3JG • TEL 01242 532290 • CONTACT David Dalby • E-MAIL ddalby@chelt.ac.uk • WEB www.chelt.ac.uk/ae/ad

The Media Centre, which houses the Professional Media and Media Communications Fields, was opened by Lord Puttnam in 1993. This three-story complex comprises large photographic studios (one with drive-in facility) darkrooms, processing areas including in-house transparency processing, graphic design studios, viewing/lecture theatre, 2- and 3-machine edit suites and multi-imaging programming areas. The Atrium Gallery shows student work, exhibitions by practising professionals and touring photographic exhibitions. The Pittville Learning Centre houses a specialist Art, Design and Media Library with an impressive collection of all the latest journals, magazines and newspapers and a growing collection of films, videos and CD-ROMs. The computer facilities include a large network of Apple Macintosh machines and PCs with software for graphic design, illustration, image manipulation and design for interactive media.

CITY COLLEGE NORWICH

Learning Support Services, Ipswich Road, Norwich NR2 2LJ • TEL 01603 773010 • FAX 01603 760362 • CONTACT Steve Phillips

Large library and audio-visual materials collection including slides and some 5000 video programmes. Video production and sound/radio commissions undertaken at the Centre for Creative Arts.

HAMMERSMITH & WEST LONDON COLLEGE

Media Services, Gliddon Road, Barons Court, London W14 9BL • TEL 020 8741 1688 • FAX 020 8741 2491 • E-MAIL college@hwlc.ac.uk • WEB www.hwlc.ac.uk

The college's Media Suite offers an upgraded television studio with editing, cameras and lighting equipment, and facilities to produce multimedia materials for courses. The college has built two new sound recording studios. Students using audio technology can record their voice-overs, singing, music and oral examinations in a sound-proof environment with professional equipment and support from qualified Media Services staff.

FARNBOROUGH COLLEGE OF TECHNOLOGY

Boundary Road, Farnborough, Hampshire GU14 6SB •
TEL 01252 407270 • FAX 01252 407271 • CONTACT Alan Harding, Head
of School Media and Visual Arts • E-MAIL a.harding@farn-ct.ac.uk •
WEB www.farn-ct.ac.uk

Degree and postgraduate qualification and commercial training for all
aspects of television and video production.

GLASGOW CALEDONIAN UNIVERSITY

Audio-Visual Services, 70 Cowcaddens Road, Glasgow G4 0BA •
TEL 0141 331 3845 • FAX 0141 331 3688 • CONTACT Gerry Doyle, Head
of Audio-Visual Services

The provision of audio-visual services throughout the university; television production and editing; video-conferencing (ISDN and Scottish
MANS); equipment maintenance; production of audio-visual multimedia teaching materials; photography.

HEALTH EDUCATION BOARD FOR SCOTLAND

Woodburn House Canaan Lane, Edinburgh EH10 4SG •
TEL 0131 536 5500 • FAX 0131 536 5501 • CONTACT Steven Garrad •
E-MAIL Steve.Garrad@hebs.scot.nhs.uk • WEB www.hebs.scot.nhs.uk

Health education videos are produced to aid training and teaching of
carers and the public. Material suitable for school use is also produced.

HILLCROFT COLLEGE

South Bank, Surbiton, Surrey KT6 6DF • TEL 020 8399 2688 •
FAX 020 8390 9171 • CONTACT Hannah Kent •
E-MAIL HKENT@hillcroft.ac.uk • WEB www. hillcroft.ac.uk

Providing learning resources including off-air video and radio recordings for a small long-term adult residential college for women.

IMPERIAL COLLEGE OF SCIENCE, TECHNOLOGY AND MEDICINE

Television Studio, Level 2 Walkway, Exhibition Road, London
SW7 2BT • TEL 020 7594 8135 • FAX 020 7594 8138 •
CONTACT Colin Grimshaw, Studio Manager; Martin Sayers •
E-MAIL tvstudio@ic.ac.uk • WEB www.lib.ic.ac.uk/av

Production of any type of video recording for use within Imperial
College. In addition to supporting both postgraduate and undergraduate teaching, the Studio produces material for promotional purposes.

KEELE UNIVERSITY

Media and Communications Centre, Keele ST5 5BG • TEL 01782 583377 • FAX 01782 714832 • CONTACT Roger Phenton, Bob Sewell • E-MAIL roger@media.keele.ac.uk • WEB www.media.keele.ac.uk

Supplies audio-visual equipment and services, including equipment hire, video and audio duplication, multimedia production, video production.

LONDON GUILDHALL UNIVERSITY

Calcutta House, Old Castle Street, London E1 7NT • TEL 020 7320 1008/1012 • FAX 020 7320 1100 • CONTACT Ian Kelso, Head of Television Services • E-MAIL kelso@lgu.ac.uk • WEB www.lgu.ac.uk

Offers comprehensive audio-visual service, production of educational material (video, graphics and photography), publicity and promotional material, staff development.

LOUGHBOROUGH UNIVERSITY

Audio-Visual Services, Loughborough LE11 3TU • TEL 01509 222191 • FAX 01509 610813 • CONTACT Dr. Anne Mumford, Director • E-MAIL avs@lboro.ac.uk • WEB www.lboro.ac.uk/service/avs

The Centre undertakes video production, tape copying, design, multimedia, photography and print services, as well as lecture room AV support.

MID-KENT COLLEGE OF HIGHER AND FURTHER EDUCATION

Horsted, Maidstone Road, Chatham, Kent ME5 9UQ • TEL 01634 830633 • FAX 01634 830224 • CONTACT John Rattle • E-MAIL john.rattle@midkent.ac.uk

Audio and video production for educational and promotional purposes. The college has a four-camera studio, linear and non-linear editing facilities; and also undertakes high-quality audio work.

NAPIER UNIVERSITY

Media Services Unit, Craiglockhart Campus, 219 Colinton Road, Edinburgh EH14 1DJ • TEL 0131 455 6169 • CONTACT Andy Methven • E-MAIL a.methven@napier.ac.uk • WEB www.napier.ac.uk/depts/msuhome.htm

The Media Services Unit is split into three main sections: Audio Visual Services, Media Production Services and the Print Room. AV Services provides equipment for lecture and conference provision. Media Production Services handles: video production, including shooting and editing on Betacam SP, and high-quality programmes for education, training and promotional purposes; multimedia, assisting staff and students with CD-ROM/internet ideas and problems as well as producing original work; photo services provides colour and black-and -white service, both for location and studio work; graphics. The Print Room provides print production facilities.

NATIONAL UNIVERSITY OF IRELAND

Audio-Visual Unit/Language Centre, An Teanglann, University Road, Galway, Ireland • TEL (353) 91 524411 x 2228 • FAX (353) 91 525700 • CONTACT Sean Macíomhair, Director; Bernadette Henchy, Secretary • E-MAIL sean.maciomhair@nuigalway.ie, bernadette.henchy@nuigalway.ie • WEB www.nuigalway.ie

The Audio-Visual Unit provides a comprehensive audio-visual service for the National University of Ireland, Galway, and produces audio and video teaching and learning programmes for the university and outside bodies.

OXFORD BROOKES UNIVERSITY

Educational Media Unit, Wheatley Campus, Wheatley, Oxford OX33 1HX • TEL 01865 485990 • FAX 01865 485723 • CONTACT David Dillon • WEB www.brookes.ac.uk

Supporting teaching and learning in the institution.

PRESTON COLLEGE

Fulwood Campus, Fulwood, Preston PR2 8UR • TEL 01772 225600 OR 225571 • FAX 01772 225576 • CONTACT Liz Hart, Mick Gornall • E-MAIL Ehart@prestoncoll.ac.uk • WEB www.prestoncoll.ac.uk

The college's Media Centre provides production and technical support for a range of vocational and academic courses including: BTEC ND Media, NCFE 9770 Using Video, A-level Media Studies and A-level Film Studies, Open College North West B Unit in Media Studies and in Film Studies. It also undertakes a limited number of commissions as student projects for non-profit organisations.

QUEEN'S UNIVERSITY BELFAST

Audio Visual Services, QUB Library, Chlorine Gardens, Belfast BT9 5EQ • TEL 028 9033 5493 • FAX 028 9038 2760 • CONTACT Jonathon Brady • E-MAIL J.Brady@qub.ac.uk • WEB www.qub.ac.uk/avs

The production of educational and corporate television programmes, audio-visual presentations and interactive video materials. Facilities include a comprehensive range of post-production facilities.

ST GEORGE'S HOSPITAL MEDICAL SCHOOL

St George's Hospital Medical School, Cranmer Terrace, London SW17 0RE • TEL 020 8725 2701 • FAX 020 8725 0075 • CONTACT David Cleverly • E-MAIL d.cleverly@sghms.ac.uk • WEB www.sghms.ac.uk/depts/accserv/index.htm

Production of materials for student education, patient education, staff training and research using television, multimedia, photographic and graphics techniques.

ST MARY'S STRAWBERRY HILL

Waldegrave Road, Twickenham TW1 4SX • TEL 020 8240 4092 • FAX 020 8240 4255 • CONTACT Michael Murnane • E-MAIL murnanem@smuc.ac.uk

Provides a video support service for staff and students, as well as teaching media/television production to drama students and students following the diploma course in Heritage Interpretation.

TRINITY & ALL SAINTS COLLEGE

Media Centre, Brownberrie Lane, Horsforth, Leeds LS18 5HD • TEL 0113 283 7249 • FAX 0113 283 7200 • CONTACT Andrew Clifford, Head of Media Services • E-MAIL a.clifford@tasc.ac.uk • WEB www.tasc.ac.uk

Media production and presentation facilities for education and commercial users which include a television studio, portable video camera units, a radio station, two sound studios and extensive graphics and desktop publishing facilities. Work up to broadcast television and radio standard is undertaken.

UNIVERSITY COLLEGE LONDON

48 Riding House Street, London W1P 7PL • TEL 020 7504 9375 • FAX 020 7436 1738 • CONTACT Les Roberts • E-MAIL Images@ucl.ac.uk

UCL Images undertakes corporate and broadcast video production and is a specialist in the areas of science, technology and medicine. It has media-training studio services for 'blue-chip' clients in central London, as well as around Europe. It also undertakes the sale of broadcast material in the fields of science.

UNIVERSITY OF BATH

Audio-Visual Unit, Bath, BA2 7AY • TEL 01225 826826 x 5399 • CONTACT Pete Clark

Provides audio-visual equipment to assist with all university activities.

UNIVERSITY OF BIRMINGHAM

Television Services, Information Service, Edgbaston, Birmingham B15 2TT • TEL 0121 414 6496/6492 • FAX 0121 414 6999 • CONTACT Robert Jacobs, Pat Askey • E-MAIL r.jacobs@bham.ac.uk, p.askey@bham.ac.uk • WEB www.is.bham.ac.uk/tvs/index.htm

Television production for both academic and commercial clients plus facilities hire.

UNIVERSITY OF BRIGHTON

Media Services, Department of Learning Resources, Watts Building, Brighton BN2 4GJ • TEL 01273 642772 • FAX 01273 606093 • CONTACT Martin Hayden, Gavin Nettleton • E-MAIL G.J.Nettleton@brighton.ac.uk

Production and acquisition of video programmes and other learning materials to support university courses and research; comprehensive services in design and photography; collaborations, co-productions and distribution of generic educational and training materials.

UNIVERSITY OF CAMBRIDGE

CUMIS, 1 Bene't Place, Lensfield Road, Cambridge CB2 1EL • TEL 01223 762549 • FAX 01223 330571 • E-MAIL info@cumis.cam.ac.uk • WEB www.arct.cam.ac.uk/cumis

The Cambridge University Moving Image Studio (CUMIS), located in the Department of Architecture, has a university-wide remit to focus and co-ordinate research, teaching and production in moving image arts and sciences. Its facilities, for use by individuals and workshop groups, include digital image and sound capture and post-production.

UNIVERSITY OF CENTRAL LANCASHIRE

Centre For Learning Technologies, Preston PR1 2HE • TEL 01772 892750 OR 892752 • FAX 01772 892931 • CONTACT Andrew Marriott • E-MAIL a.s.marriott@uclan.ac.uk • WEB www.uclan.ac.uk/clt/clt.htm

The centre undertakes a wide range of audio-visual related activities.

UNIVERSITY COLLEGE CORK

Audio Visual Services, Cork, Ireland • TEL (353) 21 902279/902596 • FAX (353) 21 272642 • CONTACT W A Perrott, Director • E-MAIL a.v.services@ucc.ie • WEB www.ucc.ie/services/av.html

Acquisition and maintenance of audio-visual facilities for the college; provision of photographic, graphic and video production services for teaching and publication; provision of comprehensive conference facilities including video/data projection, simultaneous translation, interpreting and video conferencing systems; provision of medical illustration and clinical photographic services at the University Hospital for the Medical and Dental Schools.

UNIVERSITY COLLEGE DUBLIN

Audio Visual Centre, Library Building, Belfield, Dublin 4, Ireland • TEL (353) 1 706 7038 OR 7020 • FAX (353) 1 283 0060 • CONTACT Helen Guerin, Fran Malone • E-MAIL Helen.Guerin@ucd.ie • WEB www.avc.ucd.ie

This Academic Support Centre for University College Dublin is concerned with promoting the use of educational technology. Services include multimedia, photography, video and television. Professional facilities are also available for the production of teaching materials and the delivery of educational programmes. The centre supports Betacam and digital formats, has an Avid edit suite, and is equipped with a full broadcast specification studio and interactive classroom.

UNIVERSITY OF DUNDEE

Video Services, Caird House, Dundee DD1 4HN • TEL 01382 345599 • FAX 01382 345575 • CONTACT Peter H Bartlett • E-MAIL p.h.bartlett@dundee.ac.uk • WEB www.dundee.ac.uk/itservices/videoser.htm

Video production of teaching materials, mainly medical. External projects accepted.

UNIVERSITY OF EAST ANGLIA

Audio-Visual Services, Norwich NR4 7TJ • TEL 01603 592833 x 2488 • FAX 01603 593859 • CONTACT Chris Browne, Manager • WEB www.uea.ac.uk/avc

The Audio Visual Service maintains over £1 million of AV equipment for schools and centres at 150 sites across the university, providing support to teaching and research; lecture rooms; public lectures and events; conferences and short courses, as well as television, video and multimedia production and video conferencing.

UNIVERSITY OF EDINBURGH

Media and Learning Technology Service (MALTS), 55/57 George Square, Edinburgh EH8 9JU • TEL 0131 650 4097 • FAX 0131 650 4101 • E-MAIL malts@ed.ac.uk • WEB www.malts.ed.ac.uk

MALTS delivers a range of services for local university needs and outside contracts at competitive rates. The areas covered by MALTS are: teaching room services, conference services, equipment loan, computer-based learning materials, studio and location video production, copying media and off-air recording, training, video-conferencing, design and support for departmental and faculty AV equipment, multi-media library and resource collection, information and co-ordination.

UNIVERSITY OF ESSEX

Teaching Services, Wivenhoe Park, Colchester CO4 3SQ • Tel 01206 873220 • Fax 01206 872523 • Contact PA Brown • Web www2.essex.ac.uk/tsu

Comprehensive media services including television, 16mm and 35mm film projection, slide-making and off-air television recording.

UNIVERSITY OF GLASGOW

Media Services, 64 Southpark Avenue, Glasgow G12 8LB • Tel 0141 330 5676 • Fax 0141 330 5674 • Contact Ann Drummond, Director • E-mail a.drummond@udcf.gla.ac.uk • Web www.gla.ac.uk/Otherdepts/Media

Provides a full range of production services in television, audio, photography, graphics and medical illustration. Multimedia development, production and digitisation facilities (to MPEG-2 standard). Installation and maintenance of equipment in lecture theatres. Advisory and technical services, equipment loan, conference support. Media training courses. The department is currently developing its delivery of moving images online.

UNIVERSITY OF HERTFORDSHIRE

Learning Technology Unit, Learning and Information Services, College Lane, Hatfield AL10 9AB • Tel 01707 284734 • Fax 01707 284666 • Contact Steve Bennett, LTDU Manager; Mike Hare, Media Consultant • E-mail S.J.Bennett@herts.ac.uk, M.Hare@herts.ac.uk • Web www.herts.ac.uk/lis

Materials production services for university staff; advice and training for university staff and students in using learning technologies.

UNIVERSITY OF LEEDS

University Media Services, Leeds LS2 9JT • Tel 0113 233 2656 • Fax 0113 233 2655 • Contact Sally Driver • E-mail s.i.driver@leeds.ac.uk • Web http://mediant.leeds.ac.uk

The range of products and services is being developed constantly as customers' demands and expectations change and grow, and new technology is introduced. The range of products and services is also diverse, and includes general and medical photography services; poster and display making services; television and sound production and training services; self-access television facilities; television programme sales; copying from videotape, audiotape, film and off-air; audio-visual equipment purchase and advice. Digital media are at the forefront of developments in new technology, with the major role of supporting and educating the consumer in new media technology.

UNIVERSITY OF LUTON

Park Square, Luton, LU1 3JU • Tel 01582 489260 • Fax 01582 489259 • Contact Mark Gamble • E-mail mark.gamble@luton.ac.uk

Provides support for audio-visual teaching and learning requirements of university; part of Central Learning Resources. Also undertakes production for external clients.

UNIVERSITY OF MANCHESTER

Media Centre, Coupland II Building, Coupland Street, Oxford Road, Manchester M13 9PL • Tel 0161 275 2525 • Fax 0161 275 2529 • Contact Edward Poole • E-mail media-centre@man.ac.uk • Web www.media.man.ac.uk

The Media Centre aims to provide the university with all its audio-visual needs. The centre is involved in all forms of video, sound and graphics, including supporting a huge number of lecture theatres and seminar rooms around the campus.

UNIVERSITY OF NEWCASTLE UPON TYNE

Audio-Visual Centre, Framlington Place, Newcastle upon Tyne NE2 4HH • Tel 0191 222 6951 • Fax 0191 222 7696 • Contact Paul Down, Julie Leath • E-mail p.h.down@ncl.ac.uk, J.E.Leath@ncl.ac.uk • Web www.avc.ncl.ac.uk

An integrated centre providing graphics, lecture room, photographic and television services. Digital imaging is well established in the centre's photography, graphics and television work. The centre produces television programmes in the studio and on location for the university and teaching hospitals. A video catalogue is available. The UKERNA-funded Video Conferencing Advisory Service (UCAS) is managed by the department.

UNIVERSITY OF NORTH LONDON

166-220 Holloway Road, London N7 8DB • Tel 020 7607 2789 • Fax 020 7607 2789 • Web http://nemo.unl.ac.uk/media

The university has a number of media centres providing a range of different services.

UNIVERSITY OF NOTTINGHAM

Audio Visual Educational Services, Queen's Medical Centre, Nottingham NG7 2UH • TEL 0115 924 9924 x 43576 • FAX 0115 970 9917 • CONTACT Geoffrey Yarnall • E-MAIL Geoff.Yarnall@nottingham.ac.uk • WEB www.nottingham.ac.uk/AVES

Provision of a wide range of photographic, video and graphics services to the University of Nottingham and local hospitals.

RSITY OF OXFORD

edia Production Unit, Public Relations, 37 Wellington Square, ford OX1 2JF • TEL 01865 270531 • FAX 01865 270527 • CONTACT ren Watts • E-MAIL karen.watts@etrc.ox.ac.uk • www.etrc.ox.ac.uk

Media Production Unit provides a comprehensive range of services h incorporate the use of audio-visual and video equipment with ienced staff to deal with the university's needs and requirements.

TY OF PAISLEY

ment of Educational and Staff Development (E&SD), Paisley s, Paisley PA1 2BE • TEL 0141 848 3820 • FAX 0141 848 3822 • Robert W Rowatt • E-MAIL esd@paisley.ac.uk • w.paisley.ac.uk/units/ed-index.htm

sual resources provided by the department to the whole uni- clude overhead projection, video replay, slide, film and data . Camcorders and monitors for training in communication also available. E&SD is licensed to record any broadcast tel- gramme for educational purposes. Satellite broadcasts can corded, which mainly students learning languages use. are made in French, German and Spanish. Programmes d on request and held in the E&SD video library. Details of held can be accessed through the university library com- . Students and academic staff can book viewing facilities. elevision studios at Paisley Campus and University Photographic, design and graphics services are also

The BUFVC handbook
BUFVC....

ISBN 0-901299-70-7

UNIVERSITY OF PORTSMOUTH

Media Development Centre, Museum Road, Portsmouth PO1 2QQ • TEL 02392 843902 • FAX 02392 843299 • CONTACT Richard Hackett • E-MAIL richard.hackett@port.ac.uk • WEB www.port.ac.uk/mdc

The Media Development Centre is a multimedia production facility serving the university's teaching, research and communications activities. It also acts as a commercial visual communications company specialising in the development of digital media solutions for corporate training and distance learning. It operates to broadcast standards and outputs on analogue and digital tape, CD-ROM and Web-based video on demand. AVID In Sync editing facilities are also available.

UNIVERSITY OF SHEFFIELD

Learning Media Unit, 5 Favell Road, Sheffield S3 7QX • TEL 0114 222 0400 • FAX 0114 276 2106 • CONTACT John Stratford, Director • E-MAIL learningmedia@sheffield.ac.uk • WEB www.shef.ac.uk/~learnmed

The Learning Media Unit is the internal production unit of the University of Sheffield. It produces video, audio and multimedia resources to support teaching, research and promotion within the institution. The Learning Media Unit operates to high-level production standards, and undertakes its own marketing of over 100 video titles reflecting expertise in education, medicine, science and technology.

UNIVERSITY OF SOUTHAMPTON

Teaching Support and Media Services, Highfield, Southampton SO17 1BJ • TEL 023 8059 3785 • FAX 023 8059 3005 • CONTACT Dr. Haydn S. Mathias • E-MAIL h.s.mathias@soton.ac.uk

Educational development, technology and media department organised as three divisions. The Interactive Learning Centre provides training and consultancy for lecturers in teaching and learning, and undertakes development work in the use of learning technologies. The Audio-Visual Division provides a comprehensive audio-visual support service for the university, including the design and refurbishment of teaching spaces. The Media Services Division offers services in photography, graphics, video, digital media, black-and-white and colour copying, and printing.

UNIVERSITY OF STIRLING

Media Services, The University of Stirling, Stirling FK9 4LA •
TEL 01768 467253 • FAX 01786 466850 • CONTACT Gordon Brewster •
E-MAIL gab1@stir.ac.uk • WEB www.stir.ac.uk/infoserv/media

Media Services was established to provide a complete, centralised service, ranging through graphics, photography, audio and video production and printing. It offers a range of facilities including television and video, graphic design and desktop publishing, photography, printing and equipment hire.

UNIVERSITY OF STRATHCLYDE

AV Media Services, 155 George Street, Glasgow G1 1RD •
TEL 0141 548 2567 • FAX 0141 552 5182• CONTACT Sheila MacNeill •
E-MAIL s.macneill@strath.ac.uk • WEB www.avms.strath.ac.uk

AV Media Services supplies a comprehensive television and media production service for the University of Strathclyde. The emphasis is on the production of educational material, ranging from short video inserts to educational programmes with considerable budgets. Programmes are also produced for a range of clients from both the higher education and commercial sectors. AV Media Services is committed to the emerging technologies. Programmes are produced in a digital environment using AVID editing systems and, building on the established skills, interactive programmes are produced for delivery via the Internet and CD-ROM.

UNIVERSITY OF ULSTER

School of Media and the Performing Arts, Coleraine BT52 1SA•
TEL 028 7032 4196 • FAX 028 7032 4964 • CONTACT Professor John Hill
• E-MAIL wj.hill@ulst.ac.uk • WEB www.ulst.ac.uk

Undergraduate and postgraduate courses in media studies and journalism involving the combination of theoretical, critical and production-based approaches. Well equipped television and sound studio, edit suites and photographic facilities are also available.

UNIVERSITY OF WALES SWANSEA

Media Services, Singleton Park, Swansea SA2 8PP • TEL 01792 295010 •
E-MAIL aamedia@swan.ac.uk • WEB www.swan.ac.uk/media/index.htm

Media Services are responsible for providing audio-visual services across the campus for lectures, seminars and conferences. There is a variety of equipment available for use, and the staff of the centre have the knowledge and expertise in the equipment and its applications, as well as in-depth knowledge of the lecture theatres and seminar rooms around the campus.

UNIVERSITY OF WARWICK

Audio-Visual Services, University of Warwick, Coventry CV4 7AL • TEL 024 7652 3360 • CONTACT Bal Dhesi, Manager • E-MAIL cudcc@warwick.ac.uk • WEB www.warwick.ac.uk/ETS/MM-AV/av.htm

The audio-visual services in university-controlled areas, including centrally timetabled rooms, are co-ordinated by staff in Senate House and supported operationally from the Audio Visual Centre. Most departments, however, also have some audio-visual equipment of their own which is under departmental control.

UNIVERSITY OF THE WEST OF ENGLAND

Media Centre, Coldharbour Lane, Bristol BS16 1QY • TEL 0117 965 6261 • MINICOM 0117 976 3806 • CONTACT Richard Egan, Head of Centre • E-MAIL Rich.Egan@uwe.ac.uk • WEB www.uwe.ac.uk

The Media Centre exists to provide a focus for the development and application of media and new media in education. It supports students, staff and other teaching professionals with resources, development activity and new research, and provides consultancy and development services both across the university and on a commercial or partnership basis. The centre includes specialists in multimedia and graphic design, video production, Web and print publishing, photography, sound and music technology and audio-visual support for classroom activity. Dedicated multimedia teaching and open learning facilities are available within the centre.

UNIVERSITY OF YORK

Audio-Visual Centre, Wentworth College, Heslington, York YO10 5DD • TEL 01904 433031 • FAX 01904 433033 • CONTACT Rob Whitton • E-MAIL rw8@york.ac.uk • WEB www.york.ac.uk/univ/conf/admin/av.htm

The Audio-Visual Centre is responsible for providing equipment and technical staff to support teaching in term-time and conference business in vacation. The range of services provided includes the provision of audio-visual equipment in lecture theatres and seminar rooms on the Heslington campus and at the King's Manor; recording, editing, copying and conversion of videos; audio recording; and technical advice for drama productions, conferences, concerts and special events.

EDUCATION OFFICERS IN TELEVISION

Both the BBC and Channel Four provide education officers as support for their educational broadcasts. Queries relating to educational broadcasts on the ITV Network channels should be addressed to the Duty Officer at the appropriate regional company listed below.

BBC EDUCATION OFFICERS

The BBC's Education Information Unit (TEL 020 8746 1111) will be able to answer most questions relating to its educational broadcasts. A wealth of information about the BBC and education can also be found at www.bbc.co.uk/education.

The BBC produces a number of useful publications that can be obtained by contacting the telephone number given above.

BBC Education Officers are in regular contact with schools, teachers, advisers and teacher-training establishments.

ENGLAND

BBC Education, Room 2312, 201 Wood Lane, London W12 7TS

Julie Cogill (Chief Education Officer)	020 8752 5611
E-MAIL julie.coghill@bbc.co.uk	or 020 8752 5622
Jenny Towers (Lower Primary)	020 8752 5447
E-MAIL jenny.towers@bbc.co.uk	
Shelagh Scarborough (Middle Primary)	020 8752 4845
E-MAIL shelagh.scarborough@bbc.co.uk	
Samina Miller (Science Technology)	020 8752 5776
E-MAIL samina.miller@bbc.co.uk	
Steven Fawkes (Languages/Special Needs)	020 8752 5359
E-MAIL steven.fawkes@bbc.co.uk	

EDINBURGH

BBC Education, Room 305, Broadcasting House, 5 Queen Street, Edinburgh EH2 1JF

John Russell (Senior Education Officer)	0131 248 4261
E-MAIL john.russell@bbc.co.uk	
Donald Gunn (Education Officer)	0131 248 4261
E-MAIL donald.gunn@bbc.co.uk	

GLASGOW

BBC Education, Room B21, Broadcasting House, Queen Margaret Drive, Glasgow G12SDG

David Smith (Education Officer)   0141 338 2488
E-MAIL david.a.smith@bbc.co.uk

NORTHERN IRELAND

Educational Broadcasting Services, Room 201, BBC, Ormeau Avenue, Belfast BT2 8HQ

No named officer   028 9033 8437
E-MAIL Education.NI@bbc.co.uk

WALES

BBC Wales Education, Broadcasting House, Llandaff, Cardiff CF5 2YQ
Dr. Eleri Wynn-Lewis   029 2032 2838
E-MAIL lewise60@bbc.co.uk

CHANNEL FOUR EDUCATION OFFICERS

Channel Four Education Officers are contacted through Channel Four Learning, c/o Channel Four Television, 124 Horseferry Road, London SW1P 2TX, TEL 020 7396 4444 (switchboard) or 01926 436 4444 (sales and information), FAX 020 7306 5599 or 5630, WEB www.channel4.com. Education Officers are distributed by region as follows:

Education Director, based in London:
Simon Fuller   020 7291 8708

South West England: Malcolm Ward   01962 777888

South East: Adrienne Jones   020 8402 3227

North West: John Austin   01270 759514

Midlands: Rick Hayes   01926 864719

East Anglia: Mary Ellwood   01502 710519

North East: Liz Meenan   0113 2305019

Northern Ireland: Peter Logue   028 9446 9222

Wales: Chris Alford   01633 450596

Scotland: Anne Fleck   0141 568 7111

ITV NETWORK COMPANIES

Most non-BBC schools programmes are now broadcast by Channel Four. However, as users of this handbook may have cause to communicate with the network companies, basic contact details are provided below. The ITV homepage is on www.itv.co.uk; the range of information offered at the regional companies' Web sites varies considerably.

ANGLIA TELEVISION

Anglia House, Norwich NR1 3JG   TEL 01603 615151
www.anglia.tv.co.uk   FAX 01603 631032

BORDER TELEVISION

Television Centre, Carlisle CA1 3NT   TEL 01228 525101
www.border-tv.com   FAX 01228 541384

CARLTON TELEVISION

101 St Martin's Lane, London WC2N 4AZ   TEL 020 7240 4000
www.carltontv.co.uk   FAX 020 7240 4171

CENTRAL INDEPENDENT TELEVISION

Central Court, Gas Street, Birmingham B1 2JP   TEL 0121 643 9898
www.centraltv.co.uk   FAX 0121 634 4898

CHANNEL TELEVISION

Television Centre, La Pouquelaye, St Helier,
Jersey, Channel Islands JE2 3ZD   TEL 01534 816816
www.channeltv.co.uk   FAX 01534 816817

GRAMPIAN TELEVISION

Queen's Cross, Aberdeen AB9 2XJ   TEL 01224 846846
www.grampiantv.co.uk   FAX 01224 846800

GRANADA TELEVISION

Granada Television Centre, Quay Street, Manchester M60 9EA
www.granadatv.com   TEL 0161 832 7211

HTV WALES

The Television Centre, Culverhouse Cross, Cardiff CF5 6XJ
www.htv.co.uk/wales   TEL 029 2059 0590
     FAX 029 2059 7183

HTV WEST

The Television Centre, Bath Road, Bristol BS4 3HG
www.www.htv.co.uk/west   TEL 0117 972 2722
     FAX 0117 971 7685

LONDON WEEKEND TELEVISION
The London Television Centre, Upper Ground, London SE1 9LT
www.lwt.co.uk   TEL 020-7620 1620

MERIDIAN BROADCASTING (NEWBURY)
Unit 1-3 Brookway, Hambridge Lane, Newbury RG14 5UZ
www.meridiantv.co.uk   TEL 01645 522322

MERIDIAN BROADCASTING (MAIDSTONE)
West Point, New Hythe, Kent ME20 6XX
www.meridiantv.co.uk   TEL 01622 882244

MERIDIAN BROADCASTING (SOUTHAMPTON)
Television Centre, Southampton SO14 0PZ
www.meridiantv.co.uk   TEL 023 8022 2555

S4C
Parc Ty Glas, Llanishen, Cardiff CF4 5DU
www.s4c.co.uk   TEL 029 2074 7444

SCOTTISH TELEVISION
Cowcaddens, Glasgow G2 3PR   TEL 0141 300 3000
www.scottishmediagroup.com   FAX 0141 300 3030

TYNE TEES TELEVISION
The Television Centre, City Road, Newcastle upon Tyne, NE1 2AL
www.g-wizz.net/tttv   TEL 019 261 0181
                                                   FAX 0191 261 2302

UTV
Havelock House, Ormeau Road, Belfast BT7 1EB
www.utvlive.com   TEL 028 9032 8122
                                                   FAX 028 9024 6695

WESTCOUNTRY TELEVISION
Western Wood Way, Langage Science Park, Plymouth PL7 5BG
www.carlton.com/westcountry   TEL 01752 333333
                                                   FAX 01752 333444

YORKSHIRE TELEVISION
The Television Centre, Leeds LS3 1JS   TEL 0113 243 8283
www.g-wizz.net/ytv   FAX 0113 244 5107

ORGANISATIONS

This section offers a selection of contacts which are likely to be useful to those interested in the BUFVC, its publications and services. Further, comprehensive listings can be found in the *Directory of British Associations*, or sector-specific publications such as the *British Film Institute Film and Television Handbook*.

ADVERTISING STANDARDS AUTHORITY (ASA)

2 Torrington Place, London WC1E 7HW • TEL 020 7580 5555 • FAX 020 7631 3051 • WEB www.asa.org.uk

The ASA was set up in 1962 to ensure that non-broadcast advertisements appearing in the UK are legal, decent, honest and truthful. The Authority protects the public by ensuring that the rules in the British Codes of Advertising and Sales Promotion are followed by everyone who prepares and publishes advertisements. Independent of both the advertising industry and government, the ASA's work is funded by a small levy on display advertising and direct mail expenditure. The ASA aims to promote the highest standards in advertising, by a programme of industry information and training with some 70 presentations and seminars each year. It actively promotes its work and role through a co-ordinated media relations strategy to the advertising industry and consumers.

ART LIBRARIES SOCIETY (ARLIS)

18 College Road, Bromsgrove, Worcestershire B60 2NE • TEL 01527 579298 • FAX/TEL 01527 579298 • WEB http://arlis.nal.vam.ac.uk

ARLIS/UK & Ireland is an independent body, founded in 1969, which became an educational charity in 1995. It aims to promote all aspects of the librarianship of the visual arts, including architecture and design. The Society welcomes as members all those involved in the documentation of these fields and represents the profession to the outside world.

ARTS & HUMANITIES DATA SERVICE (AHDS)

King's College LondonLibrary, Strand, London WC2R 2LS • TEL 020 7848 2935 • FAX 020 7848 2939 • WEB www.ahds.ac.uk • E-MAIL info@ahds.ac.uk

The AHDS is a national service funded by the Joint Information Systems Committee (JISC) of the UK's Higher Education Funding Councils and the Arts and Humanities Research Board to collect, preserve and promote re-use of the electronic resources which result from research in the arts and humanities.

ARTS & HUMANITIES RESEARCH BOARD (AHRB)

10 Carlton House Terrace, London SW1Y 5AH • TEL 020 7969 5256 • FAX 020 7969 5413; Northavon House, Coldharbour Lane, Bristol BS16 1QD • TEL 0117 931 7417 • FAX 0117 931 7157 • WEB www.ahrb.ac.uk

The AHRB is the first UK-wide body to fund research in both the arts and humanities. It was established in October 1998 by the Higher Education Funding Council for England (HEFCE), the British Academy and the Department for Education in Northern Ireland (DENI), which have now been joined by the Scottish and Welsh Funding Councils. The AHRB provides funding and support in three programmes: advanced research; postgraduate research and training; and special funding for university museums and galleries. The Chief Executive and the post-graduate division (inherited from the former Humanities Research Board of the British Academy) are based in London, the research division in Bristol.

Postgraduate Programme: The AHRB operates two schemes – both inherited from the HRB: Studentships in the Humanities, and Postgraduate Professional and Vocational Awards.

Advanced Research Programme: The AHRB has a budget of just under £20 million to support advanced research in all fields of the arts and humanities. Applications are accepted from academic staff in higher education institutions in all parts of the UK and are assessed through a rigorous process of peer review.

University Museums and Galleries: The Board has taken over responsibility of HEFCE's scheme of special funding for university museums and galleries. Allocations to individual institutions are fixed until 2001 and the Board is currently considering its strategy in developing its future support for university museums and galleries.

ARTS COUNCIL OF ENGLAND

14 Great Peter Street, London SW1P 3NQ • TEL 020 7333 0100 • FAX 020 7973 • E-MAIL enquiries@artscouncil.org.uk • WEB www.artscouncil.org.uk

The Arts Council of England is the national funding body for the arts in England. It is responsible for developing, sustaining and promoting the arts through the distribution of public money from central government and revenue generated by the National Lottery. The Arts Council exists to help people enjoy the arts by supporting drama, music, dance and touring companies, contemporary art galleries and exhibitions, literature, film, and multimedia projects. The Government funds national galleries and museums. The Arts Council is a fully independent, non-political body operating at arm's length from Government. Originally founded in 1946 as the Arts Council of Great Britain, autonomous arts councils for England, Scotland and Wales were set up in 1994.

ARTS COUNCIL OF NORTHERN IRELAND

77 Malone Road, Belfast BT9 6AQ • TEL 028 9038 5200 • FAX 028 9066 1715

The Council distributes government and National Lottery funds for the arts throughout Northern Ireland.

ARTS COUNCIL OF WALES

9 Museum Place, Cardiff CF1 3NX • TEL 029 2037 6500 • FAX 029 2022 1447 • WEB www.ccc-acw.org.uk

The Council distributes government and National Lottery funds for the arts throughout Wales.

ASLIB – THE ASSOCIATION FOR INFORMATION MANAGEMENT

Staple Hall, Stone House Court, London EC3A 7PB • TEL 020 7903 0000 • FAX 020 7903 0011 • E-MAIL aslib@aslib.co.uk • WEB www.aslib.co.uk

Aslib, founded in 1924, is a corporate membership organisation with over 2000 members in some 70 countries. Aslib actively promotes best practice in the management of information resources, represents its members and lobbies on all aspects of the management of and legislation concerning information at local, national and international levels. Aslib provides consultancy and information services, professional development training, conferences, specialist recruitment, and publishes primary and secondary journals, conference proceedings, directories and monographs, and special interest groups.

ASSOCIATION OF COMMONWEALTH UNIVERSITIES (ACU)

John Foster House, 36 Gordon Square, London WC1H 0PF • TEL 020 7387 8572 • FAX 020 7387 2655 • E-MAIL pubinfo@acu.ac.uk • WEB www.acu.ac.uk

The ACU is a voluntary association of over 460 universities throughout the Commonwealth. Its aim is to promote contact and co-operation between member universities; to support the movement of academic staff and students between member universities; to provide information about Commonwealth universities; to host the consultancy, the Commonwealth Higher Education Management Service (CHEMS). Only universities and approved institutions of higher learning in the Commonwealth may become members. (With the council's approval, universities may remain members if the country leaves the Commonwealth.) New members are admitted only with the approval of the council. Affairs are controlled by the council of 31 vice-chancellors, university presidents or principals, representing member universities in the different regions of the Commonwealth.

ASSOCIATION FOR DATABASE SERVICES IN EDUCATION & TRAINING (ADSET)

Chancery House, Dalkeith Place, Kettering NN16 0BS •
TEL 01536 410500 • FAX 01536414274 •
E-MAIL info@adset-plus.co.uk • WEB www.adset-plus.co.uk

ADSET promotes the effective use of information related to career opportunities by: promoting coherence and compatibility of standards for recording such information and ensuring those standards meet the needs of current and prospective users; managing and maintaining support for a network of individuals and organisations who form an Association facilitating a forum for exchange of, support for, and research into, best practice in the delivery of information for or about individual career choice; providing advice and guidance (either directly or through Association members) on liability, copyright, data protection security, licensing, collection and indexing of information and other relevant issues; promoting and providing links with other national and international information service providers and to encourage the support of computer hardware and software suppliers; representing the interests of Association members to government, employers, trade unions, and other organisations; and publishing information in the form of reports and directories which will assist information services to provide coherent information to their clients.

ASSOCIATION FOR LEARNING TECHNOLOGY (ALT)

ALT Administration, University of Oxford, Suite 6, Littlegate House, 16/17 St Ebbes Street, Oxford OX1 1PT • TEL 01865 286923 •
FAX 01865 286930 • E-MAIL alt@conted.ox.ac.uk •
WEB www.csv.warwick.ac.uk/alt-E/index.html

ALT is a membership organisation, launched in 1993, which seeks to bring together all those with an interest in the use of learning technology in higher and further education. ALT aims to promote good practice in the use and development of learning technologies in higher and further education; facilitate interchange between practitioners, developers, researchers and policy-makers in education and industry; and represent the membership in areas of policy such as infrastructure provision and resource allocation.

ASSOCIATION FOR THE STUDY OF MEDICAL EDUCATION (ASME)

4th Floor, Hobart House, 80/82 Hanover Street, Edinburgh EH2 1EL • TEL 0131 225 9111 • FAX 0131 225 9444 • E-MAIL info@asme.org.uk • WEB www.asme.org.uk

ASME is a membership organisation which doctors and medical educators from any speciality and level are invited to join. ASME is unique in that it draws its members from all areas of medical education – undergraduate, postgraduate and continuing – and from all specialities. It has a function as a forum for debate and exchange of information, and is building on its contacts in medicine and teaching in the UK and among other networks, to promote knowledge and expertise in medical education.

AUDIO-VISUAL ASSOCIATION

Herkomer House, 156 High Street, Bushey, Watford WD2 3DD • TEL 020 8959 5959 • FAX 020 8950 7560

The Association is the only professional body established to protect and enhance the interests of people – creative, technical, administrative and supply – involved in the non-broadcast sector of the UK audio-visual conference and multimedia industry.

THE BRITISH ACADEMY

10 Carlton House Terrace, London SW1Y 5AH • TEL 020 7969 5200 • FAX 020 7969 5300 • E-MAIL secretary@britac.ac.uk • WEB www.britac.ac.uk

The British Academy was established by Royal Charter in 1902, under the full title of The British Academy for the Promotion of Historical, Philosophical and Philological Studies. It is an independent and self-governing fellowship of scholars. It is the national academy for the humanities and the social sciences, the counterpart to the Royal Society, which exists to serve the natural sciences. The Academy aims to represent the interests of scholarship nationally and internationally; to give recognition to excellence; to promote and support advanced research; to further international collaboration and exchange; to promote public understanding of research and scholarship; and to publish the results of research. The Academy's primary purpose is to promote research and scholarship in the humanities and social sciences; since 1999, following the establishment of the Arts & Humanities Research Board, its activities and programmes cover the social sciences equally with the humanities. It receives a Parliamentary grant-in-aid and administers its own private funds arising from gifts and legacies, from contributions made by the Fellows themselves, and from grants made by research foundations.

BRITISH ACADEMY OF FILM & TELEVISION ARTS (BAFTA)

195 Piccadilly, London W1V 5DE • TEL 020 7734 0022 • FAX 020 7734 1792 • WEB www.bafta.org

BAFTA is the UK's leading organisation promoting and rewarding the best in film, television and interactive media. A membership-led organisation, it runs a wide range of events covering topical issues on all areas which are not only open to Academy members but non-members as well. Based in central London, the Academy provides meeting place for members as well as being a unique venue which hosts many prestigious events organised through its conference facilities department.

BRITISH BOARD OF FILM CLASSIFICATION (BBFC)

3 Soho Square, London W1V 6HD • TEL 020 7439 7961 • WEB www.bbfc.co.uk

The BBFC is an independent, non-governmental body. It was established in 1912 by the film industry when local authorities started to impose their own, widely varying, censorship on films under legislation originally designed only to give them controls over safety standards in cinemas. By the mid-1920s it had become the general practice for local authorities to accept the decisions of the Board, which had already become entirely independent of the industry. In 1984 Parliament passed the Video Recordings Act and the following year the principal officers of the Board were designated as the body to implement the Act by classifying videos for sale, rent or loan. At this point the Board's title was changed to reflect the fact that classification plays a far larger part in the Board's work than censorship.

BRITISH COMPUTER SOCIETY (BCS)

1 Sanford Street, Swindon, Wilts. SN1 1HJ • TEL 01793 417417 • FAX 01793 480270 • E-MAIL bcshq@hq.bcs.org.uk • WEB www.bcs.org.uk

As the only chartered professional Institution for the field of information systems (IS) engineering, the British Computer Society exists to provide service and support to the IS community, including individual practitioners, employers of IS staff and the general public. Formed in 1957, the Society operates under a Royal Charter granted in 1984 which requires it, among other things, to: 'promote the study and practice of Computing and to advance knowledge therein for the benefit of the public'. The BCS is also an Engineering Institution, fully licensed by the Engineering Council to nominate Chartered and Incorporated Engineers and to accredit university courses and training schemes.

THE BRITISH COUNCIL

10 Spring Gardens, London SW1A 2BN • TEL 0161 957 7755 (general), 020 7389 4383 (education) • FAX 0161 957 7762 (general), 020 7389 4292 (education) • E-MAIL general.enquiries@britcoun.org OR education.enquiries@britcoun.org • WEB www.britcoun.org/arts/film/bc.htm

The British Council is the United Kingdom's international organisation for educational and cultural relations. Its purpose is to enhance the UK's reputation in the world as a valued partner. It does this by creating opportunities for people worldwide with programmes in education, English language teaching, the arts, science, governance and information through a network of 230 offices and teaching centres in 109 countries. It receives a grant-in-aid from the Foreign and Commonwealth Office and earns income from teaching English, conducting British examinations and managing development and training contracts. The Council's Film & Television Department exists to: select British shorts, documentaries and animated films for festivals all over the world; work with festivals and cinemas and other British Council offices around the world to organise showcase events for British feature films; provide an information service about British films both within the UK and at international festivals. It also produces the *British Film Catalogue*, a free annual publication with information on new British films (also freely available online at www.britfilms.com/britfilms99/index.html), and *The Directory of International Film and Video Festivals*, published every two years, with details of how to enter festivals worldwide.

BRITISH EDUCATIONAL COMMUNICATIONS & TECHNOLOGY AGENCY (BECTa)

Milburn Hill Road, Science Park, University of Warwick, Coventry CV4 7JJ • TEL 024 7641 6994 • FAX 024 7641 1418 • WEB www.becta.org.uk

Formerly the National Council for Educational Technology (NCET), BECTa ensures that technology supports the Department for

Education and Employment's (DfEE) drive to raise educational standards, and provides professional expertise to support the future development of the National Grid for Learning (NGfL). BECTa has been tasked by the Minister to work closely with the DfEE, other government departments and agencies and LEAs to provide advice and support to assist the Government in meeting its objectives of: ensuring that technology supports closely the Department's efforts to drive up standards in core curriculum subjects, in the teaching of key skills, in school effectiveness, and more widely in the development of lifelong learning; ensuring that young people leave school and college with the information and communication technology skills that they will need for the 21st century; and in both of these areas, ensuring that the needs of people with special educational needs are addressed.

BRITISH FEDERATION OF FILM SOCIETIES (BFFS)

PO Box 1DR, London W1A 1DR • TEL 020 7734 9300 • FAX 020 7734 9093 • E-MAIL info@bffs.org.uk • WEB www.bffs.org.uk

The BFFS is a national body which promotes voluntary film exhibition and represents the interests of film societies in the United Kingdom. It receives some financial support from the British Film Institute and works with other bodies such as local Arts Boards and the National Lottery Commission to support film societies.

BRITISH FILM INSTITUTE (BFI)

21 Stephen Street, London W1P 2LN • TEL 020 7294 1444 • FAX 020 7436 7950 • WEB www.bfi.org.uk

The BFI exists to promote greater understanding and appreciation of, and access to, film and moving image culture in the UK. In July 1998 the BFI underwent a major structural review which resulted in four new operational departments: Exhibition, Collections, Production and Education. These will help the Institute reach out to fresh audiences and connect with the millions of children and adults who may be unaware of the BFI's existence. The departments' functions are:

Collections: Films, television programmes, computer games, museum artefacts, stills, posters and designs have become part of the Collections Department. It includes the National Film and Television Archive (NFTVA), which now holds over 400,000 films and television programmes from 1894 to the present day.

Education and Training: Learning about film and television, at any level of formal education or vocational training, is the Department's responsibility. It is concerned with: research – to find out what is taught, where, to whom, and how; teacher training – for people teaching media in schools and colleges; policy and lobbying – for clearer and better curricular provision for the teaching of moving image media; working with other BFI departments to develop resources and policy for education about film and television

Exhibitions: The creation of a national exhibition strategy reaching out to film festivals, regional cinemas and the under-valued film society movement, but also encompassing the National Film Theatre, is the aim of the Exhibition Department. The department develops opportunities for cinemagoers everywhere to choose from, and learn about, the broadest possible range of British and world cinema.

Production: Although not currently financing feature films, the Production Department will administer a substantial regional production fund and continue the highly successful New Directors Fund, which has seen a steady stream of shorts produced since it was launched a decade ago.

BRITISH INTERACTIVE MULTIMEDIA ASSOCIATION (BIMA)

"Briarlea", Southend Road, South Green, Billericay CM11 2PR •
TEL 020 7436 8250 • FAX 01277 658107 • E-MAIL info@bima.co.uk •
WEB www.bima.co.uk

BIMA is the trade association for the UK's interactive media sector. It provides its members with a forum for the exchange of information and views on the market and promotes the sector to government, industry and education. The Association has representatives on many committees and steering groups including the Government's Creative Industries Export Promotion Group, Digital Media Alliance, New Media Knowledge, Skillset, and the London Digital Media School. It also has strong relationships with associations and governments internationally including Canada, USA, Australia, Japan, Korea and throughout Europe.

BRITISH KINEMATOGRAPH, SOUND & TELEVISION SOCIETY (BKSTS) AKA THE MOVING IMAGE SOCIETY – BKSTS

63-71 Victoria House, Vernon Place, London WC1B 4DA •
TEL 020 7242 8400 • FAX 020 7405 3560 •
E-MAIL movimage@bksts.demon.co.uk • WEB www.bksts.com

The BKSTS exists to encourage, sustain, educate, train and represent all those who, creatively or technologically, are involved in the business of providing moving images and associated sound in any form, through any medium; to encourage and promote excellence in all aspects of moving image and associated sound technology; to promote these aims throughout the world, while remaining independent of all governments and commercial organisations.

BRITISH LIBRARY NATIONAL SOUND ARCHIVE (NSA)

96 Euston Road, London NW1 2DB • TEL 020 7412 7440 • FAX 020 7412 7441 • E-MAIL nsa@bl.uk • WEB www.bl.uk

The NSA is one of the largest sound archives in the world. It now holds more than a million discs, 170,000 tapes and a growing number of videos. The collections come from all over the world and cover the entire range of recorded sound from music, drama and literature to oral history and wildlife sound from the end of the 19th century to the present day.

BRITISH SCREEN ADVISORY COUNCIL (BSAC)

19 Cavendish Square, London W1M 9AB • TEL 020 7499 4177 • FAX 020 7306 0329 • E-MAIL BSAC@BSACouncil.co.uk

The BSAC is an independent, advisory body to government and policy makers at national and European level. It is a source of information and research for the screen media industries. The BSAC provides a unique forum for the audio-visual industry to discuss major issues which affect the industry. Its membership embraces senior management from all aspects of television, film, and video. The BSAC regularly commissions and oversees research on the audio-visual industry and uses this research to underpin its policy documents. In addition to regular monthly meetings, it organises conferences, seminars and an annual reception in Brussels. The BSAC is industry-funded.

BRITISH VIDEO ASSOCIATION (BVA)

167 Great Portland Street, London W1N 5FD • TEL 020 7436 0041 • FAX 020 7436 0043 • WEB www.bva.org.uk

The BVA is the trade body that represents the interests of publishers and rights owners of video home entertainment. Its members account for 90% of the industry, which has grown since the early 1980s into a £1.42 billion rental and retail business. It liaises with government, the media, other industry bodies and carries out extensive market research.

BRITISH VIDEO HISTORY TRUST (BVHT)

c/o British Universities Film & Video Council (BUFVC), 77 Wells Street, London W1P 3RE • TEL 020 7393 1500 • FAX 020 7393 1555 • E-MAIL ask@bufvc.ac.uk • WEB www.bufvc.ac.uk

The BVHT was set up by the BBC and the BUFVC in 1988 to meet the need for videotaped documentation of everyday life in Britain. It enables non-professional people to record aspects of British life and culture which might otherwise be lost. By lending high-quality video equipment to groups, the Trust aims to record 'raw footage' suitable for use by future researchers and programme-makers. However, it does not provide facilities for producing complete documentary programmes for broadcast purposes. Groups from local history societies to trades unions have applied to record projects ranging from oral history (recollections of industries and communities to accounts of dying skills such as silversmithing) to footage of clashes between the police and New Age travellers. Priority is given to ideas which will collect the experience of ordinary people, or which will record some unusual aspect of British society or social history.

BROADCASTING STANDARDS COMMISSION

7 The Sanctuary, London SW1P 3JS • TEL 020 7233 0544 • FAX 020 7233 0397 • E-MAIL bsc@bsc.org.uk • WEB www.bsc.org.uk

The Broadcasting Standards Commission was formed from the Broadcasting Standards Council and the Broadcasting Complaints Commission. It is the statutory body for standards and fairness in broadcasting, and the only organisation within the regulatory framework of UK broadcasting to cover all television and radio. This includes BBC and commercial broadcasters as well as text, cable, satellite and digital services. The Commission has three main tasks, set out in the 1996 Broadcasting Act: to produce codes of practice relating to standards and fairness; consider and adjudicate on complaints; monitor, research and report on standards and fairness in broadcasting.

BROADCASTING, ENTERTAINMENT & CINEMATOGRAPH TECHNICIANS UNION (BECTU)

111 Wardour Street, London W1V 4AY • TEL 020 7437 8506 • FAX 020 7437 8268 • E-MAIL bectu@geo2.poptel.org.uk • WEB www.bectuorg.uk

BECTU is the independent trade union for those working in broadcasting, film, theatre, entertainment, leisure and allied industries who are primarily based in the UK. BECTU represents permanently employed, contract and freelance workers within these industries. BECTU was founded in 1991 after a series of mergers among separate unions during the 1980s, the history of which can be traced back to 1890. The union offers a wide range of services to its 32,000 members, including advice on tax, legal, and safety matters, as well as negotiating wages and contracts with employers throughout the industry. BECTU also publishes *Stage Screen and Radio* magazine ten times a year. Membership is voluntary, and anyone working or seeking employment in the industries covered by BECTU can apply for membership. The union is financed entirely by individual subscriptions from members.

CAMPAIGN FOR PRESS & BROADCASTING FREEDOM

8 Cynthia Street, London N1 9JF • TEL 020 7278 4430 • FAX 020 7837 8868 • E-MAIL cpbf@architechs.com • WEB www.architechs.com/cpbf

CAMPAIGNS FOR DIVERSITY AND DEMOCRACY IN THE MEDIA

Centre for Information on Language Teaching and Research (CILT) 20 Bedfordbury, London WC2N 4LB; Resources Library & Information Services • TEL 020 7379 5110 • FAX 020 7379 5082 • E-MAIL library@cilt.org.uk • WEB www.cilt.org.uk

CILT was established in 1966 as an independent charitable trust supported by central government grants, with the aim of collecting and disseminating information on all aspects of modern languages and the teaching of modern languages. CILT is not a membership organisation; and anyone concerned with language teaching and learning is welcome to visit the Centre or write for information. CILT's prime objectives are firstly to promote a greater national capability in languages, and also to support the work of all those concerned with language teaching and learning.

CIMTECH (NATIONAL CENTRE FOR INFORMATION MEDIA & TECHNOLOGY)

University of Hertfordshire, 45 Grosvenor Road, St Albans, Herts. AL1 3AW • TEL 01727 813651 • FAX 01727 813649 • E-MAIL c.cimtech@herts.ac.uk • WEB http://cimtech.herts.ac.uk

Cimtech Limited is the UK's centre of expertise on all aspects of information management and technology. It was established in 1967 and numbers among its members and clients over 1000 of the UK and Europe's leading organisations in both the public and private sectors. It has advised a wide range of organisations on how to take advantage of the latest developments in information management and technology to re-engineer their processes and meet their corporate objectives more effectively. Cimtech carries out strategy studies, helps users to define their information management requirements and procure the most cost-effective solutions.

COMBINED HIGHER EDUCATION SOFTWARE TEAM (CHEST)

CHEST & NISS Centre, University of Bath, Computing Services, Claverton Down, Bath BA2 7AY • TEL 01225 826282 • FAX 01225 826177 • E-MAIL chest@chest.ac.uk • WEB www.chest.ac.uk

CHEST acts as a focal point for the supply of software, data, information, training materials and other IT related products to the Higher and Further Education sectors. It is a not-for-profit organisation within, and part of, UK Higher Education, with its headquarters at the University of Bath. Although CHEST is now substantially self-funding, it is strongly supported by the Department for Education and Employment (DfEE) through the joint committee of its funding councils. It is advised by the CHEST Policy Group. CHEST's role and remit have expanded considerably since it was set up in 1988. It now serves both Higher Education (post-18 graduate level) and Further Education (post-16 non-degree level) institutions in the UK, UK research councils and the Republic of Ireland. CHEST agreements, where CHEST focuses most of its energies, are formal contracts between CHEST and the suppliers of IT products. These agreements are usually for up to five years and almost all are for site licences, where the staff and students of the institution may use the products covered at no charge other than a single, fixed annual fee. CHEST establishes many other arrangements as well. At the basic level it agrees educational discount prices for more than a thousand products, and publishes these in the form of the *CHEST Directory*. The *CHEST Directory* is held online, updated daily, and available for free access to the community.

COMMITTEE OF VICE-CHANCELLORS AND PRINCIPALS OF THE UNIVERSITIES OF THE UNITED KINGDOM (CVCP) – see Universities UK

COMMONWEALTH INSTITUTE

Kensington High Street, London W8 6NQ • TEL 020 7603 4535 • FAX 020 7602 7374 • E-MAIL info@commonwealth.org.uk • WEB www.commonwealth.org.uk

The Institute's mission is promoting awareness and knowledge of the Commonwealth. It is an independent statutory body funded by the UK Government, other Commonwealth governments, business partners and through its own activities. It is controlled by a Board of Governors which includes the High Commissioners of all Commonwealth countries represented in London. It is a registered charity and a registered museum, and is overseen by the UK's Foreign and Commonwealth Office as a non-departmental public body. The Institute provides education with a particular focus on young people, and an authoritative and accessible source of knowledge and resources on the Commonwealth available throughout UK and in other member countries.

COUNCIL FOR BRITISH ARCHAEOLOGY (CBA)

Bowes Morrell House, 111 Walmgate, York YO1 2UA • TEL 01904 671417 • FAX 01904 671384 • WEB http://britac3.ac.uk//cba/cba/cba.html

The CBA works to improve and promote public interest in and understanding of Britain's past, and concerns itself with conservation, information, research, publishing, education and training in archaeology. The CBA Education Department works with the BUFVC on a joint Working Party to review and co-ordinate the listing of films, videos and new media on archaeology suitable for use in education. This work has contributed to the audio-visual section of the CBA publication *Teaching Archaeology: a United Kingdom Directory of Resources*, produced in conjunction with English Heritage. The CBA also runs, again in conjunction with the BUFVC, the biennial Channel 4 Awards for the best video and television programme on an archaeological subject. These awards are presented under the auspices of the British Archaeological Awards.

DIGITAL TELEVISION GROUP (DTG)

Liss Mill, Liss, Hampshire GU33 7BD • TEL 01730 893144 • FAX 01730 895460 • WEB www.dtg.org.uk

The DTG was set up in the spring of 1995. It acts as a technical clearing house, resolving the many complex issues which will determine the successful launch of digital television. Technical and regulatory issues that are managed within the group include: designs for a common receiver, interoperability and common interface; transmission issues – coverage, frequency allocations and international co-ordination; new services – Electronic Programme Guides, the Application Programming Interface, content decoder and interactivity; widescreen formats and compatibility; services for the disadvantaged – subtitling, audio description and signing services.

EAST ANGLIAN FILM ARCHIVE (EAFA)

University of East Anglia, Norwich NR4 7TJ • TEL 01603 592 664 • FAX 01603 458 553

The East Anglian Film Archive aims to collect and preserve moving images relating to East Anglia and to provide a service of access and presentation where copyright allows. Established in 1976, it was the first regional film archive in the UK. EAFA is a non-profit making organisation based at the University of East Anglia (UEA). Since 1990, EAFA has run the unique Film Archiving Masters course with the Film Studies sector at UEA. It is a member of the UK Film Archive Forum.

EDUCATIONAL BROADCASTING SERVICES TRUST (EBS TRUST)

36-38 Mortimer Street, London W1N 7RB • TEL 020 7765 5714 • FAX 020 7580 6246 E-MAIL mail@ebstrust.u-net.com

Established in 1988 by the BBC, the EBS Trust is an independent trust company dedicated to the development of education at all levels using electronic technologies, principally those traditionally associated with broadcasting. It specialises in facilitating projects where consortia of interests prevail and where the techniques of distance education are needed. EBS is an independent producer in its own right but draws on a network of experts in the television and radio industries to work on specific projects.

EDUCATIONAL RECORDING AGENCY (ERA)

New Premier House, 150 Southampton Row, London WC1B 5AL • TEL 020 7837 3222 • FAX 020 7837 3750 • E-MAIL era@era.org.uk • WEB www.era.org.uk

An ERA Licence enables an educational establishment to record for educational purposes any radio broadcast, television broadcast and cable output of ERA's members, apart from Open University programmes, which come under a separate licensing scheme. Certain rights may not be covered by ERA members; recordings may be made of this material outside the ERA licence or under a separate licence. Copyright affords legal protection to the creators of material so that they can control the way in which work may be exploited. The law of copyright provides a basis on which to strike a balance between the legitimate interests of the creators who wish to be rewarded for the use or reproduction of their works and the needs of the educator to have access to these works.

EDUCATIONAL TELEVISION AND MEDIA ASSOCIATION (ETMA) –
see Society for Screen-based Learning Technology

EDUSERV – see National Information Services & Systems (NISS)

FEDERATION AGAINST COPYRIGHT THEFT (FACT)

7 Victory Business Centre, Worton Road, Isleworth, Middlesex
TW7 6DB • TEL 020 8568 6646 • FAX 020 8560 6364

FACT is an investigative organisation funded by its members to combat video counterfeiting. It is a non-profit making organisation limited by guarantee.

FEDERATION AGAINST SOFTWARE THEFT (FAST)

1 Kingfisher Court, Farnham Road, Slough, Berkshire SL2 1JF •
TEL 01753 527999 • FAX 01753 532100 • E-MAIL fast@fast.org •
WEB www.fast.org.uk

FAST was created in 1984 by the software industry to lobby Parliament for changes to the copyright law. It works on behalf of the software industry and also alongside corporates who require advice and guidance to achieve a legally sustainable software environment.

FEDERATION OF COMMERCIAL AUDIO-VISUAL LIBRARIES (FOCAL)

Pentax House, South Hill Avenue, Northolt Road, South Harrow,
Middlesex HA2 0DU • TEL 020 8423 5853 • FAX 020 8933 4826 •
E-MAIL info@focalint.org • WEB www.focalint.org

FOCAL was formed in 1985 as an international professional trade association to represent commercial film and audio-visual libraries, professional film researchers, producers and others working in the industry. FOCAL holds regular seminars and workshops on a variety of industry related subjects and is represented at the leading international trade fairs including MIPTV, MIPCOM, MILIA, RTNDA, NATPE and the London Television Show. It publishes a quarterly journal *Focal International*.

FÉDÉRATION INTERNATIONALE DES ARCHIVES DU FILM (FIAF)

1 Rue Defacqz, B-1000 Brussels, Belgium • TEL (32 2) 538 3065 •
FAX (32 2) 534 4774 • E-MAIL fiaf@mail.interpac.be •
WEB www.cinema.ucla.edu/FIAF/Text/default.html

FIAF, the International Federation of Film Archives, brings together institutions dedicated to rescuing films both as cultural heritage and as historical documents. Founded in Paris in 1938, FIAF is a collaborative association of the world's leading film archives whose purpose has always been to ensure the proper preservation and showing of motion pictures. Today, more than 100 archives in over 63 countries collect, restore, and exhibit films and cinema documentation spanning the entire history of film.

FILM COUNCIL

10 Little Portland Street, London W1N 5DF • TEL 020 7861 7861 • E-MAIL info@filmcouncil.org.uk • WEB www.filmcouncil.org.uk

The Film Council, which came into existence on 1 April 2000, was set up by government to be the lead organisation for the UK film industry. Its creation is seen to be a particularly important initiative from both industry and government viewpoints because for the first time there is one organisation in the UK responsible for encouraging both cultural and commercial film activity. As a Lottery funding distributor, the Film Council will channel all public money for film production with the exception of the support provided to the National Film and Television School. The main objective of the Film Council is to develop a coherent strategy for film culture, the development of the film industry and the encouragement of inward investment. This breaks down into two equally important but distinct aims which can be summarised as: developing film culture by improving access to, and education about, the moving image; and developing a sustainable UK film industry.

FILM EDUCATION

Alhambra House, 27-31 Charing Cross Road, London WC2H 0AU • TEL 020 7976 2291 • FAX 020 7839 5052 • E-MAIL postbox@filmeducation.org • WEB www.filmeducation.org

Film Education is a registered charity funded by the film industry in the UK. Its aim is to encourage and promote the use of film and cinema within the National Curriculum. This states that teachers should give pupils the opportunity to analyse and evaluate a wide range of media, including film. Since 1985, Film Education has expanded the range of its publications and services to respond to the growing importance of Media in the National Curriculum, and to meet the demand for current educational material on film and filmmaking. In addition to providing a range of free educational materials, Film Education organises events, INSET courses, workshops, seminars and an annual National Schools Film Week. The study materials are written by teachers who specialise in the teaching of film, within the curriculum, from primary level to GCSE, A Level and GNVQ. Study resources include film specific study guides, generic study guides, BBC Learning Zone programmes, study videos, CD-ROMs and educational Internet pages, plus an information booklet for cinema managers working with schools.

THE GRIERSON MEMORIAL TRUST

WEB http://ds.dial.pipex.com/town/plaza/dg40/griersontrust/trust.htm

In 1974, the Grierson Memorial Trust was founded as a registered charity, primarily to assume responsibility for the Grierson Award for the best documentary film. In 1980, administration of the Grierson Trust passed over to the British Film Institute (BFI), and the Award became one of the most coveted of the annual BFI Awards presentations. Following cessation of the BFI Awards night, administration is currently undertaken by Ivan Sopher & Co, the film industry accountants.

HIGHER EDUCATION DIGITISATION SERVICE (HEDS)

University of Hertfordshire, College Lane, Hatfield, Herts. AL10 9AB • TEL 01707 286078 • FAX 01707 286079 • E-MAIL heds@herts.ac.uk • WEB http://heds.herts.ac.uk

HEDS is funded by the Joint Information Systems Committee (JISC) and managed by the University of Hertfordshire. It provides advice, consultancy and a comprehensive production service for digitisation and digital library development. HEDS supports project development from initial feasibility assessments to final delivery of the client's digitised materials. The service is provided for the educational sector as well as museums, archives and other non-profit making organisations.

IMPERIAL WAR MUSEUM FILM AND VIDEO ARCHIVE (IWMFVA)

Lambeth Road, London SE1 6HZ • TEL 020 7416 5291/2 (commercial users), 0207 416 5293/4 (non-commercial users) • FAX 020 7416 5299

The collection of the Imperial War Museum Film and Video Archive was founded in 1919 when copies of the official films made in Britain during World War I were handed over to the Museum (itself founded in 1917) for preservation. The Archive now holds some 120 million feet of film and 6500 hours of videotape, relating primarily to official records of the British armed services in the two World Wars, but also including newsreels, amateur film, and more recent footage such as the former library of NATO, and UNTV Zagreb film documenting the conflict in former Yugoslavia and United Nations peace-keeping efforts. The Archive is a member of the International Federation of Film Archives (FIAF) and a member of the UK Film Archive Forum.

INDEPENDENT TELEVISION COMMISSION (ITC)

33 Foley Street, London W1P 7LB • TEL 020 7255 3000 •
FAX 020 7306 7800 • WEB www.itc.org.uk

Under its powers, derived from the Broadcasting Acts of 1990 and 1996, the ITC issues licences that allow commercial television companies to broadcast in and from the UK – whether the services are received by conventional aerials, cable or satellite, or delivered by analogue or digital means. These licences vary according to the type of service, but they all set out conditions on matters such as standards of programmes and advertising. The ITC regulates these services by monitoring broadcasters' performance against the requirements of the ITC's published licences and codes and guidelines on programme content, advertising and sponsorship and technical performance; there is a range of penalties for failure to comply.

The ITC also has a duty to ensure that a wide range of television services is available throughout the UK (and that, taken as a whole, these are of a high quality and appeal to a range of tastes and interests), as well as a duty to ensure fair and effective competition in the provision of these services. The ITC also investigates complaints and regularly publishes its findings.

Under proposals in the Government White Paper 'A new future for communications' (Cm 5015, Stationery Office, 2000), the ITC, along with other regulators of the electronic communications sector, will combine to form a new unified regulator, OFCOM.

THE INDUSTRIAL SOCIETY

Principal Office, Peter Runge House, 3 Carlton House Terrace, London SW1Y 5DG • TEL 020 7479 1000 020 7479 1111 •
WEB www.indsoc.co.uk

The Industrial Society campaigns to improve working life and is the UK's leading authority on best practice at work. The Society believes that sustainable business results go hand-in-hand with fair people-management practices. All its activities focus on the creation of an effective partnership between employers and employees, a partnership based on the acknowledgement of mutual responsibilities.

INTERNATIONAL ASSOCIATION FOR MEDIA & HISTORY (IAMHIST)

Box 1216, Washington, CT 06793, USA • WEB
www.leeds.ac.uk/ics/iamhist/index.htm

The International Association for Media and History is a family of professional film and television broadcasters, scholars, and others who are passionately concerned about film, radio and television and their relation to history. It organises conferences, publishes *The Historical Journal of Film, Radio and Television*, and offers a forum for discussion about related news and events.

INTERNATIONAL ASSOCIATION FOR MEDIA IN SCIENCE (IAMS)

c/o British Universities Film & Video Council (BUFVC), 77 Wells Street, London W1P 3RE • TEL 020 7393 1500 • FAX 020 7393 1555 • E-MAIL ask@bufvc.ac.uk • WEB www.bufvc.ac.uk

Established in 1992 as the successor to the International Scientific Film Association, IAMS's interests are centred in three main aspects of the use of film, television and multimedia in science and technology – namely, their use in science education (including distance learning), in certain specialised areas of research, and in the wider popularisation of science. Membership is open to academic institutions, charitable organisations, professional associations, public bodies, film and television companies, distributors and private individuals. IAMS is supported entirely from membership fees and receives no public or corporate funding.

INTERNATIONAL VISUAL COMMUNICATIONS ASSOCIATION (IVCA)

19 Pepper Street, Glengall Bridge, Docklands, London E14 9RP • TEL 020 7512 0571 • FAX 020 7512 0591 • E-MAIL info@ivca.org • WEB www.ivca.org

The IVCA works to promote the role of commissioners, producers and the support industries which provide corporate visual communication. With roots in video, film, business events, equipment and hire industries, the IVCA has developed significant representation of the new, fast-growing technologies, notably business television, digital communications, interactive media and the Internet. The industry has a £2.2 billion turnover, and the IVCA is the largest association of its kind in the world, with sister organisations throughout Europe. It operates eight business streams and provides over 30 direct member services.

INTERUNIVERSITY HISTORY FILM CONSORTIUM (IUHFC)

c/o British Universities Film & Video Council, 77 Wells Street, London W1P 3RE • TEL 020 7393 1500 • FAX 020 7393 1555 • E-MAIL ask@bufvc.ac.uk • WEB www.bufvc.ac.uk

The IUHFC comprises 15 British university history departments. For over 20 years, it has produced films and organised conferences to bring film in its historical context to the attention of historians and students.

The films, which are designed specifically for use in education, deal with some of the major issues in 20th century history which occurred during the period when sound film became a significant part of the mass media. They have been compiled using original contemporary documentary and feature film material from British and foreign archive sources.

JOINT ACADEMIC NETWORK (JANET)

JANET Customer Service, UKERNA, Atlas Centre, Chilton, Didcot, Oxon. OX11 0QS • TEL 01235 822212 • FAX 01235 822397 • E-MAIL service@ukerna.ac.uk • WEB www.ja.net/welcome.html

JANET is the UK's academic and research network, funded by the JISC of the Higher Education Funding Councils for England (HEFCE), Scotland (SHEFC), Wales (HEFCW) and the Department of Education for Northern Ireland (DENI). JANET is managed and developed by UKERNA under a Service Level Agreement from the JISC. JANET connects several hundred institutions, including all universities, most colleges of higher education, most research council establishments and other organisations that work in collaboration with the academic and research community. JANET is fully connected to other Internet service providers in the UK and also to the National Research Networks in Europe. It forms part of the global Internet, providing access to the US and the rest of the world. As a computer network JANET facilitates the exchange of data and information between connected institutions. SuperJANET is the name used for the broadband, or high-speed, part of JANET. The name was coined in 1989 for a new initiative aimed at providing an advanced optical fibre broadband network for the HE community at an affordable price. SuperJANET was envisaged as a network of networks formed by a national network complemented by a number of regional networks (called Metropolitan Area Networks or MANs) serving areas where several HE institutions are located closely together. The SuperJANET project has transformed the JANET network from one primarily handling data to a network capable of simultaneously transporting video and audio as well as data.

JOINT INFORMATION SYSTEMS COMMITTEE (JISC)

JISC Secretariat, Northavon House, Coldharbour Lane, Bristol BS16 1QD • TEL 0117 931 7403 • FAX 0117 931 7255 • E-MAIL jisc@jisc.ac.uk • WEB www.jisc.ac.uk

Funded by the Scottish Higher Education Funding Council (SHEFC), the Higher Education Funding Council for England (HEFCE), the

Higher Education Funding Council for Wales (HEFCW) and the Department of Education Northern Ireland (DENI), JISC's mission is to 'stimulate and enable the cost effective exploitation of information systems and to provide a high quality national network infrastructure for the UK higher education and research councils communities'.

KRASZNA-KRAUSZ FOUNDATION

122 Fawnbrake Avenue, London SE24 0BZ • TEL /FAX 020 7738 6701 • WEB http://dialspace.dial.pipex.com/town/plaza/dg40/k-k/index.htm

The Kraszna-Krausz Awards, sponsored by the Kraszna-Krausz Foundation, are made annually, with prizes for books on still photography alternating with those for books on the moving image. Entries in each year cover books published in the previous two years. The winning books are those which make original and lasting educational, professional, historical, technical, scientific, social, literary or cultural contributions to the field.

LIBRARY ASSOCIATION

7 Ridgmount Street, London WC1E 7AE • TEL 020 7255 0500 • FAX 020 7255 0501 • E-MAIL info@la-hq.org.uk • WEB www.la-hq.org.uk

The Library Association is the leading professional body for librarians and information managers. It has over 25,000 members who work in all sectors, including business and industry, further and higher education, schools, local and central government departments and agencies, the health service, the voluntary sector and national public libraries. It has members throughout the UK and in more than 100 countries overseas.

MANCHESTER VISUALIZATION CENTRE (MVC)

Manchester Computing, University of Manchester, Manchester M13 9PL • TEL 0161 275 6095 • FAX 0161 275 6800/6040 • E-MAIL mvc-info@mcc.ac.uk • WEB www.man.ac.uk/MVC

The MVC was established in 1974 as the Computer Graphics Unit. MVC: provides graphics, visualisation, multimedia, image processing and World Wide Web services to the University of Manchester and all the machines operated by Manchester Computing (about 7000 computers from PCs to supercomputers); undertakes research and development in high-performance and cluster computing, interactive computer graphics, multimedia, image processing and visualisation; provides a range of training and education courses.

MECHANICAL COPYRIGHT PROTECTION SOCIETY (MCPS)

Elgar House, 41 Streatham High Road, London SW16 1ER •
Tel 020 8769 4400 • Fax 020 8378 7300 • E-mail info@mcps.co.uk •
Web www.mcps.co.uk

Collects 'mechanical' royalties due to publisher and composer members from the recordings of their copyright musical works. MCPS issues licences to the producers of CDs, records, tapes, videos, audio-visual, multimedia, broadcast and film productions.

MEDIA ARCHIVE FOR CENTRAL ENGLAND (MACE)

c/o Birmingham Central Library, Chamberlain Square, Birmingham
B3 3HQ • Tel 0121 464 1533

MACE is the newest of the regional film archives in the UK, and forms the final part of a network of national and regional moving image archives. Established in 2000, MACE is to collect films and television programmes recording the life and experience of the Midlands. It is an observer member of the UK Film Archive Forum.

MEDIA, COMMUNICATION & CULTURAL STUDIES ASSOCIATION (MECCSA)

Faculty of Arts and Media, Surrey Institute of Art & Design, Falkner
Road, Surrey GU9 7DS • E-mail hdavis@surrart.ac.uk

MeCCSA represents individual academics and departments within higher education institutions across the UK, in the field of media, communication and cultural studies. It seeks to promote the field of media, communication and cultural studies and make the case for its work and its enhancement with funding bodies such as the Arts & Humanities Research Board, and the Economic & Social Research Council, the media, schools and colleges and any other appropriate forum. The Association seeks to consult with organisations such as the Quality Assurance Council and the National Advisory Committee on Creative and Cultural Education.

MENTAL HEALTH MEDIA

356 Holloway Road, London N7 6PA • Tel 020 7700 8171 • Fax 0171
686 0959 • E-mail info@mhmedia.com • Web www.mhmedia.com

The aim of Mental Health Media is to bring together media and the fields of mental health and learning difficulties to challenge discrimination. It works to help journalists print and broadcast the voices of people who have experienced mental health problems. Through video journalism training it helps people with learning difficulties record their own stories, wishes and demands. The organisation also produces video, television, radio, audio and interactive programmes, CD-ROMs and Websites about learning difficulties, mental distress and well-being.

THE MOVING IMAGE SOCIETY – see British Kinematograph, Sound & Television Society (BKSTS)

NATIONAL ACQUISITIONS GROUP (NAG)

Westfield House, North Road, Horsforth, Leeds LS18 5HG • TEL/FAX 0113 259 1447 • WEB www.bic.org.uk/bic/nag.html

NAG was established in 1986 as a forum to stimulate, co-ordinate and publicise developments in library acquisitions and the book trade. Its members include individuals and organisations within publishing, bookselling and library systems supply, in addition to librarians from all kinds of libraries. NAG has two main aims: to bring together all those in any way concerned with library acquisitions, to assist them in exchanging information and comment and to promote understanding and good practice between them; and to seek to influence other organisations and individuals to adopt its opinions and standards. It also works on behalf of its members to define the market for publishers, stimulate sales for booksellers, improve acquisitions practice for librarians, promote and co-ordinate technological advances, develop mutual understanding and co-operation for all. The Group organises a highly successful and dynamic education, training and research programme, including an annual conference in September, a quarterly newsletter and semi-annual journal.

NATIONAL COMPUTING CENTRE (NCC)

Oxford House, Oxford Road, Manchester M1 7ED • TEL 0161 242 2200 • FAX 0161 242 2400• E-MAIL webster@ncc.co.uk • WEB www.ncc.co.uk

NCC is an independent IT services group which has been solving business problems through IT for over 30 years. The key focus of its work is to harness the power of IT to meet the business objectives of organisations across the world. It is not only the independent voice of the IT user but a leading provider of solutions for its clients.

NATIONAL FILM AND TELEVISION ARCHIVE – see British Film Institute (BFI)

NATIONAL FILM & TELEVISION SCHOOL (NFTS)

Beaconsfield Studios, Station Road, Beaconsfield HP9 1LG •
Tel 01494 671234 • Fax 01494 674042 • Web www.nftsfilm-tv.ac.uk

The NFTS is one of the leading European centres for professional training in the screen entertainment and media industries. Its graduates have a high record of employment in a competitive freelance industry and their work can be seen regularly on terrestrial, satellite and cable television, at the cinema and on commercial video. NFTS courses are predominantly practical and geared to the needs of people who plan to make their careers in the screen industries. The school's unique partnership with government and industry – both in funding and in liaison and consultation – ensures that its courses meet the present and future needs of the industry.

NATIONAL INFORMATION SERVICES & SYSTEMS (NISS)

Computing Services, University of Bath, Claverton Down, Bath BA2 7AY • Tel 01225 826036 • Fax 01225 826177 • E-mail niss@niss.ac.uk • Web www.niss.ac.uk

NISS, a division of Eduserv, operates within the UK education sector and provides online information services for the education and research community. Although NISS's primary target audience is higher education, the reach of computers and networked information grows ever wider, and users in further education and schools may also find valuable information via the NISS Website. NISS manages a substantial collection of information and information resources, as well as offering links to a wide range of information services on the Internet and other networks worldwide. The aims of NISS services are to provide: access to quality, selected information; detailed descriptions in a resource descriptions database; information delivered to the desktop; services which are information-driven rather than technology-driven; continued support for a wide user base.

NATIONAL INSTITUTE OF ADULT CONTINUING EDUCATION (NIACE)

21 de Montfort Street, Leicester LE1 7GE • Tel 0116 204 4200/4201 • Fax 0116 285 4514 • E-mail niace@niace.org.uk • Web www.niace.org.uk

NIACE's formal aim is to 'promote the study and general advancement of adult continuing education'. Its strategic plan commits NIACE to 'support an increase in the total numbers of adults engaged in formal and informal learning in England and Wales; and at the same time to take positive action to improve opportunities and widen access to learning opportunities for those communities under-represented in current provision'. NIACE undertakes this work through: advocacy to national and local government, funding bodies, industry and providers of education and training; collaboration with providers across all sectors of post-compulsory education and training; and through fostering progression routes for adults seeking to develop pathways as learners; a commitment to supporting evaluation and monitoring and to high quality service; securing informed debate – through research, enquiry, publication and through arranging seminars and conferences; effective networking – to ensure that lessons learned in one part of the system can be drawn on elsewhere; ensuring that the best of international practice is available to its members and users a commitment to being itself a well-managed learning organisation.

NATIONAL MUSEUM OF PHOTOGRAPHY, FILM & TELEVISION (NMPFT)

Bradford, West Yorkshire BD1 1NQ • TEL 01274 202030 • FAX 01274 723155 • E-MAIL talk.nmpft@nmsi.ac.uk • WEB www.nmpft.org.uk • EDUCATION: TEL 01274 202040 • E-MAIL education.nmpft@nmsi.ac.uk • WEB www.nmpft.org.uk/education

Founded in 1983, the NMPFT has quickly become the most-visited British museum outside London, welcoming around 750,000 visitors each year. A dramatic redevelopment programme has transformed the Museum and a £16m expansion programme, supported by the Arts and Heritage Lottery Funds, the European Community, the Foundation for Sports and Art and the private sector, has enabled it to meet the challenges of the digital age. The Museum's renowned collection contains many items of historical, social and cultural value – notably the world's first photographic negative, the earliest television footage and what is widely regarded as the world's first example of moving pictures – Louis le Prince's 1888 film of Leeds Bridge. As home to the one of the leading photographic archives, the Museum holds over 6000 photographs by William Henry Fox Talbot, 1.3 million images contained in the Daily Herald Archive spanning 1911-1960s, and Julia Margaret Cameron's Herschel Album. Its collection of rare early film and television technology is one of the finest in the world.

NATIONAL RESOURCE CENTRE FOR DANCE (NRCD)

University of Surrey, Guildford, Surrey GU2 7XH •
TEL 01483 259316 • FAX 01483 259500 •
E-MAIL NRCD@surrey.ac.uk • WEB www.surrey.ac.uk/NRCD

The NRCD is a non-profit national archive, centre for research, and information service for dance and movement. It aims to preserve the nation's dance heritage and enables, supports, and enhances the study, research, and teaching of dance. Founded in 1982, the NRCD has a core reference collection, an archive, a publishing programme, and a short course programme. It is based at the George Edwards Library on the University of Surrey campus.

NEW PRODUCERS ALLIANCE (NPA)

9 Bourlet Close, London W1P 7PJ • TEL 020 7580 2480 •
FAX 020 7580 2484 • E-MAIL info@npa.org.uk- • WEB www.npa.org.uk

The NPA is the main forum and focus for new talent within the British film industry. It has grown from a small gathering of like-minded producers in 1993, to an internationally respected association with around 1300 members today. Its members range from highly experienced feature film-makers, major companies and industry professionals to short film-makers and first-timers, all of whom are dedicated to sharing information in the desire to promote feature film-making in the UK. Its aims are: to educate and inform feature film producers in the UK; to encourage the making of commercial feature films for an international audience; to seek creative partnerships with producers worldwide; to provide a forum for like-minded film-makers to meet; to share industry information and experience; to support specific initiatives which encourage film-making in the UK.

NORTHERN REGION FILM & TELEVISION ARCHIVE (NRFTA)

Blanford House, Blanford Square, Newcastle Upon Tyne NE1 4JA •
TEL 0191 232 6789 • FAX 0191 230 2614

The Northern Region Film and Television Archive was founded in 1998 to collect, protect and project moving images from the Northern Region of England, covering Cumbria, Northumberland, Teesside, Durham and Tyne and Wear. The Archive is based on two sites – Tyne and Wear Archives in Newcastle and Teesside University in Middlesbrough – and contains material from all of the broadcasters in the region, regionally based production companies and gifted amateurs.

NORTH WEST FILM ARCHIVE (NWFA)

Manchester Metropolitan University, Minshull House, 47-49 Chorlton Street Manchester M1 3EU • TEL 0161 247 3097 • FAX 0161 247 3098

The North West Film Archive was set up in 1977 and is the professionally recognised home for moving images made in or about Greater Manchester, Lancashire and Cheshire. The Archive works closely with colleagues in national and regional film archives throughout the country. In 1994 it became a member of the International Federation of Film Archives (FIAF) and is a member of the UK Film Archive Forum.

ORAL HISTORY SOCIETY

The Secretary, Oral History Society, c/o Department of Sociology, University of Essex, Colchester C04 3SQ • TEL 020 7412 7405 • WEB www.sx.ac.uk/sociology/oralhis.htm

The Oral History Society is a national and international organisation dedicated to the collection and preservation of oral history. It encourages people of all ages to tape, video or write their own and other people's life stories. It offers practical support and advice about how to get started, what equipment to use, what techniques are best, how to look after tapes, and how to make use of what is collected. The Society's members come from all backgrounds with different occupations and interests but share a common love of the past. Through twice-yearly journals and conferences it brings together a network of individuals and local groups from all over Britain and Europe to share ideas, problems and solutions. Recent successful oral history conferences have examined topics such as cinema, health, sport, religion, broadcasting, politics, migration and the lives of women.

PERFORMING ARTS DATA SERVICE (PADS)

Gilmorehill Centre, University of Glasgow, Glasgow G12 8QQ • TEL 0141-330 4357 • FAX 0141-330 3659 • E-MAIL info@pads.ahds.ac.uk • WEB www.pads.ahds.ac.uk

The PADS collects and promotes the use of digital resources to support research and teaching across the broad field of the performing arts – music, film, broadcast arts, theatre, dance. Its target audience is performing arts researchers, teachers and students in UK higher education. The PADS has an interest in all types of resources related to the performing arts from digital versions of works themselves, representations or constituents of the works, materials about the performing arts and catalogue data. The PADS takes responsibility within the AHDS for researching, implementing and promoting best practices appropriate to the storing and delivery of time-based media (both sound and moving images).

PERFORMING RIGHTS SOCIETY (PRS)

29-33 Berners Street, London W1P 4AA • TEL 020 7580 5544 • FAX 020 7306 4455 • E-MAIL info@prs.co.uk • WEB www.prs.co.uk

The PRS is the UK association of composers, songwriters and music publishers, which administers the 'performing right' in their music. Whenever copyright music is heard in public, the people who own the copyright in the work are entitled by law to give permission and should get paid by the music user; but, the people who create and publish music need help to give that permission (license their music) and to collect the fees due, and so give PRS the right to do both on their behalf.

PRESS COMPLAINTS COMMISSION (PCC)

1 Salisbury Square, London EC4Y 8AE • TEL 020 7353 1248 • FAX 020 7353 8355

The PCC succeeded the Press Council as the press regulatory body in 1991. It is charged to enforce a code of practice that is framed by the newspaper and periodical industry and published by the PCC.

PRODUCERS ALLIANCE FOR CINEMA & TELEVISION (PACT)

45 Mortimer Street, London W1N 7TD • TEL 020 7331 6000 • FAX 020 7331 6700 • E-MAIL enquiries@pact.co.uk • WEB www.pact.co.uk

Founded in 1991, PACT has established itself as the only trade association in the UK representing independent television, feature film, animation and new media production companies. Representing over a thousand independent production companies, with a collective turnover exceeding £1.5 billion, PACT is governed by a Council elected by and from its membership to ensure that it represents their interests and aspirations. It also represents the interests of companies providing finance, distribution, facilities and other commercial services related to production. PACT's core policy aim is to promote and protect the commercial and cultural interests of its membership. It also seeks to encourage the development of new production companies and producers. It informs its members of the business and creative opportunities available within Europe, endeavours to present a coherent voice over policy issues to the European Union and continues to lobby for a properly structured and funded UK film industry.

QUALIFICATIONS & CURRICULUM AUTHORITY (QCA)

29 Bolton Street, London W1Y 7PD • Tel 020 7509 5555 • E-MAIL webinfo@qca.org.uk • WEB www.qca.org.uk

The QCA came into being in October 1997, bringing together the work of the National Council for Vocational Qualifications and the School Curriculum and Assessment Authority, with additional powers and duties. The Education Act 1997 gave QCA a core remit to promote quality and coherence in education and training. QCA's prime duty is to advise the Secretary of State for Education and Employment on all matters affecting the school curriculum, pupil assessment and publicly funded qualifications offered in schools, colleges and workplaces.

THE RADIO AUTHORITY

Holbrook House, 14 Great Queen Street, Holborn, London WC2B 5DG • Tel 020 7430 2724 • Fax 020 7405 7062 • E-MAIL reception@radioauthority.org.uk • WEB www.radioauthority.org.uk

The Radio Authority licenses and regulates all commercial radio services, comprising national, local, cable, national FM subcarrier, satellite, digital and restricted services (including all short-term, freely radiating services such as 'special event' radio, and highly localised permanent services such as hospital and student radio). The Authority is responsible for monitoring the obligations on its licensees required by the Broadcasting Acts 1990 and 1996. The Authority has three main tasks: to plan frequencies; to appoint licensees with a view to broadening listener choice; and to regulate programming and advertising. It is required, after consultation, to publish codes to which licensees must adhere. These cover programmes, advertising and sponsorship, and engineering. There are also rules on ownership. The Authority can apply sanctions to licensees who break the rules. Sanctions include broadcast apologies and/or corrections, fines and the shortening or revocation of licences. Licensees pay annual fees to the Authority and application fees are charged to applicants applying for licences. These fees are the Authority's only source of income and cover all its operating costs.

THE ROYAL ANTHROPOLOGICAL INSTITUTE (RAI)

50 Fitzroy Street, London W1P 5HS • Tel 020 7387 0455 • Fax 020 7383 4235 • E-MAIL rai@cix.compulink.co.uk • WEB www.rai.org.uk

The RAI is a non-profit-making registered charity. It is entirely independent, with a director and a small staff accountable to the council, who give their services without remuneration. The Institute has its own freehold building in central London. It is funded partly from the income on endowments, but mostly from subscriptions. The Royal Anthropological Institute publishes journals, has a privileged link with the Museum of Mankind Library at the British Museum, has a film lending library and an extensive photographic collection, gives awards for outstanding scholarship, organises lectures and meetings, and manages a number of trust funds for research. The journals circulate all over the world, and about 70% of subscriptions revenue comes from outside the UK.

THE ROYAL SOCIETY

6 Carlton House Terrace, London SW1Y 5AG • TEL 020 7839 5561 • FAX 020 7930 2170 • WEB www.royalsoc.ac.uk

The Royal Society is an independent academy promoting the natural and applied sciences. It was founded in 1660. The Society has a dual role, as the UK Academy of Science, acting nationally or internationally, and as the provider of a broad range of services for the scientific community in the national interest, responsive to individual demand with selection by merit, not by field. The Society consists of 1150 Fellows, and is governed by a Council headed by the President and Officers.

ROYAL TELEVISION SOCIETY (RTS)

Holborn Hall, 100 Grays Inn Road, London WC1X 8AL • TEL 020 7430 1000 • FAX 020 7430 0924 • E-MAIL info@rts.org.uk • WEB www.rts.org.uk

The Television Society was formed on 7 September 1927, nine years before the first public service broadcast from Alexandra Palace. What began with a small group of television enthusiasts intent on furthering this new scientific discovery has today become the Royal Television Society, representing the most important communications medium in the world. The Society was granted its Royal title in 1966 and now represents over 4000 members from the entire spectrum of the broadcasting industry. No longer just an engineering society, RTS members can now be found in all parts of the ever widening industry. The RTS is the only Society exclusively devoted to television and, as the industry undergoes significant change, it stands as a unique, central, independent forum where the art, science, business, craft and politics of television can be discussed by representatives from every branch of the industry.

SCOTTISH ARTS COUNCIL

12 Manor Place, Edinburgh EH3 7DD • Tel 0131 226 6051 • Fax 0131 225 9833 • E-mail help.desk.sac@artsfb.org.uk • Web www.sac.org.uk

The Scottish Arts Council is the principal channel for Government funding of the contemporary arts in Scotland. It receives an annual grant from the Scottish Office, most of which is then distributed to Scottish artists and arts organisations. Seventy-three organisations, including Scotland's national companies – Scottish Ballet, Scottish Opera, the Royal Scottish National Orchestra and the Scottish Chamber Orchestra – are funded on an ongoing basis. It also distributes National Lottery funds to the arts in Scotland (over £100 million since 1994). It supports galleries, festivals, theatres, arts centres, touring companies, contemporary dance, promoters, service organisations and artist resource centres. It also provides awards, bursaries, fellowships, travel and research grants to visual artists, craftspeople, writers, musicians, playwrights, dancers and arts administrators.

SCOTTISH FILM & TELEVISION ARCHIVE – see Scottish Screen Archive

SCOTTISH SCREEN ARCHIVE

1 Bowmont Gardens, Glasgow G12 9LR • Tel 0141 337 7400 • Fax 0141 337 7413 • Web www.scottishscreen.com

Established in 1976 as the Scottish Film and Television Archive, with a remit to locate and preserve Scotland's indigenous film heritage, the Archive's collection comprises some 23,000 reels including documentary, newsreels and topicals, shorts, television news material, advertising and promotional films. This collection has been built up largely though donations. Those wishing to deposit or donate material to the Archive are invited to discuss conditions with the Acquisitions Officer or Curator. Detailed information on all titles shortlisted is available from a computer database. A printed reference catalogue with synopsis entries for 3000 titles is available for purchase. From its viewing collection of 16mm and 35mm prints and a growing library of video copies, the Archive can provide access for academic and historical research and for educational and museum use. Enquiries concerning prints for festival screenings and retrospectives are also welcome. The Archive can also offer a service to those producing programmes for commercial or broadcast use. The Archive's cataloguing and preservation activities are supported by the Heritage Lottery Fund.

SCOTTISH SCREEN

249 West George Street, Glasgow G2 4RB • TEL 0141 302 1700 • FAX 0141 302 1711 • E-MAIL info@scottishscreen.com • WEB www.scottishscreen.com

Scottish Screen is responsible to the Scottish Parliament for developing all aspects of screen industry and culture in Scotland through script and company development, short film production, training, education, exhibition funding, the Film Commission locations support and the Scottish Film and Television Archive.

SGRÎN – MEDIA AGENCY FOR WALES

The Bank, 10 Mount Stuart Square, Cardiff Bay, Cardiff CF1 6EE • TEL 029 2033 3300 • FAX 029 2033 3320 • E-MAIL sgrin@sgrinwales.demon.co.uk • WEB www.sgrinwales.demon.co.uk

Sgrîn, Media Agency for Wales, is the primary organisation for film, television and new media in Wales. Sgrîn is responsible for the formulation of a strategic vision for the development of the industrial and cultural aspects of these industries to their full potential. Sgrîn is committed to enhancing the Welsh economy and Welsh culture by encouraging industrial growth, cultural development and public involvement in all its forms. Its aims are to: champion the development of film, television and new media in Wales to its full potential; raise the profile and awareness of Welsh film, television and new media in Wales and beyond; support cultural development and encourage participation in all aspects of film, television and new media in Wales; encourage the art of filmmaking in Wales; acquire, preserve and make available Wales' film and television heritage; to uphold the principles of equality of opportunity, supporting the Welsh language, cultural diversity and ethnicity and rejecting discrimination on grounds of disability and geographical distribution.

SKILLSET

2nd Floor, 91-101 Oxford Street, London W1R 1RA • TEL 020 7534 5300 • FAX 020 7534 533 • E-MAIL info@skillset.org • WEB www.skillset.org

Skillset is the National Training Organisation for Broadcast, Film, Video and Multimedia. It exists to encourage the delivery of informed training provision so that the British broadcast, film, video and multimedia industry's technical, creative and economic achievements are maintained and improved. Skillset is a strategic, all-industry organisation and is supported by key employers and unions.

SOCIETY FOR RESEARCH INTO HIGHER EDUCATION (SRHE)

3 Devonshire Street, London W1N 2BA • Tel 020 7637 2766 • Fax 020 7637 2781 • E-mail srheoffice@srhe.ac.uk • Web www.srhe.ac.uk

The SHRE was established in 1965 to stimulate and co-ordinate research into all aspects of higher education. It aims to improve the quality of higher education through the encouragement of debate and publication on issues of policy, on the organisation and management of higher education institutions, and on the curriculum, teaching and learning methods. The Society's income is derived from subscriptions, sales of its books and journals, conference fees and grants. It receives no subsidies, and is wholly independent. Its individual members include teachers, researchers, managers and students. Its corporate members are institutions of higher education, research institutes, professional, industrial and governmental bodies. The Society's membership is international with members in every continent and it regards its international work as amongst its most important activities.

SOCIETY FOR SCREEN-BASED LEARNING TECHNOLOGY

9 Bridge Street, Tadcaster, North Yorkshire, LST4 9AW• Tel/Fax 01937 530520 • E-mail josie.key@learningonscreen-u-net.com • Web www.learningonscreen.org.uk

Learning on Screen (LOS) is the new identity of the Educational Television and Media Association (ETmA), which was founded in 1967 to bring together institutions, individuals and organisations using television and other forms of media in education and training. Membership of Learning on Screen is open to individuals, educational and commercial organisations. The Society for Screen-based Learning (the registered company name of Learning on Screen) is a Registered Charity which receives no central funding, but which is formally recognised by the Department for Education, the Welsh Office Education Department and the Scottish Executive Education and Lifelong Learning Department, all of which, along with the BBC, Channel 4, ITC, NCET, the British Council and the Open University, are represented on its National Executive.

SOUTH EAST FILM & VIDEO ARCHIVE (SEFVA)

University of Brighton, Grand Parade, Brighton BN2 2JY • Tel 01273 643 213 • Fax 01273 643 214

The South East Film and Video Archive was established in 1992. Its function is to locate, collect, preserve and promote films and videos made in the counties of Surrey, Kent, East Sussex and West Sussex. It is based at the University of Brighton. It is a member of the UK Film Archive Forum.

STAFF & EDUCATIONAL DEVELOPMENT ASSOCIATION (SEDA)

Selly Wick House, 59/61 Selly Wick Road, Selly Park, Birmingham B29 7JE • TEL 0121 415 6801 • FAX 0121 415 6802 • E-MAIL office@seda.demon.co.uk • WEB www.seda.demon.co.uk

SEDA is the professional association for staff and educational developers in the UK, promoting innovation and good practice in higher education, formed in 1993 by the merger of the Standing Conference on Educational Development and the Staff Development Group of the Society for Research into Higher Education. The Association for Education and Training Technology merged with SEDA in 1996.

TECHNICAL ADVISORY SERVICE FOR IMAGES (TASI)

Institute for Learning & Research Technology, University of Bristol, 8-10 Berkeley Square, Bristol BS8 1HH • TEL 0117 928 7060 • FAX 0117 928 7112 • E-MAIL info@tasi.ac.uk • WEB www.tasi.ac.uk

TASI is a service funded by the JISC set up to advise and support the academic community on the digital creation, storage and delivery of image-related information. Its objectives are to: share and promote technical expertise and standards within the academic and public sectors; enable the academic community to develop digital archives of good quality image-related materials to support effective teaching and research by providing comprehensive information and advice.

TSW FILM & TELEVISION ARCHIVE FOR THE SOUTH WEST

Royal William Yard, Stonehouse, Plymouth PL1 3RP • TEL 01752 202 650 • FAX 01752 205 025

The TSW Film and Television Archive is a registered charity which is the official film archive for the South West of England. It is supported by the British Film Institute, The South West Media Development Agency and many other bodies. It is the largest regional film archive in the UK. The archive holds the Westward Television, Television South West and BBC South West collections which cover virtually every newsworthy event in the region from 1961 to 1992. It is a member of the UK Film Archive Forum.

UK FILM ARCHIVE FORUM (UKFAF)

c/o British Universities Film & Video Council, 77 Wells Street, London W1P 3RE • TEL 020 7393 1500 • FAX 020 7393 1555 • E-MAIL ask@bufvc.ac.uk • WEB www.bufvc.ac.uk/faf/faf.htm

Established in 1987 with the object of creating a network of public sector moving image archives in the UK. The Forum has an interest in all the archival aspects of the moving image, and has particular interest in the preservation of nitrate film, acetate film, and videotape; the training of archivists, acquisitions policy, standards for archives, copyright, co-operation with film laboratories, and contacts with foreign archives. Membership is institutional, although others can be invited to attend Forum meetings as Observing Members.

THE UK OFFICE FOR LIBRARY & INFORMATION NETWORKING (UKOLN)

The Library, University of Bath, Bath BA2 7AY • TEL 01225 826580 • FAX 01225 826838 • WEB www.ukoln.ac.uk

UKOLN is a national centre for support in network information management in the library and information communities. It provides awareness, research and information services and has the following goals: to promote awareness of emergent issues at technical, service and policy levels; to provide a focal point for research, development, and performance measurement; to influence policy makers and service providers in the interests of the communities it serves; to demonstrate high-quality information services.

UNITED KINGDOM EDUCATION & RESEARCH NETWORKING ASSOCIATION (UKERNA)

Atlas Centre, Chilton, Didcot, Oxon. OX11 0QS • TEL 01235 822 200 • FAX 01235 822 399 • WEB www.ukerna.ac.uk

UKERNA manages the operation and development of the JANET networks under a Service Level Agreement from the JISC of the UK Higher Education Funding Councils.

UNIVERSITIES UK

Woburn House, 20 Tavistock Square, London WC1H 9HQ • TEL 020 7419 4111 • FAX 020 7388 8649 • E-MAIL info@cvcp.ac.uk • WEB www.cvcp.ac.uk

Universities UK is the new name of the Committee of Vice-Chancellors and Principals of the Universities of the United Kingdom (CVCP). Universities UK's vision for higher education in the UK is for a system that is adequately funded from a diversity of sources, that provides access for all those UK citizens who would benefit from it, is at the leading edge of research and promotes good practice in teaching and learning. Its mission is to be the leading voice of UK universities. It aims to support the university sector by: promoting public understanding of the objectives, achievements, needs and diversity of UK universities; improving the funding, regulatory and marketing environment within which UK universities pursue their diverse missions; assisting in the development of good practice in all spheres of university activity by sharing ideas and experience; championing the independence and autonomy of UK universities.

VEGA SCIENCE TRUST

CPES, University of Sussex, Falmer, Brighton BN1 9QJ • TEL 01273 678726 • FAX 01273 677196 • E-MAIL g.e.watson@vega.org.uk • WEB www.vega.org.uk

The Vega Science Trust produces programmes for network television which treat science as cultural activity, so complementing present media coverage of science. It aims to bridge the gap between professional and public understanding of science by creating programmes in which the state-of-the-art understanding of our leading scientists is made more accessible.

VERA MEDIA

30-38 Dock Street, Leeds LS10 1JF • TEL 0113 242 8646 • FAX 0113 242 8739 • E-MAIL vera@vera-media.co.uk • WEB www.networking-media.org

Vera Media is a video/multimedia production and training organisation. It produces programmes for education, arts, voluntary and public sector, and community documentaries with women's, youth and similar groups. It also runs accredited, European-financed training for individuals and groups, and publishes the Directory of Film, Video and Multimedia Courses in Yorkshire and Humber. Vera Media has an information and resources library on media careers, equal opportunities, film festivals, employment rights, women's representation on screen and more. Visits by appointment.

VIDEO STANDARDS COUNCIL (VSC)

Kinetic Business Centre, Theobald Street, Borehamwood, Herts. WD6 4PJ • Tel 020 8387 4020 • Fax 020 8387 4004 • E-mail vsc@videostandards.org.uk • Web www.videostandards.org.uk

VSC was established 1989 as a non-profit making body to develop and administer a Code of Practice designed to promote high standards within the video industry. In 1993, its brief was expanded to promote high standards within the computer games industry. VSC membership represents all segments of the video and games industries and on the retail side has over 8000 registered retail outlets across the country.

THE VISUAL ARTS DATA SERVICE (VADS)

Surrey Institute of Art & Design, University College, Falkner Road, Farnham , GU9 7DS • Tel 01252 892723 • Fax 01252 892725 • E-mail info@vads.ahds.ac.uk • Web www.vads.ahds.ac.

The VADS began operation in March 1997 and is part of the AHDS funded by JISC and AHRB. Its two main goals are: to build a searchable on-line archive of digital resources for use by the visual arts community especially higher education for teaching, learning and research and to establish and promote good practice in the creation, management and preservation of digital resources through an advisory, training and publications programme.

VOICE OF THE LISTENER & VIEWER (VLV)

101 King's Drive, Gravesend, Kent DA12 5BQ • Tel 01474 352835 • Fax 01474 351112 • E-mail vlv@btinternet.com

The VLV is a non-profit-making society with the aims of supporting high standards in broadcasting. It has no political, sectarian or commercial affiliations and speaks for listeners and viewers on the whole range of broadcasting issues.

WALES FILM AND TELEVISION ARCHIVE (WFTA)

Unit 1, The Science Park, Aberystwyth SY23 3AH • Tel 01970 626 007 • Fax 01970 626 008

In 1989 the Wales Film and Television Archive was established as a pilot project, entering a new and permanent phase in 1992. It is now part of Sgrîn – Media Agency for Wales. The WFTA selects, preserves and where possible makes available films and television programmes relating to Wales, and now holds over 3,000,000 feet of film, and 2,500 hours of videotape. It is a member of the International Federation of Film Archives (FIAF) and is a member of the UK Film Archive Forum.

WESSEX FILM AND SOUND ARCHIVE (WFSA)

Hampshire Record Office, Sussex Street, Winchester SO23 8TH •
TEL 01962 847 742 • FAX 01962 878 681

The archive collects and preserves film, video and sound recordings of interest to Hampshire and the surrounding counties. It is a member of the UK Film Archive Forum.

WOMEN'S AUDIO-VISUAL EDUCATION SCHEME (WAVES)

The Wheel, 4 Wild Court, off Kingsway, London WC2B 5AU •
TEL 020 7430 1076 • FAX 020 7242 2765 • WEB www.waves.org.uk

WAVES aims to promote and train women to work in the audio and visual media industries and to produce their own independent work.

WRITERS & SCHOLARS INTERNATIONAL

33 Islington High Street, London N1 9LH • TEL 020 7278 2313 •
FAX 020 7278 1878 • WEB www.indexoncensorship.org

Writers and Scholars International publishes the magazine *Index on Censorship*. It aims to help the victims of censorship, to inform the world about the issues of censorship and freedom of expression, and to promote discussion and debate.

YORKSHIRE FILM ARCHIVE (YFA)

College of Ripon & York St John, College Road, Ripon HG4 2QX •
TEL 01765 696 264 • FAX 01765 606 267

The Yorkshire Film Archive is the professionally recognised public access film archive for the region. It is based at the College of Ripon & York St John, in Ripon, and provides a wide range of services including professional advice and expertise, specialist facilities for the long term care and conservation of the film collections, and programmes of outreach work to ensure that these images are constantly accessible to audiences across the region. It is a member of the UK Film Archive Forum.

HE LEARNING & TEACHING SUPPORT NETWORK (LTSN) & SUBJECT CENTRES

BACKGROUND

The Learning and Teaching Support Network (LTSN) is a network of 24 subject centres based in higher education institutions throughout the UK. It is funded by the four higher education funding bodies in England, Scotland, Wales and Northern Ireland. The Network aims to promote high-quality learning and teaching through the development and transfer of good practice in all subject disciplines, and to provide a 'one-stop shop' of learning and teaching resources for the higher education community.

The LTSN offers subject-specific expertise through the 24 subject centres, as well as generic expertise on learning and teaching issues that cross subject boundaries through a Generic Learning and Teaching Centre (GLTC), based in York. The LTSN is managed and co-ordinated by an executive based within the Institute for Learning and Teaching (ILT) in York.

ACTIVITIES

The LTSN's core activities are:
- setting up, supporting and developing learning and teaching networks
- promoting and sharing good practices in learning, teaching and assessment
- brokering the transfer of knowledge between users, experts, developers and innovators.

THE SUBJECT CENTRES

The 24 subject centres, listed at the end of this section, are a mix of single site and consortium-based centres, all located within relevant subject departments and hosted by higher education institutions. Many of the new subject centres build on previous Computers in Teaching Initiative (CTI) centres and the Fund for the Development of Teaching and Learning (FDTL) projects, thus providing some continuity of knowledge and expertise.

The subject focus recognises that, for many staff in higher education, it is at this level where most networking and exchange of learning, teaching and assessment practice takes place. The centres will aim to have high visibility within their subjects and ensure they provide a proactive and responsive service to the needs of their communities. The core activities of each subject centre will include:

- collation of information on all aspects of teaching, learning and assessment
- provision of staff development opportunities
- advisory service to practitioners and departments
- support through maintenance of networks and effective contacts
- liaison with relevant professional bodies and subject associations
- advice on the implementation of communication and information technologies in learning and teaching
- ensuring that all practitioners and disciplines are aware of current and future developments in learning and teaching
- collaboration with cognate subject centres to support interdisciplinary and multidisciplinary activity
- collaboration with the Generic Learning and Teaching Centre to ensure that subject centre staff are aware of broader issues

THE GENERIC LEARNING AND TEACHING CENTRE (GLTC)

There are also many learning and teaching issues and practices common to all subjects which will be disseminated and promoted by the GLTC. It will build links between the subject centres and become a major national source of information and expertise on learning and teaching practice. It will assist the subject centres, and higher education providers more generally, to make the best use of a wide range of approaches to learning and teaching.

Launched in the summer of 2000, the GLTC is located in York together with the Joint Information Systems Committee's (JISC) new Technology Integration Centre (TIC). The GLTC's core activities will include:

- collating information on generic developments in teaching, learning and assessment
- advising subject centres and HE institutions on generic teaching, learning and assessment issues, including the use of new technologies
- maintaining an international outlook on generic learning and teaching developments
- liaison with institutional learning and teaching bodies
- staff development activity

- liaison with the JISC and other organisations managing research and development projects in learning and teaching
- making available evaluations of generic communication and information technologies and teaching materials

THE TECHNOLOGY INTEGRATION CENTRE (TIC)

The Technology Integration Centre (TIC) is funded by the JISC and will work closely with the LTSN. It will investigate, develop and prove the applicability of new technologies in support of the whole education process in higher and further education. These will include technologies relevant to learning and teaching and their integration into wider student support and administrative systems.

WHO CAN BENEFIT FROM THE LTSN?

Individuals: the LTSN offers all staff involved in learning and teaching in higher education, including academic staff, senior managers, learning technologists, educational development staff, and staff developers, the opportunity to share their ideas and develop them with like-minded colleagues in their own subject area. The LTSN will become the primary information and advice resource on learning and teaching matters for all academic and related staff in higher education.

Departments: departments in HE institutions will benefit from the subject expertise and state-of-the-art information available from the relevant subject centres.

Institutions: the 'user communities' – staff in HE institutions and, ultimately, students – will benefit as they are made aware of and use good practices and new developments in learning and teaching. Institutions will also benefit from the professional development of their staff and be able to use the support services offered by the GLTC.

LTSN SUBJECT CENTRES

ACCOUNTANCY, BUSINESS AND MANAGEMENT
University of East Anglia   01603 593343

ART, DESIGN AND COMMUNICATION
Art and Design; Communication; Media; Film and Television Studies
University of Brighton   01273 643119

BIOSCIENCE
Biosciences; Agriculture; Forestry; Agricultural; Food Sciences
University of Leeds   0113 2233 3100

ECONOMICS
University of the West of England   0117 928 7071

EDUCATION (ESCALATE)
Education Studies
University of Nottingham   0117 9256283

EDUCATION IN THE BUILT ENVIRONMENT
Architecture; Building and Surveying; Town and Country Planning; Landscape
Cardiff University   029 20 874600

ENGINEERING
Loughborough University   01509 22 7170

ENGLISH
Royal Holloway, University of London

GEOGRAPHY, EARTH AND ENVIRONMENTAL SCIENCES
University of Plymouth   01752 233051

HEALTH SCIENCES AND PRACTICE
Subjects Allied to Medicine; Nursing and Midwifery
King's College London   020 7848 3141

HISTORY, CLASSICS AND ARCHAEOLOGY
University of Glasgow   0141 330 4942

HOSPITALITY, LEISURE, SPORT AND TOURISM
Hospitality; Leisure; Recreation; Sports; Tourism
Oxford Brookes University   01603 592312

INFORMATION AND COMPUTER SCIENCES
Librarianship and Information Studies; Computer Science
University of Ulster   028 9036 8020

LANGUAGES AND AREA STUDIES
Linguistics; Area Studies; Languages and Related Studies
University of Southampton   023 80 594814

LAW
University of Warwick   024 7652 3117

MATERIALS
University of Liverpool   0151 794 5006

MATHS, STATS AND OR NETWORK
Mathematics; Statistics; Operational Research
University of Birmingham   0121 414 7095

MEDICINE, DENTISTRY AND VETERINARY MEDICINE
University of Newcastle   0191 222 5888

PERFORMING ARTS (PALATINE)
Drama; Dance; Performing Arts; Music
University of Lancaster   01273 643004

PHILOSOPHY AND RELIGIOUS STUDIES
Philosophy; Theology; Religious Studies
University of Leeds   0113 233 4184

PHYSICAL SCIENCES
Physics; Astronomy; Chemistry
University of Hull   01482 465418

PSYCHOLOGY
University of York   01904 433154

SOCIAL POLICY AND SOCIAL WORK (SWAP)
Social Policy and Administration; Social Work
University of Southampton   023 8059 7800

SOCIOLOGY, ANTHROPOLOGY AND POLITICS
University of Birmingham   0121 414 6063

For further information, contact the LTSN Executive team at:

Genesis 3, Innovation Way, York Science Park
Heslington, York YO10 5DQ
TEL 15501904 434249 • FAX 01904 434247
E-MAIL ltsnenquiries@ilt.ac.uk • WEB www.ltsn.ac.uk

JISC REGIONAL SUPPORT CENTRE MANAGERS (RSC)

Since Spring 2000, the Further Education Funding Councils (FEFCs) of England, Northern Ireland, Scotland and Wales have become full funding partners of the Joint Information Systems Committee (JISC). To ensure that the Further Education community may take full advantage of the JISC's services and as part of the JISC's involvement in the National Learning Network, a number of JISC Regional Support Centres (RSCs) have been established across the country.

There is one RSC for each FEFC region: nine in England, one in Wales, one in Northern Ireland and two in Scotland. All are being run by a partnership/consortium of a Higher Education Institution(s) and a Further Education Institution(s). The RSCs will primarily connect FE colleges to JANET. The second phase will focused on awareness raising and training activities. For further information, see www.jisc.ac.uk:8080/assist/rsc.html.

EAST MIDLANDS

Loughborough College, Radmoor, Loughborough, Leics. LE11 3BT

CONTACT Lesley Price • TEL 01509 618114 (direct), 07799470288 (mobile) • FAX 01509 618109 • E-MAIL pricel@loucoll.ac.uk

EASTERN

RSC-EAST, Regional Office, Anglia Polytechnic University, Bishop Hall Lane, Chelmsford, Essex CM1 1SG

CONTACT Gerard Hayes • TEL 01268 638601 • FAX 01268 638631 E-MAIL g.hayes@rsc-eastern.ac.uk

LONDON

ULCC, 20 Guilford Street, London WC1N 1DZ

CONTACT Mick Kahn • TEL 020 7692 1177 • E-MAIL M.Kahn@ulcc.ac.uk

NORTH WEST

JISC Project Office, Elswick Building, Blackpool & The Fylde College, Ashfield Rd, Bispham, Blackpool FY2 0HB

CONTACT Jonathan Day • TEL 01253 504071 E-MAIL jday@blackpool.ac.uk

NORTHERN IRELAND

Queen's University Belfast, 6 College Park East, Belfast BT7 1LQ

CONTACT Sandra McKillop • TEL 028 9027 38841 • FAX 028 9033 5051
E-MAIL s.mckillop@qub.ac.uk

NORTHERN

Northern Colleges Network Ltd., The Gardener's Lodge, Neville's
Cross Campus, Darlington Road, Durham DH1 4SY

CONTACT Gareth Davies • TEL 0191 3754119, 07710 679620 (mobile)
FAX 0191 3754250 • E-MAIL gareth.davies@newdur.ac.uk

IT and Communication Services, Unit 1, Technology Park, Chester
Road, Sunderland SR2 7PS

CONTACT Dave Webster • TEL 0191 515 2990
E-MAIL dave.webster@sunderland.ac.uk

SCOTLAND NORTH AND EAST

Institute for Computer-Based Learning, Heriot-Watt University,
Edinburgh EH14 4AS

CONTACT Sarah Price • TEL 0131 451 3281 • FAX 0131 451 3283
E-MAIL sprice@icbl.hw.ac.uk

SCOTLAND SOUTH AND WEST

North Glasgow College, 110 Flemington Street, Glasgow G21 4BX

CONTACT Charles Sweeney • TEL 0141 5589001 ext. 295
FAX 0141 5583804 • E-MAIL cswee001@udcf.gla.ac.uk

SOUTH EAST

RSC South East Centre, Cornwallis South, The University, Canterbury,
Kent CT2 7NF

CONTACT Adam Blackwood • TEL 07748 960088
E-MAIL a.blackwood@ukc.ac.uk

SOUTH WEST

Babbage 301, University of Plymouth, Drake Circus, Plymouth PL4 8AA

CONTACT Jon Taylor • TEL 01752 233899 • FAX 01752 233839
E-MAIL jtaylor@rsc-south-west.ac.uk

WALES

Library and Information Services, University of Wales, Swansea SA2 8PP

CONTACT Enid O'Shea • TEL 01792 295164 • FAX 01792 295851
E-MAIL e.oshea@swansea.ac.uk

WEST MIDLANDS

IT Services, University of Wolverhampton, Wulfruna Street, Wolverhampton WV1 1SB

CONTACT Greg Vivash • TEL 01902 322546

E-MAIL greg.vivash@wlv.ac.uk

YORKSHIRE AND HUMBER

York College, Tadcaster Road, York, YO2 1UA

CONTACT Nicholas Hart • TEL 01904 770424

E-MAIL nicholas.hart@dial.pipex.com

MEDIA LEGISLATION AND REPORTS

This annotated bibliography comprises mainly government publications, but also diverse reports published by industry bodies, trade unions and independent pressure groups. The Editors would like to thank the staff of the *British Film Institute Film & Television Handbook* for their assistance in the compilation of this section.

1909   CINEMATOGRAPH ACT 1909

6 pages, HMSO, 1909. Sets out the law concerning the licensing of cinema premises by local authorities and fire safety.

1923   BROADCASTING COMMITTEE REPORT

Chairman: Sir Frederick Sykes (Cmd 1951), 46 pages, HMSO, 1923. The earliest comprehensive review of the scope and potentialities of broadcasting.

1926   REPORT OF THE BROADCASTING COMMITTEE 1926

Chairman: Earl of Crawford and Balcarres (Cmd 2599), 22 pages, HMSO, 1926. The Committee was appointed to advise on arrangements subsequent to the expiring of the British Broadcasting Company's licence in 1926. It recommended that the broadcasting service should be conducted by a public corporation.

1927   CINEMATOGRAPH FILMS ACT 1927

ii 24 pages, HMSO, 1927. An Act to restrict blind booking and advance booking of cinematograph films, and to secure the renting and exhibition of a certain proportion of British films, and for purposes connected therewith.

1932   THE FILM IN NATIONAL LIFE: BEING THE REPORT OF AN ENQUIRY CONDUCTED BY THE COMMISSION ON EDUCATIONAL AND CULTURAL FILMS INTO THE SERVICE WHICH THE CINEMATOGRAPH MAY RENDER TO EDUCATION AND SOCIAL PROGRESS

Chairman: B S Gott, xii, 204 pages, George Allen and Unwin, 1932. The principal recommendation of the report, 'that a National Film Institute be set up in Great Britain financed in part by public fund', led to the founding of the British Film Institute (BFI).

1935   REPORT OF THE TELEVISION COMMITTEE

Chairman: Lord Selsdon (Cmd 4793), 27 pages, HMSO, 1935. The Committee was appointed in 1934 to consider the development of television and to advise the Postmaster General on the relative merits of the several systems and the conditions under which any public service of television should be provided.

1936   REPORT OF THE BROADCASTING COMMITTEE 1935

Chairman: Viscount Ullswater (Cmd 5091), 77 pages, HMSO, 1936. A report on conditions generally within the broadcasting service.

1936   REPORT OF A COMMITTEE APPOINTED BY THE BOARD OF TRADE TO CONSIDER THE POSITION OF BRITISH FILMS

Chairman: Lord Moyne (Cmd 5320), 41 pages, HMSO, 1936

1936   A PRE-WAR VIEW OF THE INDUSTRY AND OF THE PROTECTIVE USE OF THE QUOTA: 'A STATISTICAL SURVEY OF THE CINEMA INDUSTRY IN GREAT BRITAIN IN 1934'

S Rowson in *The Journal of the Royal Statistical Society*, vol. 99, part 1, 1936, pages 67-129. Gives figures on cinema seats available, films passed by censor, film supply and distribution, etc.

1938   CINEMATOGRAPH FILMS ACT 1938

iii, 48 pages, HMSO, 1938. An Act to make further provision for securing the renting and exhibition of a certain proportion of British cinematograph films, and for restricting blind booking and advance booking of cinematograph films.

1944   TENDENCIES TO MONOPOLY IN THE CINEMATOGRAPH FILM INDUSTRY: REPORT OF A COMMITTEE APPOINTED BY THE CINEMATOGRAPH FILMS COUNCIL

Chairman: Albert Palache, 41 pages, HMSO, 1944. Discusses the value of the industry to the nation, the strength of the big circuits, the position of the independent producer, barring practices, etc.

1945   REPORT OF THE TELEVISION COMMITTEE 1943

Chairman: Lord Hankey (29054), 25 pages, HMSO, 1945. The report of the committee appointed in 1943 to prepare plans for the reinstatement and development of the television service after the Second World War.

1947   THE FACTUAL FILM: A SURVEY SPONSORED BY THE DARTINGTON HALL TRUSTEES

260 pages, PEP (Political and Economic Planning on behalf of the Arts Enquiry of the Dartington Hall Trustees), 1947. 'The Factual Film' is the second report of the Arts Enquiry initiated in autumn 1941, and deals with British documentary film, newsfilm, films of record, and the use of film in education. Appendices cover the British feature film industry, film censorship and the educational film movement in Scotland.

1948   REPORT OF THE COMMITTEE ON THE BRITISH FILM INSTITUTE

Chairman: Sir Cyril J Radcliffe (Cmd 7361), 13 pages, HMSO, 1948. The Committee was appointed in 1947. Discusses the functions and purposes of the Institute.

1948   REPORT OF THE FILM STUDIO COMMITTEE

Chairman: G H Gater, 17 pages, HMSO, 1948. The Committee was appointed by the President of the Board of Trade to consider and review the suggestion that a studio, owned and/or managed by the State, might make an important contribution to solving the difficulties of independent producers.

1949   DISTRIBUTION AND EXHIBITION OF CINEMATOGRAPH FILMS: REPORT OF THE
            COMMITTEE OF INQUIRY APPOINTED BY THE PRESIDENT OF THE BOARD OF TRADE

Chairman: Sir Arnold Plant (Cmd 7837), 63 pages, HMSO, 1949. Completes the picture of the industry in the 1940s begun in the Palache Report (1944).

1949   REPORT OF THE WORKING PARTY ON FILM PRODUCTION COSTS

Chairman: Sir George Gater, 32 pages, HMSO, 1949. Discusses problems of labour relations and analyses the costs of film-making.

1950   THE FILM INDUSTRY IN GREAT BRITAIN: SOME FACTS AND FIGURES

vi, 41 pages, The British Film Academy, 1950. A report of the facts and figures which were made available by others. Contains information on production, distribution, sponsorship, Quota regulations, etc. The booklet was originally compiled for the convenience of the British Film Academy staff and was later given wider distribution.

1951   REPORT OF THE BROADCASTING COMMITTEE 1949

Chairman: Lord Beveridge (Cmd 8116), 327 pages, HMSO, 1951 The Committee was appointed in 1949 to consider the constitution, control, finance and other general aspects of the sound and television broadcasting services of the United Kingdom … and to advise on the conditions under which these services and wire broadcasting should be conducted after 31 December 1951.

1951   REPORT OF THE BROADCASTING COMMITTEE 1949

Appendix H. Memoranda submitted to the Committee (Cmd. 8117), viii, 583 pages, HMSO, 1951. Evidence presented by most organisations and individuals is included. The lengthy BBC submission is followed by evidence from government departments; BBC advisory bodies; 'disinterested outsiders' (*e.g.* The British Film Institute and the Labour Party); 'minorities with a message'; 'inside interests' (*e.g.* ACTT and BBC Staff Association); 'outside interests' (*e.g.* Paramount Pictures and Granada theatres); and commercial broadcasting.

1951   BROADCASTING MEMORANDUM ON THE REPORT OF THE BROADCASTING
        COMMITTEE 1949

        (Cmd. 8291), 12 pages, HMSO, 1951. Comment by the Attlee
        Government on the 1949 Report.

1952   THE BRITISH FILM INDUSTRY: A REPORT ON ITS HISTORY AND PRESENT
        ORGANISATION, WITH SPECIAL REFERENCE TO THE ECONOMIC PROBLEMS OF
        BRITISH FEATURE FILM PRODUCTION

        307 pages, PEP (Political and Economic Planning), 1952. The results of
        a study carried out at the suggestion of the British Film Institute. Aims
        to give a comprehensive account of the development, organisation and
        problems of the British film industry.

1952   BROADCASTING: MEMORANDUM ON THE REPORT OF THE BROADCASTING
        COMMITTEE 1949

        (Cmd. 8550), 10 pages, HMSO, 1952. Recommendations by the Churchill
        Government for the renewal of the BBC's Charter. Includes the govern-
        ment's conclusion that, in the expanding field of television, provision
        should be made to permit some element of competition.

1952   CINEMATOGRAPH ACT 1952

        6 pages, HMSO, 1952. Sets out the law concerning the licensing of cin-
        ema premises by local authorities and fire safety. (See also 1909 Act.]

1953   BROADCASTING: MEMORANDUM ON TELEVISION POLICY

        (Cmd 9005), 7 pages. HMSO, 1953. Statement by the Churchill govern-
        ment redefining the policy stated in the Memorandum of 1952 and
        outlining proposals for the setting up of an independent television
        authority.

1954   TELEVISION ACT 1954

        21 pages, HMSO, 1954. An Act to make provision for television broad-
        casting services in addition to those provided by the British
        Broadcasting Corporation, and to set up a special authority for that
        purpose.

1956   COPYRIGHT ACT 1956

        iii, 92 pages, HMSO, 1956. Part 2, 13, deals with copyright in cinemato-
        graph films and Part 2, 14, with copyright in television broadcasts and
        sound broadcasts.

1957   CINEMATOGRAPH FILMS ACT 1957

        ii, 12 pages, HMSO, 1957. Deals with the Levy and the mandate of the
        National Film Finance Corporation.

1958   'THE BRITISH FILM INDUSTRY'

In PEP (Political and Economic Planning), vol. 24, Nº 424, Planning, 23 June 1958, pages 131-170. In two sections. Section 1 discusses decline in cinema attendance, films on television, impact of wide screens, the Government and the industry. Section 2 discusses exhibition, Quota regulations, distribution, production, etc.

1960   FILMS ACT 1960

iii, 33 pages, HMSO, 1960. Consolidates the earlier Acts and sets out the principal laws governing film business.

1962   REPORT OF THE COMMITTEE ON BROADCASTING 1960

Chairman: Sir Harry Pilkington (Cmnd 1753), xii, 342 pages, HMSO, 1962. The Committee was appointed to consider the future of the broadcasting services in the United Kingdom, the dissemination by wire of broadcasting and other programmes, and the possibility of television for public showing; and to advise on the services which should in future be provided in the United Kingdom by the BBC and the ITA.

1963   TELEVISION ACT 1963

25 pages, HMSO, 1963. The Act extended the period for which the ITA was to provide television services.

1964   REPORT ON THE DEPARTMENTAL COMMITTEE ON THE LAW ON SUNDAY OBSERVANCE

Chairman: Lord Crathorne (Cmnd 2528), v, 81 pages, HMSO, 1964. Part 2, Chapter 5, pages 18-21; Part 4, Chapter 17, pages 58-59; and Appendix C, page 72, deal specifically with cinemas and conditions of Sunday employment in cinemas.

1964   RECOMMENDATIONS OF THE CINEMATOGRAPH FILMS COUNCIL

Chairman of the Cinematograph Films Council: Sir Sydney C Roberts (Cmnd 2324), 31 pages, HMSO, 1964. Discusses the decline in cinema admissions, the changing patterns of attendance, and the distribution circuits. Includes the 'Roberts Committee Report of the Structure and Trading Practices Sub-Committee of the Cinematograph Films Council', which detailed the complaints of independent exhibitors and independent producers and assessed the solutions proposed.

1964   TELEVISION ACT 1964

ii, 37 pages, HMSO, 1964. Consolidates the Television Acts of 1954 and 1963.

1964   SURVIVAL OR EXTINCTION? A POLICY FOR BRITISH FILMS

47 pages, Association of Cinematograph, Television and Allied Technicians, 1964. Includes the 'Roberts Committee Report of the Structure and Trading Practices Sub-Committee of the Cinematograph Films Council' which detailed the complaints of independent exhibitors and independent producers and assessed the solutions proposed.

1966   BROADCASTING

(Cmnd 3169), 11 pages, HMSO, 1966. Conclusions reached by the Government on the finances of the BBC, the future fourth television service, local sound radio, etc.

1966   FILMS: A REPORT ON THE SUPPLY OF FILMS FOR EXHIBITION IN CINEMAS

Chairman: Ashton Roskill (House of Commons paper, 206), v, 113 pages, HMSO, 1966. The Monopolies Commission's report.

1967   NATIONAL FILM SCHOOL: REPORT OF A COMMITTEE TO CONSIDER THE NEED FOR A NATIONAL FILM SCHOOL

49 pages, HMSO, 1967. The Committee, under the Chairmanship of Lord Lloyd of Hampstead, was appointed by Jennie Lee in October 1965 with the following terms of reference: 'To consider the need for a National Film School and to advise, if necessary, on the objects and size of such a school, its possible location and form of organisation, and the means by which it might be financed'. The Committee decided that a National Film School 'should be established at the earliest possible moment'. (The School opened in 1971.)

1971   ITV2: A SUBMISSION TO THE MINISTER OF POSTS AND TELECOMMUNICATIONS BY THE INDEPENDENT TELEVISION AUTHORITY

24 pages, Independent Television Authority, 1971. Gives the Authority's views about the use of the fourth television channel.

1972   REPORT OF THE TELEVISION ADVISORY COMMITTEE 1972

Chairman: Sir Robert Cockburn, 21 pages, HMSO, 1972. The Committee was appointed to advise the Minister on questions on the technical development of television and sound broadcasting and related matters.

1972   SOUND BROADCASTING ACT 1972

20 pages, HMSO, 1972. Extended the functions of the ITA, renamed the Independent Broadcasting Authority (IBA), so as to include the provision of local sound broadcasting services.

1973   TELEVISION ADVISORY COMMITTEE 1972

Papers of the Technical Sub-Committee, ix, 87 pages, HMSO, 1973. Deals with matters relating to the extension of the 625-line service and the closure of the 405–line service.

1973   INDEPENDENT BROADCASTING AUTHORITY ACT 1973

ii, 52 pages, HMSO, 1973. Consolidates the Television and Sound Broadcasting Acts 1964 and 1972.

1973   NATIONALISING THE FILM INDUSTRY: REPORT OF THE ACTT NATIONALISATION FORUM

59 pages, Association of Cinematograph, Television and Allied Technicians, 1973. An ACTT special publication in two sections with appendices. Section 1, 'The Film Industry Today', analyses the position of the British film industry in the early 1970s; Section 2, 'A Publicly Owned Film Industry', lays down guidelines for the creation, structure and operation of a nationalised industry. The appendices assemble the statistical material and research data.

1973   TELEVISION IN WALES: THE FIFTH CHANNEL SOLUTION: A POLICY DOCUMENT ON THE FUTURE OF TELEVISION IN WALES

29 pages, Association of Cinematograph, Television and Allied Technicians, HTV Cardiff Shop, 1973. Supports a separate Welsh language television channel for Wales.

1974   INDEPENDENT BROADCASTING AUTHORITY ACT 1974

11 pages, HMSO, 1974

1974   AN ACT TO MAKE FURTHER PROVISION AS TO THE PAYMENTS TO BE MADE TO THE INDEPENDENT BROADCASTING AUTHORITY BY TELEVISION PROGRAMME CONTRACTORS.

Report of the Committee on Broadcasting Coverage. Chairman: Sir Stewart Crawford (Cmnd 5774), v, 96 pages, HMSO, 1974. Investigation into the broadcasting needs of Scotland, Wales, Northern Ireland and rural England.

1975   REPORT OF THE WORKING PARTY ON A FOURTH TELEVISION SERVICE IN WALES: ADRODDIAD Y GWEITHGOR AR BEDWERYDD GWASANAETH TELEDU YNG NGHYMRU

Chairman: J W N Siberry (Cmnd 6209), v, 143 pages, HMSO, 1975 (English text to page 69, Welsh text, pages 70-143). The Working Party was appointed to work out arrangements required to provide a fourth television service in Wales, including timing and estimates of cost, on the basis of the Report of the Crawford Committee on Broadcasting Coverage (1974).

1976   FUTURE OF THE BRITISH FILM INDUSTRY: REPORT OF THE PRIME MINISTER'S WORKING PARTY

Chairman: Mr John Terry (Cmnd 372), v, 33 pages, HMSO, 1976. The Working Party was established in 1975 to consider the requirements of a viable and prosperous British film industry over the next decade with special reference to scale of production, financial needs and resources, and the desirability of a closer integration between the cinematograph and television industries in respect of the resources and the film entertainment and information which they can afford. Recommended that a new public body, to be called the British Film Authority, should be created to assume responsibility for film functions fulfilled up to that time, in the main, by two Government departments.

1976   SUPPORT FOR THE ARTS IN ENGLAND AND WALES: A REPORT TO THE CALOUSTE GULBENKIAN FOUNDATION BY LORD REDCLIFFE MAUD

201 pages, Calouste Gulbenkian Foundation, UK and Commonwealth Branch, 1976. The enquiry was initiated in 1974 by the Foundation at the request of the Standing Conference of Regional Arts Associations and the Arts Council of Great Britain to study the future pattern of national, regional and local patronage of the arts in England and Wales, including the work of regional arts associations and the role of local authorities, and to make recommendations. Chapter 3, pages 76-80, discusses the funding of the British Film Institute.

1977   COPYRIGHT AND DESIGNS LAW: REPORT OF THE COMMITTEE TO CONSIDER THE LAW ON COPYRIGHT AND DESIGNS

Chairman: The Honourable Mr Justice Whitford (Cmnd 6732), xiv, 272 pages, HMSO, 1977. The Committee was appointed in 1974 to consider and report whether any (and, if so, what) changes were desirable in the law relating to copyright as provided in particular by the Copyright Act 1956 and the Design Copyright Act 1968, including the desirability of retaining the system of protection of industrial designs provided by the Registered Designs Act 1949. Chapter 5, pages 75-84, discusses audio and video recording. Chapter 19, pages 224-229, discusses cinematography films and broadcasts.

1977   REPORT OF THE ALL-INDUSTRY COMMITTEE (CONVENED BY THE ASSOCIATION OF INDEPENDENT PRODUCERS) OF THE FILM INDUSTRY 1977

Chairman: Robert Bolt, 12 pages, Association of Independent Producers, 1977. The report of an ad hoc body, comprising people directly and currently working in the British film industry and drawn from every branch of it, in the light of the proposals of the Terry Committee.

1977   REPORT OF THE COMMITTEE ON THE FUTURE OF BROADCASTING

Chairman: Lord Annan (Cmnd 6753), xv, 522 pages, HMSO, 1977. The Committee was appointed in 1974 to consider the future of the broadcasting services in the United Kingdom, including the dissemination by wire of broadcast and other programmes and of television for public showing; to consider the implications for present of any recommended additional services of new techniques; and to propose what constitutional, organisational and financial arrangements and what conditions should apply to the conduct of all these services.

1977   REPORT OF THE COMMITTEE ON THE FUTURE OF BROADCASTING

Chairman: Lord Annan. Appendices E-I: Research papers commissioned by the Committee (Cmnd 76753-1), iii, 168 pages, HMSO, 1977. Contents: J G Blumler, 'The Intervention of Television in British Politics'; J D Halloran and P Croll, 'Research Findings on Broadcasting'; B V Hindley, 'The Profits of Advertising-Financed Television Broadcasting'; G B G Lomas, 'The Population of Great Britain, 1961-1991'; A Smith, 'The Relationship of Management with Creative Staff'.

1978   AIP REPORT: RECOMMENDATIONS TO THE GOVERNMENT FOLLOWING THE PRIME MINISTER'S WORKING PARTY REPORT ON THE FUTURE OF THE BRITISH FILM INDUSTRY AND THE INTERIM ACTION COMMITTEE'S REPORT ON THE SETTING UP OF A BRITISH FILM AUTHORITY

31 pages, Association of Independent Producers, 1978. Analyses the UK production industry and the involvement of Government and states the AIP's proposals for change.

1978   BROADCASTING

(Cmnd 7294), 71 pages, HMSO, 1978. A White Paper setting out the Government's proposals for the future constitution, structure and organisation of broadcasting in the United Kingdom. The proposals, among which was one for establishing an Open Broadcasting Authority, were the result of the Callaghan Government's consideration of the 'Report of the Committee on the Future of Broadcasting' under the Chairmanship of Lord Annan, and of the many comments received on the Committee's recommendations.

1978   THE FOCUS REPORT: RECOMMENDATIONS TO THE GOVERNMENT FOLLOWING THE
PRIME MINISTER'S WORKING PARTY REPORT ON THE FUTURE OF THE BRITISH FILM
INDUSTRY AND THE INTERIM ACTION COMMITTEE'S REPORT ON THE SETTING UP
OF A BRITISH FILM AUTHORITY

49 pages, FOCUS, 1978. FOCUS (Film Conservation & Utilisation
Society) is a consumer group for film-goers. Its report covers marketing, monopoly, cinema admissions, and programming.

1978   PROPOSALS FOR THE SETTING UP OF A BRITISH FILM AUTHORITY. REPORT OF THE
INTERIM ACTION COMMITTEE ON THE FILM INDUSTRY

Chairman: Sir Harold Wilson (Cmnd 7071), iv, 14 pages, HMSO, 1978.
The Committee was appointed to advise, among other things, on the
achievement of a viable and prosperous British film industry over the
ensuing decade and, in doing so, to make a closer study of the appropriate constitution and operating role of the British Film Authority
recommended by the 1976 Terry Report, to assist in identifying the
statutory requirements when legislation could be introduced.

1978   REPORT OF THE WORKING PARTY ON THE WELSH TELEVISION FOURTH CHANNEL
PROJECT: ADRODDIAD Y GWEITHFOR AR Y CYNLLUN PEDWAREDD SIANEL I GYMRU

Chairman: D J Trevelyan (to Jan. 1978), Mrs S. Littler (from Jan. 1978
to May 1978), iv, 99 pages, HMSO, 1978 (English text to page 48, Welsh
text, pages 51-99). The Working Party was appointed in 1977 to consider how progress might be made with the project for a fourth television
channel in Wales, taking into account the Siberry Working Party Report
(1978) and the recommendations on the framework of broadcasting
generally and the fourth channel in particular, which are made in the
1977 report of the Annan Committee so that, once money were available, an immediate start could be made.

1979   THE FINANCING OF THE BRITISH FILM INDUSTRY. SECOND REPORT OF THE INTERIM
ACTION COMMITTEE ON THE FILM INDUSTRY

Chairman: Sir Harold Wilson (Cmnd. 7597), iv, 13 pages, HMSO, 1979.
Deals with the financial background, state support for film production
and the effect of taxation on the industry.

1979   REPORT OF THE COMMITTEE ON OBSCENITY AND FILM CENSORSHIP

Chairman: Bernard Williams (Cmnd 7772), vii, 270 pages, HMSO, 1979.
The Committee was appointed in 1977 to review the laws concerning
obscenity, indecency and violence in publications, displays and enter-
tainments in England and Wales, except in the field of broadcasting, to
review the arrangements for film censorship in England and Wales, and
to make recommendations.

1980   A BILL TO AMEND AND SUPPLEMENT THE INDEPENDENT BROADCASTING AUTHORITY ACT 1973 IN CONNECTION WITH THE PROVISION BY THE INDEPENDENT BROADCASTING AUTHORITY OF A SECOND TELEVISION SERVICE AND OTHERWISE IN CONNECTION WITH THE FUNCTIONS OF THE AUTHORITY; TO ESTABLISH A BROADCASTING COMPLAINTS COMMISSION; TO REQUIRE CONSULTATION BETWEEN THE BRITISH BROADCASTING CORPORATION AND THE AUTHORITY ABOUT THE SCHEDULING OF TELEVISION PROGRAMMES IN WELSH; AND FOR CONNECTED PURPOSES (BILL 139)

vi, 30 pages, HMSO, 1980

1980   STATISTICS, TECHNOLOGICAL DEVELOPMENTS AND CABLE TELEVISION: THIRD REPORT OF THE INTERIM ACTION COMMITTEE ON THE FILM INDUSTRY

Chairman: Sir Harold Wilson (Cmnd 7855), iv, 24 pages, HMSO, 1980. Looks at technological developments (video reproduction, satellite broadcasting, etc.) and cable television.

1980   A BILL TO PROVIDE FOR THE TELEVISING OF THE PROCEEDINGS OF THE HOUSE OF COMMONS AND ITS COMMITTEES AND TO ESTABLISH A PARLIAMENTARY TELEVISION UNIT TO CONTROL THE TELEVISING, PROVIDE FEEDS AND RECORDINGS TO OUTSIDE ORGANISATIONS AND MAINTAIN AN ELECTRONIC HANSARD

(Bill 134), iv. 2 pages, HMSO, 1980

1980   BROADCASTING ACT 1980

37 pages, HMSO, 1980. An Act to amend and supplement the Independent Broadcasting Authority Act 1973 in connection with the provision by the IBA of a second televising service ... to make provision as to the arrangements for the broadcasting of television programmes for reception in Wales ... and to establish a Broadcasting Complaints Commission; and for connected purposes.

1980   BROADCASTING ACT 1981

iv 81 pages, HMSO, 1981. An Act to consolidate the Independent Broadcasting Authority Acts 1973, 1974 and 1978 and the Broadcasting Act 1980.

1981   DIRECT BROADCASTING BY SATELLITE: REPORTS OF A HOME OFFICE STUDY

vi, 100 pages, HMSO, 1981. A study, initiated by the Home Secretary, of the implications of establishing a UK DBS service by about 1985 or 1990. Covers technical, financial and resource implications for the UK broadcasting system. Also considers European aspects of Direct Broadcasting by Satellite.

1981   FILM AND TELEVISION CO-OPERATION: FOURTH REPORT OF THE INTERIM ACTION
        COMMITTEE ON THE FILM INDUSTRY

Chairman: Sir Harold Wilson (Cmnd 8227), iv, 5 pages, HMSO, 1981. Makes recommendations for encouraging investment in production, whether of television features, film for television, or feature films intended for showing first in cinemas and subsequently by other means, including television.

1981   NATIONAL FILM FINANCE CORPORATION ACT 1981

12 pages, HMSO, 1981. An Act to consolidate the Cinematograph Film Production (Special Loans) Acts 1949 to 1980 and to repeal, as spent, certain enactments relating to the National Film Finance Corporation.

1981   A BILL TO PROHIBIT THE SALE AND SETTING ON HIRE OF VIDEOCASSETTES OF
        ADULT CATEGORY TO CHILDREN AND YOUNG PERSONS (BILL 46)

2 pages, HMSO, 1981

1982   BROADCASTING IN THE WELSH LANGUAGE AND THE IMPLICATIONS FOR WELSH
        AND NON-WELSH SPEAKING VIEWERS AND LISTENERS. SECOND REPORT FROM THE
        COMMITTEE ON WELSH AFFAIRS, SESSION 1980–81

Home Office and Welsh Office (Cmnd 8469), 24 pages, HMSO, 1982. Observations by the Secretary of State for the Home Department and the Secretary of State for Wales, the BBC, IBA and the Welsh Fourth Channel Authority.

1982   THE CABLE BROADCAST DEBATE: MORE CHANNELS – MORE CHOICE? IMPLICATIONS
        OF THE PROPOSALS OF THE HUNT INQUIRY: THE VIEWS OF THE INDEPENDENT
        BROADCASTING AUTHORITY

8 pages, Independent Broadcasting Authority, 1982.

1982   THE CABLE DEBATE: THE BBC'S RESPONSE TO THE HUNT REPORT

43 pages, British Broadcasting Corporation, Information Division, 1982 Contains four essays by members of the BBC Directorate with an appendix giving the BBC's evidence to the Hunt inquiry.

1982   CINEMATOGRAPH (AMENDMENT) ACT 1982

14 pages, HMSO, 1982. Extends and amends the Cinematograph Acts 1909 and 1952.

1982   THE DISTRIBUTION OF FILMS FOR EXHIBITION IN CINEMAS AND BY OTHER MEANS:
        FIFTH REPORT OF THE INTERIM ACTION COMMITTEE ON THE FILM INDUSTRY

Chairman: Sir Harold Wilson (Cmnd 8530), iv, 29 pages, HMSO, 1982. Deals with distribution and exhibition of films, making reference to the significant technological advances that were made from the time the Committee was first set up.

1982   THE HANDLING OF THE PRESS AND PUBLIC INFORMATION DURING THE FALKLANDS CONFLICT. FIRST REPORT FROM THE DEFENCE COMMITTEE, HOUSE OF COMMONS. VOLUME I: REPORT AND MINUTES OF PROCEEDINGS. SESSION 1982-83

Chairman: Sir Timothy Kitson. lxxviii pages, HMSO, 1982. Considers the problems bearing in mind two principles about the reporting of the war – the public's right to information and the Government's duty to withhold information for reasons of operational security.

1982   THE HANDLING OF THE PRESS AND PUBLIC INFORMATION DURING THE FALKLANDS CONFLICT. FIRST REPORT FROM THE DEFENCE COMMITTEE, HOUSE OF COMMONS. VOLUME II: MINUTES OF EVIDENCE. SESSION 1982-83

Chairman: Sir Timothy Kitson. viii, 493 pages, HMSO, 1982. Minutes of evidence taken on 21, 22, 27, 28 July, 20, 27 October, 9, 10 November.

1982   PUBLIC AND PRIVATE FUNDING OF THE ARTS: INTERIM REPORT ON THE NITRATE PROBLEM AT THE NATIONAL FILM ARCHIVE. TOGETHER WITH A MEMORANDUM. FOURTH REPORT FROM THE EDUCATION, SCIENCE AND ARTS COMMITTEE, HOUSE OF COMMONS

Chairman: Christopher Price. v, 6 pages, HMSO, 1982. Examines with some urgency the situation developing at the NFA with regard to its holdings on nitrate film stock.

1982   PUBLIC AND PRIVATE FUNDING OF THE ARTS: TOGETHER WITH THE MINUTES OF EVIDENCE AND APPENDICES. EIGHTH REPORT FROM THE EDUCATION, SCIENCE AND ARTS COMMITTEE, HOUSE OF COMMONS. VOLUME I

Chairman: Christopher Price. cxii pages, HMSO, 1982. Report of a Select Committee. Investigates methods by which the arts are funded. Chapter xii deals with the media arts and commercial provision and includes proposals for the creation of a single ministry to be responsible for all the performing arts.

1982   PUBLIC AND PRIVATE FUNDING OF THE ARTS: TOGETHER WITH THE MINUTE OF EVIDENCE AND APPENDICES. EIGHTH REPORT FROM THE EDUCATION, SCIENCE AND ARTS COMMITTEE, HOUSE OF COMMONS. VOLUME II: MINUTES OF EVIDENCE. SESSION 1980-81

Chairman: Christopher Price. xxi, 485 pages, HMSO, 1982.

1982   PUBLIC AND PRIVATE FUNDING OF THE ARTS: TOGETHER WITH THE MINUTE OF
        EVIDENCE AND APPENDICES. EIGHTH REPORT FROM THE EDUCATION, SCIENCE AND
        ARTS COMMITTEE, HOUSE OF COMMONS. VOLUME III: MINUTES OF EVIDENCE.
        SESSION 1981-82

Chairman: Christopher Price. xxi, pages 486-933. HMSO, 1982.

1982   REPORT OF THE BROADCASTING COMPLAINTS COMMISSION 1982

29 pages, HMSO, 1982. The first report of the Commission recommended by the Annan Committee and set up under the Broadcasting Act 1980. Covers the period 1 June 1981 to 31 March 1982 and considers 23 complaints. During the period under review 114 complaints were received, 91 of which were considered to be outside the Commission's jurisdiction.

1982   REPORT OF THE INQUIRY INTO CABLE EXPANSION AND BROADCASTING POLICY

Chairman: Lord Hunt of Tanworth. (Cmnd 8679), vi, 46 pages, HMSO, 1982. The Home Secretary announced on 22 March 1982 that this Inquiry was to be established with the following terms of reference: 'To take as its frame of reference the Government's wish to secure the benefits for the United Kingdom which cable technology can offer and its willingness to consider an expansion of cable systems which would permit cable to carry a wider range of entertainment and other services (including when available services of direct broadcasting by satellite), but in a way consistent with the wider public interest, in particular the safeguarding of public service broadcasting; to consider the questions affecting broadcasting policy which would arise from such an expansion, including in particular the supervisory framework; and to make recommendations by 30 September 1982.'

1982   REPORT ON CABLE SYSTEMS. CABINET OFFICE: INFORMATION TECHNOLOGY
        ADVISORY PANEL

54 pages, HMSO, 1982. Considers the potential role of cable systems in the UK and the desirability of a major programme of cable installation.

1982   A BILL (AS AMENDED ON REPORT) INTITLED AN ACT TO EXTEND AND AMEND THE
        CINEMATOGRAPH ACTS 1909 AND 1952 (194)

14 pages, HMSO, 1982. Intended to bring under the cinema licensing system any form of moving picture exhibition other than BBC and IBA television transmissions, licensed cable relays and private performances.

1983   A BILL TO MAKE PROVISION FOR REGULATING THE DISTRIBUTION OF VIDEO
        RECORDINGS AND FOR CONNECTED PURPOSES (BILL 14)

iv, 16 pages, HMSO, 1983.

1983   A BILL INTITLED AN ACT TO PROVIDE FOR THE ESTABLISHMENT AND FUNCTIONS OF A CABLE AUTHORITY AND TO MAKE OTHER PROVISIONS WITH RESPECT TO CABLE PROGRAMME SERVICES; TO AMEND THE BROADCASTING ACT 1981 AND TO MAKE FURTHER PROVISION WITH RESPECT TO BROADCASTING SERVICES; AND FOR CONNECTED PURPOSES (83)

viii, 55 pages, HMSO, 1983.

1983   CHOICE BY CABLE: THE ECONOMICS OF A NEW ERA IN TELEVISION

C G Veljanovski and W D Bishop, 115 pages, Institute of Economics Affairs, 1983 (Hobart Paper 96). Chapter 7 is devoted to a critique of the Hunt Report.

1983   COPYRIGHT (AMENDMENT) ACT 1983

4 pages, HMSO, 1983. An Act to amend section 21 of the Copyright Act 1956 so as to provide new penalties for offences relating to infringing copies of sound recordings and cinematograph films; and to provide for the issue and execution of search warrants in relation to such offences.

1983   THE DEVELOPMENT OF CABLE SYSTEMS AND SERVICES. HOME OFFICE AND DEPARTMENT OF INDUSTRY (CMND 8866)

90 pages, HMSO, 1983. Sets out the Government's proposals for a framework for the development of cable systems and services.

1983   FILMS: A REPORT ON THE SUPPLY OF FILMS FOR EXHIBITIONS IN CINEMAS.

Monopolies and Mergers Commission (Cmnd 8858), v, 123 pages, HMSO, 1983. The first report on the supply of films in Britain since 1966.

1983   INTELLECTUAL PROPERTY RIGHTS AND INNOVATION

Chief Scientific Officer, Cabinet Office (Cmnd 9117), x, 46 pages, HMSO, 1983. Considers how best to support the commercialisation of ideas and in particular how to help small but enterprising firms. Recommends a number of changes to the intellectual property rights system.

1983   THE PROTECTION OF MILITARY INFORMATION: REPORT OF THE STUDY GROUP ON CENSORSHIP

Chairman: General Sir Hugh Beach (Cmnd 9112). viii, 92 pages, HMSO, 1983. Considers, in the light of the Falklands conflict, how the Government should protect military information immediately prior to or during the conduct of operations.

1983   REPORT OF THE BROADCASTING COMPLAINTS COMMISSION 1983

v, 59 pages, HMSO, 1983. The second report of the Commission. Covers the period 1 April 1982 to 31 March 1983. 234 complaints were received of which 188 were outside and 46 fell within the Commission's jurisdiction.

1984   A BILL INTITLED AN ACT TO PROVIDE FOR THE ESTABLISHMENT AND FUNCTIONS OF A CABLE AUTHORITY AND TO MAKE OTHER PROVISION WITH RESPECT TO CABLE PROGRAMME SERVICES; TO AMEND THE BROADCASTING ACT 1981 AND TO MAKE FURTHER PROVISION WITH RESPECT TO BROADCASTING SERVICES; AND FOR CONNECTED PURPOSES (BILL 127)

vii, 54 pages, HMSO, 1984.

1984   FILM POLICY

(Cmnd 9319), 27 pages, HMSO, 1984. White Paper outlining the Government's plans for investing in the British film industry (through a privatised version of the National Film Finance Corporation) to the end of the 1980s.

1984   PUBLIC AND PRIVATE FUNDING OF THE ARTS: OBSERVATIONS BY THE GOVERNMENT ON THE EIGHT REPORT FROM THE EDUCATION, SCIENCE AND ARTS COMMITTEE. SESSION 1981-82. OFFICE OF ARTS AND LIBRARIES

(Cmnd. 9127), 26 pages, HMSO, 1984. Chapter 6, 'Film and Television and the British Film Institute', deals with the recommendations concerned with films and television, including the Committee's consideration of the activities of the BBC and the independent television companies.

1984   VIDEO RECORDINGS ACT 1984

17 pages, HMSO, 1984. Makes provision for regulating the distribution of video recordings.

1984   REPORT OF THE BROADCASTING COMPLAINTS COMMISSION 1984

vi, 85 pages, HMSO, 1984. Third report of the Commission covering the period 1 April 1983 to 31 March 1984; 228 complaints were received of which 181 were outside and 47 fell within the Commission's jurisdiction.

1985   THE PROTECTION OF MILITARY INFORMATION: GOVERNMENT RESPONSE TO THE REPORT OF THE STUDY GROUP ON CENSORSHIP

(Cmnd. 9499), 10 pages, Ministry of Defence, 1985. The response to the 1983 Beach Report (Cmnd 9112).

1985   REPORT OF THE BROADCASTING COMPLAINTS COMMISSION 1985

vi, 78 pages, HMSO, 1985. Fourth report of the Commission covering the period 1 April 1984 to 31 March 1985. 218 complaints were received of which 185 were outside and 33 fell within the Commission's jurisdiction.

1985   THE RECORDING AND RENTAL OF AUDIO AND VIDEO COPYRIGHT MATERIAL: A
        CONSULTATIVE DOCUMENT

Department of Trade and Industry (Cmnd 9445), iv, 14 pages, HMSO, 1985. Green Paper inviting comments on the proposition that 'copyright holders are entitled to payment for the home taping of their material and that a levy on blank audio and video tape is the only practicable way of providing such payment.'. Discusses also the recording of broadcasts for educational purposes.

1986   INTELLECTUAL PROPERTY AND INNOVATION. DEPARTMENT OF TRADE AND
        INDUSTRY

(Cmnd 9712), iv, 78 pages, HMSO, 1986. White Paper: response to Intellectual property and innovation (Cmnd 9117, 1983) and other reports on copyright.

1986   REPORT OF THE BROADCASTING COMPLAINTS COMMISSION 1986

vi, 79 pages, HMSO, 1986. Fifth report of the Commission covering the period 1 April 1985 "to 31 March 1986. 208 complaints were received of which 161 were outside and 47 fell within the Commission's jurisdiction.

1986   REPORT OF THE COMMITTEE ON FINANCING THE BBC

Chairman: Professor Alan Peacock (Cmnd 9824), xx, 219 pages, HMSO, 1986. The Home Secretary announced on 27 March 1985 that this Committee was to be established with the following terms of reference: 'To assess the effect of the introduction of advertising or sponsorship on the BBC's Home Services, either as an alternative or a supplement to the income now generated through the licence fee'.

1987   A BILL INTITLED AN ACT TO RESTATE THE LAW OF COPYRIGHT, WITH AMENDMENTS

'A Bill Intitled an Act to Restate the Law of Copyright, with Amendments; to Make Fresh Provision as to the Rights of Performers and Others in Performances; to Confer a Design Right in Original Designs; to Amend the Registered Designs Act 1949; to Make Provision with Respect to Patent Agents and Trade Mark Agents; to Confer Patents and Designs Jurisdiction on Certain County Courts; to Amend The Law of Patents; to Make Fresh Provision Penalising the Fraudulent Reception of Programmes; to Make the Fraudulent Application or Use of a Trade Mark an Offence; to Enable Financial Assistance to Be Given to Certain International Bodies; And For Connected Purposes' (HL Bill 12), xxviii, 192 pages HMSO, 1987.

1987 REPORT OF THE BROADCASTING COMPLAINTS COMMISSION 1987

vi, 74 pages, HMSO, 1987. Sixth report of the Commission covering the period 1 April 1986 to 31 March 1987. 222 complaints were received of which 174 were outside and 48 fell within the Commission's jurisdiction.

1988 BROADCASTING IN THE '90S: COMPETITION, CHOICE AND QUALITY

Home Office (Cm 517), iv, 46 pages, HMSO, 1988. White Paper setting out the Government's proposals for broadcasting in the UK in the 1990s. Includes proposals for satellite broadcasting, radio and programme standards.

1988 COPYRIGHT, DESIGNS AND PATENTS ACT 1988

ix, 238 pages, HMSO, 1988. An Act to restate the law of copyright, with amendments; to make fresh provision as to the rights of performers and others in performances; to confer a design right in original designs; to amend the Registered Designs Act 1949; to make provision with respect to patent agents and trade mark agents; to confer patents and designs jurisdiction on certain county courts; to amend the law of patents; to make provision with respect to devices designed to circumvent copy-protection of works in electronic form; to make fresh provision penalising the fraudulent reception of transmissions; to make the fraudulent application or use of a trade mark an offence; to make provision for the benefit of the "Hospital for Sick Children, Great Ormond Street, London; to able financial assistance to be given to certain international bodies; and for connected purposes.

1988 REPORT OF THE BROADCASTING COMPLAINTS COMMISSION 1988

HMSO, 1988. Seventh report of the Commission covering the period 1 April 1987 to 31 March 1988. 152 complaints were received of which 93 were outside the Commission's jurisdiction and 59 fell within it.

1988 3RD REPORT: THE FUTURE OF BROADCASTING VOLUME II

Minutes of evidence and appendices. Home Affairs Committee (House of Commons Paper 262-II), x, 372 pages, HMSO, 1988. (Volume I, House of Commons Paper 262-I, Session 1987-88, also gives minutes of evidence.)

1989 A BILL TO MAKE NEW PROVISION WITH RESPECT TO THE PROVISION AND REGULATION OF INDEPENDENT TELEVISION AND SOUND PROGRAMME SERVICES...

'A Bill to Make New Provision with Respect to the Provision and Regulation of Independent Television and Sound Programme Services and of Other Services Provided on Television or Radio Frequencies; to Make Provision with Respect to the Provision and Regulation of Local

Delivery Services; to Amend in Other Respects the Law Relating to Broadcasting and the Provision of Television and Sound Programme Services; to Make New Provision Relating to the Broadcasting Complaints Commission; to provide for the Establishment and Functions of a Broadcasting Standards Council; to Amend the Wireless Telegraphy Acts 1949 to 1967 and The Marine, &C., Broadcasting (Offences) Act 1967; and for connected purposes' [Bill 9]. viii, 159 pages, HMSO, 1989.

1989	BROADCASTING STANDARDS COUNCIL ANNUAL REPORT AND CODE OF PRACTICE 1988-89

56 pages, Broadcasting Standards Council, 1989. First annual report of the Council which was set up 'to consider the portrayal of violence, of sex, and matters of taste and decency in broadcast and video works'. Its code of practice is appended.

1989	REPORT OF THE BROADCASTING COMPLAINTS COMMISSION 1989

vi, 139 pages, HMSO, 1989. Eighth report covering the period 1 April 1988 to 31 March 1989. 348 complaints were received, more than twice as many as the preceding year. Of those within the Commission's jurisdiction formal decisions on 89 were made, 39 being full adjudications.

1989	STUDY OF PRIVATISATION OPTIONS FOR THE TERRESTRIAL BROADCASTING TRANSMISSION NETWORKS

Price Waterhouse Department of Privatisation Services, Home Office/Department of Trade and Industry,. 62 pages, HMSO, 1989. The jointly-commissioned report takes account of the views of government departments, other public section bodies, selected television and radio programme companies, and equipment manufacturers. The BBC and IBA also co-operated.

1989	THE WINDLESHAM/RAMPTON REPORT ON 'DEATH ON THE ROCK'

146 pages, Faber & Faber, 1989. The report commissioned by Thames Television from Lord Windlesham and Richard Rampton QC, on the controversial 'ThisWeek' special 'Death on the Rock'. The Government had attempted to have the screening postponed until after the inquest into the shooting by the security forces of three IRA members.

1989	DIRECTIVE 89/552/EEC – ON TELEVISION WITHOUT FRONTIERS

Commonly known as the 'Television without Frontiers' Directive', it was adopted by the Council of the European Communities in 1989. Member States, including the United Kingdom, had to bring into force laws, regulations and administrative provisions to comply with the Directive not later than 3 October 1991. The Directive itself is a single market measure intended to ensure the free flow of television pro-grammes and broadcasting services throughout the European Community. It does this by setting certain minimum standards on mat-ters such as advertising and sponsorship, and the protection of minors. If a broadcast meets these standards, no Member State may prevent reception of the broadcast on its territory. The Directive also establish-es programming quotas for European and independent productions, to be met (where practicable) by all national EU television broadcasters.

1990   BROADCASTING ACT 1990

x, 291 pages, HMSO, 1990. An Act to make new provision with respect to the provision and regulation of independent television and sound programme services and of other services provided on television or radio frequencies; to make provision with respect to the provision and regulation of local delivery services; to amend in other respects the law relating to broadcasting and the provision of television and sound pro-gramme services and to make provision with respect to the supply and use of information about programmes; to make provision with respect to the transfer of the property rights and liabilities of the Independent Broadcasting Authority and the Cable Authority and the dissolution of those bodies; to make new provision relating to the Broadcasting Complaints Commission; to provide for the establishment and func-tions of a Broadcasting Standards Council; to amend the Wireless Telegraphy Acts 1949 to 1967 and the Marine, &c., Broadcasting (Offences) Act 1967; to revoke a class licence granted under the Telecommunications Act 1984 to run broadcast relay systems; and for connected purposes.

1990   BROADCASTING STANDARDS COUNCIL ANNUAL REPORT 1989-90

59 pages, Broadcasting Standards Council, 1990. Second annual report of the Council.

1990   THE EUROPEAN INITIATIVE: THE BUSINESS OF TELEVISION & FILM IN THE 1990S

ii, 40 pages, British Screen Advisory Council, 1990. Examines the busi-ness of television and film in the 1990s. Based upon a seminar held in January 1990, attended by producers, directors and others from eight European countries. Distills the main arguments emerging from that seminar.

1990   HIGH DEFINITION TELEVISION (HDTV): THE POTENTIAL FOR NON-BROADCAST
            APPLICATIONS

Department of Trade and Industry. vii, 31 pages, HMSO, 1990. Discusses the technology and its potential; criteria for assessing the potential of markets, convergence of HDTV and the computer.

1990   REPORT OF THE BROADCASTING COMPLAINTS COMMISSION 1990

iv, 151 pages, HMSO, 1990. Ninth report covering the period 1 April 1989 to 31 March 1990. 550 complaints were received compared to 348 the previous year. Most were outside the Commission's jurisdiction. Formal decisions on 94 complaints were made, of which 44 were the subject of full adjudications.

1991   ENQUIRY INTO STANDARDS OF CROSS MEDIA PROMOTION: REPORT TO THE
            SECRETARY OF STATE FOR TRADE AND INDUSTRY

John Sadler (Cm 1436), iv, 134 pages, HMSO, 1991 The terms of reference required the author to consider to what extent it was proper for media companies to promote their own, or any associate's interests in the provision of media services or products and, where such behaviour was found to be improper and, taking into account the effect on the relevant markets, to consider what remedies might be appropriate. The evidence received was mainly about three specific examples of cross media promotion; 1) the promotion of Sky Television in newspapers owned by News International, 2) the promotion on BBC Television of magazines published by the BBC, and 3) the promotion of premium rate telephone services by national newspapers which had direct or indirect financial interests in such services.

1991   REPORT OF THE BROADCASTING COMPLAINTS COMMISSION 1991

vi, 179 pages, HMSO, 1991. Tenth report covering the period 1 April 1990 to 31 March 1991; 930 complaints were received compared to 550 the previous year. Of these, 127 were within the jurisdiction of the Commission. 44 went to adjudication and a further 65 were under consideration at the end of the year

1991   TELEVISION LICENCE FEE: A STUDY FOR THE HOME OFFICE: MANAGEMENT SUMMARY

Price Waterhouse, Home Office, 14 pages, HMSO, 1991. Report by Price Waterhouse Management Consultants who were commissioned by the Home Office in October 1990 to advise how future increases in the television licence fee from April 1991 could be set below the level of inflation measured by the Retail Price Index (RPI). The consultants were asked to examine the consequences of a range of formulae for such increases while having regard to the need to maintain the BBC's cornerstone role in British broadcasting.

1992   INDEPENDENT TELEVISION COMMISSION REPORT AND ACCOUNTS 1991

Independent Television Commission, 1992. First annual report of the ITC. For earlier reports and accounts of the independent television controlling authorities consult those published by the Independent Television Authority (later Independent Broadcasting Authority) for the years 1954-1990.

1992   REPORT OF THE BROADCASTING COMPLAINTS COMMISSION 1992

vii, 204 pages, HMSO, 1992. Eleventh report covering the period 1 April 1991 to 31 March 1992; 1048 complaints were received compared to 930 the previous year. Of these, 928 were outside the Commission's jurisdiction and 120 fell within it. With the 65 complaints before the Commission at the beginning of the year the latter total amounted to 185. Decisions were given in 130 of these complaints. The remaining 55 were awaiting decision on 3 March 1992

1992   TOWARDS A NATIONAL ARTS AND MEDIA STRATEGY

vi, 172 pages, National Arts and Media Strategy Monitoring Group, 1992. Comprises a brief 'strategic framework' of principles, priorities and action points, and a comprehensive set of 'draft strategies' including a summary of conclusions and recommendations. A draft document offered for final consultation, comment and suggested amendment.

1992   PAYING FOR BROADCASTING: THE HANDBOOK

Andrew Graham, Gavyn Davies, Brian Sturgess and William B Shew. 256 pages, Routledge, 1992. Commission by the BBC to inform debate in the run-up to the 1966 Charter renewal. Drawing on examples from Britain and other worldwide broadcasting markets, the authors project future possibilities for the revenues available from different sources – advertising and sponsorship, subscription, programme sales and co-production, and various kinds of public funding.

1992   THE FUTURE OF THE BBC: A CONSULTATION DOCUMENT

Department of National Heritage (Cmnd 2098), 43 pages, HMSO, 1992. A document intended to raise discussion about the future of the BBC after the Corporation's present charter comes to an end in 1996.

1992   EXTENDING CHOICE: THE BBC'S ROLE IN THE NEW BROADCASTING AGE

88 pages, BBC, 1992. Intended by the BBC to open up public discussion in the Charter renewal debate.

1992   DIRECTIVE 92/100/EEC – ON RENTAL RIGHTS

Authors of performers have, pursuant to the Directive, an unwaiveable right to receive equitable remuneration. Member States are required to provide a right for performers in relation to the fixation of their performances, a right for phonogram and film producers in relation to their phonograms and first fixations of their films and a right broadcasters and their broadcast and cable transmissions. Member States must also provide a 'reproduction right' giving performers, phonogram producers and broadcasting organisations the right to authorise or prohibit the direct or indirect reproduction of their copyright works. The Directive also requires Member States to provide for performers, film producers, phonogram producers and broadcasting organisations to have exclusive rights to make available their work by sale or otherwise – known as the 'distribution right'.

1993   DIRECTIVE 93/83/EEC – ON SATELLITE TRANSMISSION AND CABLE RETRANSMISSION

This Directive is aimed at eliminating uncertainty and differences in national legislation governing when the act of communication of a programme takes place. It avoids the cumulative application of several national laws to one single act of broadcasting. The Directive provides that communication by satellite occurs in the member state where the programming signals are introduced under the control of a broadcaster into an uninterrupted chain of communication, leading to the satellite and down towards earth. The Directive also examines protection for authors, performers and producers of phonograms and broadcasting organisations, and requires that copyright owners may grant or refuse authorisation for cable retransmission of a broadcast only through a collecting society.

1994   HOME AFFAIRS COMMITTEE: FOURTH REPORT – VIDEO VIOLENCE AND YOUNG OFFENDERS

(HC 514), xiv, 69 pages, HMSO, 1994. As a contribution to the public debate on the impact of violent films on children, the Home Affairs Committee interviewed witnesses and sought opinion from experts as to the effect of videotapes such as CHILD'S PLAY 3. In its report the Committee voiced its concerns about the 'corrupting influence' of violent films, but added that 'the possibility ... that a child might accidentally see a few minutes of a video being watched by his or her parents ... is not in our view sufficient reason for banning the sale or rent of all such videos even to adults'.

1994   THE FUTURE OF THE BBC: SERVING THE NATION; COMPETING WORLDWIDE

55 pages, HMSO, 1994. This report was presented to Parliament on 6 July 1994. It set out the Government's plans for the structure and operation of the BBC under a new royal charter and agreement, to operate for ten years from 1 January 1997.

1996   BROADCASTING ACT 1996

194 pages, HMSO, 1996. The Act makes provision for digital terrestrial television broadcasting and contains provisions relating to the award of multiplex licences. It also provides for the introduction of radio multiplex services and regulates digital terrestrial sound broadcasting. In addition, the Act amends a number of provisions contained in the Broadcasting Act 1990 relating to the funding of Channel Four, Sianel Pedwar Cymmru, and the operation of the Gaelic Broadcasting Committee. It also dissolves the Broadcasting Complaints Commission and the Broadcasting Standards Council and replaces these with the Broadcasting Standards Commission. Other provisions relate to the transmission network of the BBC and television coverage of listed events.

1998   DIRECTIVE 98/98 – ON HARMONISING THE TERM OF PROTECTION OF COPYRIGHT AND CERTAIN RELATED RIGHTS

This Directive is aimed at harmonising the periods of copyright throughout the European Union where different states provide different periods of protection.

1999   REVIEW OF THE FUTURE FUNDING OF THE BBC

150 pages, HMSO, 1999. The Department for Culture, Media and Sport set up the Independent Review Panel in October 1998 to report on the future funding of the BBC with the following terms of reference: 'The review panel will: i) against an expectation that the licence fee will remain the principal source of funding for public services for the Charter period: consider ways in which funding to support public service output can be extended from other sources; and take a forward look at other possible mechanisms for funding the BBC in the longer term, particularly in the light of technological development; ii) consider how to secure an appropriate balance between the BBC's public and commercial services, and review the mechanisms under which the fair-trading commitment as to commercial services is delivered; iii) consider the current structure of the concessionary licence scheme and whether a suitable alternative structure could be available'.

1999   BROADCASTING IN WALES AND THE NATIONAL ASSEMBLY: REPORT, TOGETHER WITH THE PROCEEDINGS OF THE [WELSH AFFAIRS] COMMITTEE, MINUTES OF EVIDENCE AND APPENDICES

154 pages, HMSO, 1999. Published on 27 April 1999, the Report gives conclusions and recommendations.

1999   THE FUNDING OF THE BBC: MINUTES OF EVIDENCE [OF THE CULTURE, MEDIA AND SPORT COMMITTEE]

54 pages, HMSO, 1999.

1999   THE FUNDING OF THE BBC: THIRD REPORT [OF THE CULTURE, MEDIA AND SPORT COMMITTEE]

Volume II. Minutes of Evidence and Appendices. 282 pages, HMSO, 1999. Report published on 15 December 1999.

2000   THE FUNDING OF THE BBC: GOVERNMENT RESPONSE TO THE THIRD REPORT FROM THE CULTURE, MEDIA AND SPORT COMMITTEE, SESSION 1999-2000

13 pages, HMSO, 2000. Response presented to Parliament in March 2000.

2000   NTL INCORPORATED AND CABLE & WIRELESS COMMUNICATIONS PLC: A REPORT ON THE PROPOSED MERGER

199 pages, HMSO, 2000. Report of the Competition Commission presented to Parliament in March 2000.

2000   WHATEVER HAPPENED TO NEWS AT TEN?

61 pages, HMSO, 2000. Fifth Report of the Culture, Media and Sport Committee. Report, together with Proceedings of the Committee, Minutes of Evidence and Appendices. (16 March 2000). An enquiry into the timing of the Independent Television (ITV) Network's peaktime news programme News at Ten.

2000   VIVENDI SA AND BRITISH SKY BROADCASTING GROUP PLC: A REPORT ON THE MERGER SITUATION

209 pages, HMSO, 2000. Report of the Competition Commission presented to Parliament in April 2000.

2000   INDEPENDENT NEWS & MEDIA PLC AND TRINITY MIRROR PLC: A REPORT ON THE PROPOSED MERGER

112 pages, HMSO, 2000. Report of the Competition Commission presented to Parliament in July 2000.

2000   CARLTON COMMUNICATIONS PLC AND GRANADA GROUP PLC AND UNITED NEWS
AND MEDIA PLC: A REPORT ON THE THREE PROPOSED MERGERS

233 pages, HMSO, 2000. Report of the Competition Commission presented to Parliament in July 2000.

2000   A NEW CULTURE FOR COMMUNICATIONS

109 pages, HMSO, 2000. Report presented to Parliament on 12 December 2000. The paper, a blueprint for the future of communications, recognises the convergence that has already occurred in the market place between the broadcasting, telecommunications and new media industries and proposes a new legislative framework for these with a new single regulator, an Office of Communications (OFCOM).

2001   OPPORTUNITY FOR ALL IN A WORLD OF CHANGE (OR, COMPETITIVENESS WHITE
PAPER)

92 pages, HMSO, 2001. This is the Government's White Paper on enterprise, skills and innovation. It sets out the next steps for Government in helping individuals, communities and businesses to prosper.

USEFUL INTERNET ADDRESSES

An Internet search on the words 'film' or 'video' will easily produce over a million potential links. This is a small selection of addresses that BUFVC staff have found useful in the course of their work. These sites contain a variety of resources, from moving images online to sources of general film and associated media information, and lists of links to other sites. The BUFVC has now developed its own gateway to sites of interest to higher and further education, at www.bufvc.ac.uk/gateway. This selection of sites relating to moving images and sound is searchable by academic discipline.

Ain't It Cool News
www.aint-it-cool-news.com

Irreverent but well-informed movie news site, with up-to-the-minute production news, reviews, obituaries, chat forums and links.

All Movie Guide
http://allmovie.com

Comprehensive movie database, offering searches by title, name and keyword, with detailed film descriptions, actors' biographies, essays on film genres and film history, as well as a useful glossary of terms.

American Memory (Library of Congress)
http://memory.loc.gov

The incomparable 'American Memory' section of the vast Library of Congress site includes a 'Performing Arts' section, with playscripts, theatre bills, sound recordings and motion pictures, notably the American Variety 1870-1920 section at http://memory.loc.gov/ammem/vshtml/vshome.html, which includes a wide selection of early film productions, usefully categorised by theme; excellent supporting catalogue information.

Anima
http://web.inter.nl.net/users/anima/index.htm

One of the most creative and beautiful sites on the web, mostly devoted to animations of the work of 'pre-cinema' pioneers such as Donisthorpe and Le Prince, and the chronophotographs (sequence photographs) of late nineteenth-century experimenters such as Demeny, Marey and Muybridge. The section 'Chronophotographical Projections' is particularly recommended.

Archive Films
www.archivefilms.com

Stock film footage and photo site, including fiction and non-fiction material. Includes The March of Time and the Prelinger collection. Searchable by keyword, with films accessible by catalogue numbers; basic shotlists available.

ARKive
www.arkive.org.uk

ARKive is a projected digital library of films and photographs created by the Wildscreen Trust. The site aims to become 'the world's electronic archive of photographs, moving images and sounds of endangered species and habitats'. It will include moving images, still and sound recordings by species, entire films and videos of particular scientific or historic interest, interviews with wildlife filmmakers and other resources.

Art on Screen Database
www.artfilm.org/aosdb.htm

Database produced by the Program for Art on Film, offering art and architecture subjects on film from a variety of sources, designed for students, curators and film researchers; searchable by keyword, with elegant and comprehensive catalogue entries.

BBC
www.bbc.co.uk

A vast site that covers BBC1, BBC2 and BBC Radio 1, 2, 3, 4 and 5. Although sometimes difficult to negotiate due to its enormity, the BBC website is an exceptional resource for those with a lot of time to browse. The whole site is searchable and has links to other sites of interest; it includes full BBC television and radio listings (with regional variations) and links to other sites for comprehensive UK television and radio listings.

Black Star
www.blackstar.co.uk

Comprehensive and reliable online sales for British releases of videos and DVDs.

British Film Institute (BFI)
www.bfi.org.uk

The BFI site does not include online access to its film databases, but features a wide range of useful resources, including screenings at the National Film Theatre, educational resources, film and media industry information, and an online catalogue for the BFI National Library of over 42,000 books on film and television.

Britfilms.com
www.britfilms.com

This site hosts the two databases of the Film and Television Department of the British Council – the British Films Catalogue and the Directory of International Film and Video Festivals. The former is an illustrated database of the latest British films plus an archive of previous years, the latter a comprehensive directory of film and video festivals listed alphabetically and by geographical location.

British Board of Film Classification
www.bbfc.co.uk

The British Board of Film Classification website is fully searchable by film title, director, cast, distributor, date or keyword, and can also be limited by medium. This information is not particularly full, but provides details on content that may have affected the certification and the length of footage cut from the film – unfortunately, it doesn'tnot explain why footage has been censored.

British Movietone News
www.movietone.com

British newsreel library covering the period 1929-1979 (plus the TV-AM library), with online database searchable by keyword; detailed shotlists available.

British Pathé News
www.britishpathe.com

Lively, informative site with an awareness of the Pathé newsreel's history (1910-1970) as well as its present commercial potential. Keyword searchable online database, with detailed descriptions and, sometimes, useful comment or analysis of the footage. A growing collections of online clips includes a number of engaging examples of the Pathé Pictorial cinemagazine in colour.

British Universities Film & Video Council
www.bufvc.ac.uk

The BUFVC's site includes access to AVANCE, the Television Index, the Researcher's Guide Online (RGO) and British Universities Newsreel Project (see below), as well as education films for sales, a gateway to educational websites searchable by subject area, and links to the developing Television and Radio Index for Learning and Teaching (TRILT) and MAAS Media Online, the Managing Agent and Advisory Service for the online delivery of moving images and sound to UK higher and further education.

British Universities Newsreel Project Database
www.bufvc.ac.uk/newsreels

Database of 160,000 British newsreel records, accessible to UK higher education and BUFVC members only. It features the records of all the major British newsreels, with full release data and basic synopses, searchable by title, newsreel, date, library number, issue number, subject, keyword and cameraman, with simple and advanced search options offered. The site also includes biographical and background information on the newsreels which is accessible to all.

BUBL Information Service
http://bubl.ac.uk

An information centre for UK higher education, including an extensive listing of online resources divided by subject area.

Charles Urban, Motion Picture Pioneer
http://website.lineone.net/~luke.mckernan/Urban.htm

Charles Urban was a pioneer of educational, scientific and travel films, as well as the entrepreneur behind the pioneering colour film system Kinemacolor. The site gives detailed biographical information, and includes an extensive and classified list of links to other early cinema sites (covering filmmaking to 1914).

Chartbusters
www.chart-busters.co.uk

Online video store, specialising in rare and deleted titles.

CineMedia
http://afi.cinemedia.org

Massive listing of film and television weblinks, probably the most comprehensive (if scarcely manageable) of its kind on the Net.

D.FILM
www.dfilm.com

The D.FILM Digital Film Festival is an online showcase of films made digitally. The goal of the festival is both to entertain, by showing audiences the very best work done by today's new breed of digital filmmakers, and to inspire, by actively teaching them how they can do it themselves.

DigiGuide
www.digiguide.com

DigiGuide can be downloaded from the Internet for a small fee to provide a personalised television listings guide. Once installed on a desktop, DigiGuide can be viewed offline, although it must be regularly updated online. It can be customised to the users' particular tastes and to remind the user when favourite programmes are on.

Drew's Script-o-Rama
www.script-o-rama.com

Popular and extensive resource for film and television scripts.

East Anglian Film Archive
www.uea.ac.uk/eafa

Online database, still being updated, with very basic information available for this regional archive covering East Anglia. Searching by title, keyword or filmmaker.

Educational and Television Films
www.etvltd.demon.co.uk

Collection specialising in film of Russia, China, Cuba and the Left in Britain. Portions of the catalogue are given online, but with no searchable database.

Educational Recording Agency Ltd
www.era.org.uk

The ERA Licence enables an educational establishment to record for educational purposes any radio or television broadcast, apart from Open University programmes, which come under a separate licensing scheme. The website explains the legal background, the licence and the terms and conditions of the licensing scheme.

epguides.com
www.epguides.com

A fully searchable site with lists of episode titles, cast lists and original air dates for many American television shows. Some of the records have episode synopses.

FIAF
www.cinema.ucla.edu/fiaf

The International Federation of Film Archives (FIAF), with addresses and contact details for all member archives.

FIAT/IFTA
www.nb.no/fiat

> The offical site of the International Federation of Television Archives (FIAT/IFTA).

Film Archive Forum
www.bufvc.ac.uk/faf/faf.htm

> The Film Archive Forum is the representative body of the UK's public sector film archives (the NFTVA, the IWM and the various regional film archives across the country). This site is part of the BUFVC website and includes links to all member archives.

Film Images
www.film-images.com

> Extensive stockshot library with historical and contemporary footage from the 1890s onward, from collections in America and Europe, with detailed shotlists searchable by keyword. Includes the COI Footage File of British government films, as well as eclectic European libraries.

Focal International
www.focalint.org

> International professional trade association representing commercial film and audio-visual libraries and professional film researchers. The websites offers an excellent series of links to film libraries worldwide.

Footage.net
www.footage.net

> Massive collection of individual stockshot libraries, including Archive Films, Image Bank, Historic Films, CNN Image Source and many others, with global searches over all these databases possible. The first online port of call for most film researchers.

Joint Information Systems Committee (JISC)
www.jisc.ac.uk

> The Joint Information Systems Committee (JISC) promotes the application and use of information systems and information technology in higher and further education across the UK. The site carries information about the JISC, its services and development programmes. It also has links to JISC publications and carries updates on current and past calls issued to the community in the form of JISC circulars.

Haddon Home Page
www.rsl.ox.ac.uk/isca/haddon
> Online database of ethnographic archival films, many of them from the National Film and Television Archive, with its own detailed shotlists.

Intellectual Property on the Internet (UK)
www.intellectual-property.gov.uk
> The aim of this comprehensive site is to answer users' questions and provide the necessary resources to find ways through the intellectual property (IP) jungle of copyright, designs, patents and trade marks. Questions answered include 'How do I enforce my rights?', 'How do I get permission to use someone's material?' and 'How do I know/show if material is protected?'. The site also provides resources and links on subjects such as copyright and profiting from IP.

The Internet Movie Database
www.imdb.com
> Huge database of filmographic information, with links to video availability (in the USA). Its data should not always be trusted, but its sheer size and apparent comprehensiveness have made it a standard source.

I Saw It on TV: A Guide to Broadcast & Cable Programming Sources
www.library.nwu.edu/media/resources/tvguide.html
> Wide-ranging and particularly useful guide to online resources for American and Canadian networks.

ITN Archive
www.itnarchive.com
> Database of Independent Television News (ITN), searchable by keyword and date, with detailed shotlists and notes about footage sources, predominantly for 1990s TV news. The ITN Archive holds a large 1920s-1950s newsreel library (Gaumont British News, Gaumont Graphic, British Paramount News, Universal News and others) but this material is not accessible online except for a few isolated items. Also includes details of tape compilations and video clips.

Kaleidoscope
www.kaleidoscope.org.uk
> Kaleidoscope is a non-profit making organisation devoted to the appreciation of classic British television. Promotional events are arranged throughout the country, but its website is an easy way to access much of the information. The site includes small numbers of television reviews, articles, episode guides, production material and links.

The Knowledge Online
www.theknowledgeonline.com

This free online version of *The Knowledge* directory provides information for the film and television industries, with a database of over 15,600 companies and crew, searchable by keyword, company, credit, location and name.

Library of Congress Online Catalog
http://lcweb.loc.gov/catalog

The Motion Picture division of the Library of Congress has its catalogue available online as part of the general LoC catalogue, searchable by title, name, subject or special keyword.

Media Reference Sources & Information
www.lib.berkeley.edu/MRC

A useful gateway to information sources on film, television and video.

Media UK
www.mediauk.com

An online media directory covering television, radio, newspapers, magazines and 'newsfeeds'.

MovieMail
www.moviem.co.uk

Very good video and DVD source, with an emphasis on art films and world cinema.

MoviesUnlimited.com
www.moviesunlimited.com

Extensive American (NTSC only) video source, sometimes useful for tracing that which seems to be listed in no other place.

Moving Image
www.milibrary.com

Stockshot library ranging from the collections of TV-AM, the WPA Film Library and Christian Television Corporation to the National Trust, British Tourist Authority, Royal Society for the Protection of Birds (RSPB) and 1930s public information films of the Trade and Industry Development Association (TIDA). The online database, although searchable by keyword, covers only a small proportion of the total holdings of some 8000 records.

National Archives and Records Administration (NAIL catalogue)
www.nara.gov/nara/nail.html
> Invaluable catalogue to the American Federal records, including official film records.

National Film and Television Archive (BFI)
www.bfi.org.uk/collections
> The British national film collection. Officially the NFTVA is now part of BFI Collections, a gathering together of all the BFI's various film collections. There is no online database, but the site includes the contents of some individual published catalogues such as Documentary (films in distribution) and British Silent Comedy.

National Information Center for Educational Media
www.nicem.com
> Long-established US database of film, video, audio, CD-ROM, DVD and other educational and training media materials. MediaSleuth, **www.mediasleuth.com**, is NICEM's search engine for audio-visual materials.

Newsplayer
www.newsplayer.com
> Collection of 10,000 newsfilm clips from the ITN Archive and French Pathé libraries, from 1896 to the present, accessible for £25 annual fee. Newsplayer plans to add the Frost Collection of interviews in 2001.

Nielsen Media Research
www.tvratings.com
> Nielsen supplies Canada and the US with television ratings information. This site explains how representative population samples are taken, and participants' viewing patterns are monitored. A separate section devoted to ethnic viewing trends includes graphs and explains how the company ensures fair testing is carried out.

North West Film Archive
www.nwfa.mmu.ac.uk
> Online database of films, covering the North West region of England, searchable by keyword only, with good descriptions and basic technical data available.

Olympic Television Archive Bureau (OTAB)
www.otab.com
> The official agents for Olympic Games footage. Access to the database requires registration.

100 Years of Cinema in Europe
www.mediasalles.it/ybkcent/ybk95_hi.htm

A very impressive collection of histories of film production and exhibition in most European countries.

Online Classics
www.onlineclassics.com

An astonishing site streaming complete plays, operas and musical works, with lo- and hi-band access and good background information including cast lists and production details.

Online Media Guide
http://8thhouse.com/media/onlinemediaguide.htm

OnLine Media Guide is an online production resource guide for the (mainly, American) multimedia industry. It includes the Online Media Guide – Film & Video Distributors (**www.8thhouse.com/media/ production/distributors.htm**), with American film and video distributors (listed by state), and international film and video distributors in Canada, Germany and the UK.

Produxion.com
www.produxion.com

Television production site, aiming to establish itself as a portal for all those working in the industry, with news, job information, an industry directory, links and contacts. Uses data from *Broadcast* and *Production Solutions* magazines, and includes the Broadcasters' Audience Research Board's BARB ratings going back to January 1999.

Public Motion Picture Research Centers and Film Archives
http://lcweb.loc.gov/film/arch.html

Helpful list of film archives and motion picture centres worldwide, with weblinks.

Resource Discovery Network
www.rdn.ac.uk

A service provided by the Joint Information Systems Committee (JISC) for access to Internet resources for learning and teaching communities in the UK. It is organised into a series of individual gateways, or hubs, covering the areas of Heath and Life Sciences, Engineering, Mathematics and Computing, Humanities, Physical Sciences, Social Sciences, Business and Law.

QuickTime Hot Picks
www.apple.com/quicktime/hotpicks

The Apple QuickTime site links into a wide variety of online resources using QuickTime to stream moving images and sound, notably its collection of education links and its constantly changing selection of the latest movie trailers.

Scottish Screen Archive
www.scottishscreen.com/static.taf?content=c/0701

The Scottish Screen Archive holds the Scottish national collection of film and television materials. Its online catalogue is accessible through the performing Arts Data Service at www.pads.ahds.ac.uk/SFTACatalogueIntro.html.

ScreenSound Australia
www.screensound.gov.au

One of the few national film archives to have made its catalogue available online, with very impressive cataloguing detail, and facilities to narrow searches down to viewable material only.

Silents Majority
www.mdle.com/ClassicFilms

Comprehensive source of information on silent films on the Internet, with articles, picture galleries, links, news items, biographies and other information, including a UK section.

Streaming Media World
www.streamingmediaworld.com

Information source on streaming media technology. Contains current articles, tutorials and fundamentals, including the terminology of streaming media.

SURCAT
www.surcat.com/anghtml/home.htm

Database of the *Survival* natural history television programme. Registration is required, but there is a preview site to test the database. Searches by keyword, species and location.

Tanmedia
www.tanmedia.co.uk

A news and information service for commercial moving and still image libraries and archives, with news, articles, guide to film research, and links to 100 footage sources worldwide.

Television News Archive Vanderbilt University
http://tvnews.vanderbilt.edu

Outstanding database of American broadcast news, from 1968 to the present day. Data only, not film clips.

Terra Media
www.terramedia.co.uk

A reference source on audio-visual and communications media, most notable for 'Chronomedia', an extensive and growing chronology.

TV Cream
www.tv.cream.org

This site is a directory of old television shows from the UK, US, Europe, Australia and others, constructed from memories and archive material. It is searchable alphabetically and includes links to other nostalgic television websites.

UCLA Film and Television Archive
www.cinema.ucla.edu

An American film archive promoting a newsreel that it uniquely holds (Hearst Metrotone News). The holdings are traceable through the MELVYL Catalog, though as with the Library of Congress the films' holdings are combined with books and other material, making subject searching awkward (using Power Search to comb Newsreels with the subject required is the best option); shotlists available.

UK Television Adverts
www.westwood.u-net.com/ads/ads.htm

Includes information on over 2000 advertisements from ITV, Channel 4. Channel 5 and UK based satellite channels from 1996 onwards, some of which are downloaded. These are searchable by product or by the artist(s) who appeared in the advert. The site is searchable, and has links to other relevant sites.

Worldwide Video Broadcast Standards
www.alkenmrs.com/video/wwstandards1.html

This site has a list of countries and their video broadcast standards, it includes information about the frequencies and the mains electricity voltages as well.

Xtreme Information
www.registergroup.com

Online database and monitoring service for television commercials worldwide. Searching by brand or product.

INDEX – MEDIA LEGISLATION & REPORTS

GENERAL INDEX

U